LITERATURE AND ANTHROPOLOGY

LITERATURE
AND
ANTHROPOLOGY

Edited by
Philip A. Dennis
and
Wendell Aycock

TEXAS TECH UNIVERSITY PRESS
1989

Studies in Comparative Literature No. 20
ISSN 0899-2193

This book was set in 10 on 12 Baskerville and printed on acid-free paper that meets the guidelines for permanence and durability of the Committee on Production Guidelines for Book Longevity of the Council on Library Resources.

Cover and jacket art and design by Elaine Atkinson.

Library of Congress Cataloging-in-Publication Data

Literature and anthropology.

(Studies in comparative literature ; no. 20)
Based on papers presented at the Twentieth Annual Comparative Literature Symposium, held Jan. 1987 at Texas Tech University.
Includes bibliographies.
1. Literature and anthropology—Congresses.
2. Anthropology in literature—Congresses. I. Dennis, Philip Adams, 1945-   . II. Aycock, Wendell M.
III. Comparative Literature Symposium (20th : 1987 : Texas Tech University) IV. Series: Studies in comparative literature (Lubbock, Tex.) ; no. 20.
PN51.L5738 1989   809.3   89-4279
ISBN 0-89672-166-3 (alk. paper)
Library of Congress Cataloging-in-Publication Data
ISBN 0-89672-167-1 (Pbk. : alk. paper)

Texas Tech University Press
Lubbock, Texas 79409-1037 U.S.A.

STUDIES IN COMPARATIVE LITERATURE
TEXAS TECH UNIVERSITY PRESS

*Out of print

CONTENTS

PREFACE

The purpose of Studies in Comparative Literature is to explore literatures of various cultures and linguistic groups in comparison with one another, and to compare literature with other disciplines or fields of study. First published in 1968, volumes of the series derive from annual symposia founded by Wolodymyr T. Zyla, under the auspices of the Interdepartmental Committee on Comparative Literature at Texas Tech. In subsequent years, the series flourished, and volumes have been devoted to the study of authors (e.g., Kafka, Camus, Shakespeare), genres (e.g., the short story, science fiction), and movements and themes (e.g., surrealism, mythology).

This volume evolves from the Twentieth Annual Comparative Literature Symposium, held in January, 1987, on the topic, "Literature and Anthropology." Anthropologists, writers, and literary scholars have all contributed to the volume, and the papers deal with a broad variety of topics including ethnographic mystery novels, Caribbean literature, anthropological poetry, and shamanism. The papers were selected by an interdisciplinary committee at Texas Tech on the basis of their individual merits. Rather than relating to a common, well-defined theme, they attest to the broad variety of interests within the general field of humanistic anthropology.

Wendell Aycock

INTRODUCTION

Anthropology, alone among the social sciences, has always had close ties with the humanities. Literature, in particular, has been one tool used frequently by anthropologists in their efforts to understand other cultures. Anthropologists have produced literature of their own, used literature as a source of data to be analyzed, and used works of literature in teaching about other cultures. Likewise, many scholars of comparative literature have found the broad, cross-cultural approach of anthropology appealing, and have found points of contact between their own concerns and those of anthropology. In a truly comparative fashion, the papers in this volume deal with societies as far removed in time and space as Shakespearian England, the Brazilian Amazon, the Caribbean, and the contemporary Middle East.

The first chapter is by ethnographic mystery writer Tony Hillerman. Set on the Navajo Indian Reservation, Hillerman's mystery stories have as protagonists two Navajo Tribal Policemen, Joe Leaphorn and Jim Chee. Leaphorn and Chee involve us in a different cultural world as they solve local crimes. In the process, they teach us a great deal about how Navajos think and behave. In this paper Hillerman involves us in his own thought processes as he strives to make a new story not only entertaining, but accurate ethnographically. The keen insight and sense of humor found in Hillerman's books is equally apparent in his contribution here.

The chapter by James C. Pierson discusses mystery novels in general, noting the similarities between detectives and field anthropologists. Pierson considers a number of mystery writers whose books are particularly ethnographic, that is, in which descriptions of a different culture play a prominent part. Tony Hillerman and Arthur Upfield are among the authors discussed.

Two general chapters about the relationship between anthropology and literature follow. The first is by anthropologist Miles Richardson; the second, by A. Owen Aldridge, a comparative literature scholar. Richardson is editor of *Anthropology and Humanism Quarterly*, a journal that provides a forum for publication by humanistic anthropologists. In his eloquent discussion, "Point of View in Anthropological Discourse: The Ethnographer as Gilgamesh," Richardson begins by analyzing the human practice of storytelling. It varies, Richardson argues, according to the narrator's knowledge and degree of participation in the tale. The anthropologist's story, he concludes, is the entire human story, similar in its all-encompassing sweep to the ancient story of Gilgamesh. A. Owen Aldridge, who founded and continues to edit the journal *Comparative Literature Studies*, discusses structuralism, "primitivism," and various points of convergence between the two disciplines in "Literature and the Study of Man."

Two chapters focus on particular Western writers. Philip K. Bock uses Shakespeare's plays as a source to "mine" for cultural concepts related to success, and compares related concepts among the Baruya, a New Guinea group. James Whitlark discusses Kurt Vonnegut's anthropological background and training, and relates this background to important concepts in Vonnegut's later fiction.

Bernadette Bucher discusses the diary as a literary genre, comparing the somewhat scandalous personal diaries of the French novelist Stendhal and the anthropologist Bronislaw Malinowski. She concludes that the diary is a tool through which the ethnographer or the novelist discovers his "otherness." A necessary instrument of self-discovery, the writing of a diary allows the process of ethnographic fieldwork or of fiction-writing to continue.

Two chapters offer insightful considerations of Caribbean literature. John Stewart, in "The Literary Work as Cultural Document: The Caribbean Case," analyzes two novels from his home country of Trinidad. He uses Victor Turner's concept of social drama to discuss the role fiction in Trinidad plays in creating and resolving social conflict. Michael V. Angrosino provides an overview of the work of four important Caribbean writers, set in its social context. His conclusions about the significance of fiction in defining cultural identity in the Caribbean mirror the central concern in Stewart's paper.

Barbara Jo Lantz addresses the literary qualities of various kinds of everyday narrative in Mexico, in "Mexican Modernism: Narrative Risks." Specifically, she contrasts conversational storytelling with narratives of mourning, as recorded in fiction. She concludes that the second form of discourse involves considerable risks of self-revelation, as opposed to the first form, which, elaborated within its own cultural context, provides much of the enjoyment to be had from ordinary daily life.

Female characters in fiction are the subject of chapters eleven and twelve. Elizabeth Fernea, in "The Ethnographic Novel in Modern Arabic Women's Literature: The Case of *Sitt Marie Rose*," discusses a recent Lebanese novel about the abduction and murder of a young woman in war-torn Beirut. She compares the novel to an experimental ethnography and notes its place among other recent fiction by Arab women. Claudette Columbus, in "Mother Earth in Amazonia and the Andes: Darcy Ribeiro and José María Arguedas," compares the sacred earth mother concept of the Andes, the Pacha Mama, to the "sexual confusion and sexual ferocity" of femininity in the Amazon. The novels of Brazilian Darcy Ribeiro and Peruvian José María Arguedas provide the material for analysis. Both men were anthropologists as well as novelists. Columbus concludes that both see "cultural survival as dependent on the mythopoetic sensibilities of indigenous peoples."

Celia A. Daniels works in a different medium in "The Poet as Anthropologist." Herself a poet, Daniels describes some relationships between poetry and anthropology, as illustrated by excerpts from various modern poets. The paper, with its interesting interludes of poetry, provides a change of pace from literary analyses of fiction and illustrates the recent strong interest in "anthropological poetry."

Ann Daghistany provides a thoroughly cross-disciplinary contribution in "The Shaman: Light and Dark." She uses sources from literature in conjunction with anthropological analyses of shamanism to discuss what she regards as an ancient archetype or model for human behavior. She compares and contrasts figures from the American Southwest, ancient Greece, and Renaissance Europe to describe the archetype of the shaman.

The last chapter in this volume is my own contribution, "Oliver La Farge, Writer and Anthropologist." La Farge as writer summarizes, in some sense, the relationship between anthropology and literature, because he was at once a successful writer of fiction, who won the Pulitzer Prize for his novel *Laughing Boy*, and a respected anthropologist who conducted fieldwork and produced careful ethnographic descriptions. In many ways, his life and works show the creativity possible from an active interchange between the two fields.

Philip A. Dennis

MAKING MYSTERIES WITH
NAVAJO MATERIALS

Tony Hillerman

ABSTRACT

Tony Hillerman writes mystery novels set on the Navajo Reservation in the American Southwest. His protagonists are Navajo Tribal Policemen who solve crimes set on the Reservation. By following them, we learn in some small degree to think like Navajos ourselves. Hillerman is a careful student of Navajo culture who uses his own experiences among The People as well as his reading of Navajo ethnography in creating fiction. Here, in an informal and entertaining way, Hillerman tries to involve readers in the process of writing ethnographic mysteries. He explains his own thought processes, the plot choices to be made as he writes, and the secondary importance he attaches to ethnography as opposed to storytelling.

I'd like to begin by referring to a chapter in a book I'm writing where I happen to be stuck. The working title of this book is *A Thief in Time*, and it concerns those people who ransack Indian ruins and steal the pottery and sell it at considerable profit. The spot we're in, my characters and I, involves Jim Chee, my protagonist, sitting in a police car on Chaco Mesa looking down into Chaco Canyon at the Chaco Cultural Center; he's remembering his wife's funeral. I, of course, have to recreate that funeral in the memory of my character and in the minds of my readers. Here a problem arises. Jim Chee is a very modern Navajo. He's skeptical; he's cynical; he's a graduate of Arizona State University, and he's a graduate of the FBI academy. He has his doubts about some of his tribe's traditions. He's a distant descendant of Chee Dodge, one of the most famous Navajo leaders, who himself was a skeptic about a lot of Navajo beliefs. Chee's wife was, however, not only a very traditional woman, but came from a very traditional clan, the Bitter Water, and has a very tradtional family; so I think, "What kind of funeral would he be remembering?"

The situation is complicated by the fact that the funeral would be over in the Checkerboard reservation, the east side of the Navajo reservation where Navajo culture is mixed with a lot of Pueblo Indian beliefs and with the Native American Church. Well, as I do frequently in a situation such as this, I pass the buck to a friend, in this case a young man by the name of Dennis Tsosie, who lives over at Whitehorse Lake at the Checkerboard and is a pretty traditional fellow. I ask Dennis, and he tells me, "First, why don't you have her, before she dies, ask him to have a traditional funeral?" And I say, "Good idea, I'll do that." Then he tells me how they would have a traditional funeral on the Checkerboard in 1987 as opposed to how such funerals are supposed to be. I listen carefully and take notes.

Three days later, I get a letter from Dennis that says, "Dear Mr. Hillerman, after I talked to you, I went over to my mother's house and my grandfather was there, and I told him what I talked to you about and what I told you, and they said, 'Dennis, you told him all wrong.' And here is what I should have told you." The letter has three pages, front and back, about what really happens in a funeral on the Checkerboard in 1987. Dennis says that in the cases he remembers, they usually call a funeral home; then he gives me a modern description, and I'm left approximately where I started, confused about what my character is going to remember about this funeral. I will resolve it, as I usually do in a case like this, by talking to perhaps two more people and getting more confusion—confusion, thy name is Navajo! Then I will try to guess right. One of the big advantages of writing about Navajos is that it's hard to be wrong, because, with more than sixty clans, there is enough variation in Navajo culture that whatever I say, it's probably right somewhere on the Reservation.

I can get away with the memory of the funeral. Actually, I'm indulging a whim to tell people about this funeral and how the Navajo conduct it and why. I can get away with it under the rules I play by because it is germane to the plot. This book is going to be very much about graves and the vandalism of graves—the stealing of art by those who sell it—and about anthropologists who despoil graves in their own way. Very early, therefore, I want to get the character and the reader thinking about the business of graves and the body after death. I can thereby justify imposing on people who really aren't buying an anthropological text on the Navajo, but a piece of entertainment. I can tell them more about Navajo funerals than they ever intended to know.

This business of making ethnographic material germane to the plot might sound difficult, but on one level it is very simple. For example, in a book that's just been published, *Skinwalkers*, there is a scene in which my character has been to a place where a body was found and he's looking at the tracks left by either the killer or somebody who's been there. To insert my ethnographic material, I need ask only whether the person who made the tracks was a Navajo or a white man. The question gives me an excuse to say he was a Navajo and explain why he was a Navajo. In this case, the reasons were: (a) he didn't step over the body—well, a white man might not step over the body either; (b) he carefully avoided a path of water, the crossing of which is a Navajo taboo violation (probably a white man wouldn't have avoided that); and (c) when his tracks crossed the place a snake crawled, he shuffled his feet, erasing the snake's tracks, which a Navajo would do without thinking, just as we don't step on a crack in the sidewalk because, as the saying goes, "step on a crack, break your mother's back." This example is one of those peculiar cultural things that I'm always looking for an opportunity to include in my novels. It is usually very easy, but only on a very superficial level, because the rules you play by in writing a mystery don't allow footnotes, and they don't allow digressions. I'd be tempted to digress into the Navajo attitude toward snakes, or water, but I can't get away with that in writing mysteries. I have to let anthropologists deal with these deeper details. Another book provides still another example of an easy ethnographic insertion. A policeman is looking for a cave where he knows a murder has occurred. I have him in the bottom of a canyon, coming out of a small canyon into a larger one. The problem involves direction. Does he turn upstream or downstream? The plot requires that the cave be downstream, so I have to have him turn downstream. It's a fifty-fifty chance. I hate coincidences in fiction! I can have him turn upstream and run into some obstacles and come downstream and waste four or five paragraphs. I can have him guess right, but I don't like that. Here's one of those opportunities that, if you're playing the game I'm playing, enable you to utilize some Navajo ethnography. My Navajo policeman, in fact, knows something that would tell him to turn downstream. I have him hear frogs croaking. There are very few frogs in this very desert country. The frogs would be downstream where the canyon empties into Lake Powell. Now, why do the frogs croaking mean anything to him? I skip back into the first chapter where I have a dialogue between the old man who's about to be murdered and a shaman. There the old man tells the shaman of taboo violations, and I insert one more violation, killing a frog, either accidentally or not. This violation is a Navajo taboo, and it causes crippling. It appears in Chapter One, then again in Chapter Seventeen, where the policeman remembers the violation when he hears the frogs, and he knows to turn right to Lake Powell. The readers, whether they want to be or not, are informed about a Navajo belief regarding violation of a taboo. The problem is that the reader gets only a glimpse. He doesn't get as much meaning as I would like to provide. The solution to this problem is to continue writing these kinds of mysteries. If the writer lives long enough and the readers are patient, they will eventually accumulate a whole head-full of unrelated information about Navajo, Hopi, and Zuni cultures. Once in a while, the plot gives you a good opportunity. After all, because I control the plot, I can make the opportunity! A book called *The Blessing Way* turns basically on an Enemy-Way ceremony, which was the name I gave the book. However, the editor for some reason didn't like the name and called it *The Blessing Way* instead. That name had really nothing to do with the book, but several people thought it was a religious book and gave it to their aunts, who write me indignant letters. The plot of this book requires that the Navajo policeman identify a person believed to be a witch. One of them is having an Enemy-Way ceremony, which is a special cure for certain kinds of corpse-sicknesses that are caused by witches. On the climactic final day of an Enemy-Way ceremony, the reader gets a quick look inside a hogan where a singer is doing a sandpainting. I describe a little bit of the final day of the ceremony, and, most importantly for the plot, I describe the so-called scalpshooting, in which the witch is symbolically killed. The policeman sees what is used as a scalp. It is a hat, and he knows who owns the hat, so he knows who the people believe the witch to be. Plot is served, and the reader is shown what I believe to be an extremely interesting ceremony.

The plot in another book allowed me to depict another kind of ceremony that illuminates one of the characteristics I like most about the Navajo culture—its respect for women. Navajo society is matrilineal, and the woman's role in the family and in the clan, is more important than the man's. The ceremony, called a kinaaldá, is a girl's puberty rite. It's a very beautiful ceremony, and, because of my plot, I could describe some of the kinaaldá. Again, I wrote about only the last day, because nobody in his right mind, except maybe an anthropologist, wants to sit through seven days of a ceremonial. Certainly a mystery reader wouldn't;

therefore, I take the reader to the last climactic day. Because of clan relationships, I can point out that the policeman would know to come here to find a witness because he knows the witness. He knows that a member of this clan is being initiated and that any right-thinking Navajo would be present. Not only is the witness there, she's a shaman taking part in it, so I can indicate what part she is playing in the ceremony. I can also justify taking the reader inside the hogan on the last night. The plot requires me to have the policeman and the reader find a lantern that has come off a missing helicopter, and, in this final day of the ceremony, the members of the clan will bring in objects that they want to be blessed and put them on a rug in the middle of the hogan. What better place to put my lantern? Thus, I serve the purpose of the plot and get the reader inside a hogan, where he can hear some of these chants and see part of this ceremony.

I am sometimes asked how the Navajos themselves respond to my books. One reaction comes from a Navajo librarian who works on the Papago reservation south of Tucson. We were talking one day about James Welsh, the northern Indian writer who wrote *Winter in the Blood*. We were talking also about *Ceremony* and some of my books, and we were talking about N. Scott Momaday. And I said that I write category fiction— mysteries—and the other guys write mainstream; they are artists really. She said, "We read the others and say, 'Yes, this is us and this is beautiful, but terribly sad. These people are all giving you the true, sad lot of a culture caught in a real problem.' Then we read you and we say, 'Yes, this is us, and we win.'" And she said, "Because of that, with Navajo boys, especially boys, who find it difficult to find anything relevant to read about, we find it very easy to get them reading your stuff."

Another question that I'm sometimes asked is why I don't give more attention to the Pueblo culture, which surrounds the Navajo, and the other cultures. Frankly, I know much less about them. As far as the Pueblos are concerned, I'm probably not going to learn much more about them because the Pueblo philosophy makes their religious rites more secretive. The rites are diminished if an outsider finds out what's going on inside a kiva. So when I do write about the Hopis or the Zunis, the readers see them only through the eyes of a Navajo policeman, who has an interested outsider's information and in fact knows exactly as much about them as I do, no more. Even this much information allows me the opportunity to at least arouse interest for readers in Des Moines, Miami, and Sacramento in cultures that I find downright fascinating. As an example of how I use these cultures, I can refer to *The Dark Wind*, which takes place in the former joint-use area, Hopi and Navajo. In this book, I needed a witness to a crime who would not come forward and admit it, but who would have to be found. I managed to arrange the plot so that this witness was an extraordinary elder member of the probably extinct Hopi Fog Clan, of which members were initiated into the sorcery society. This made him rather fearsome in the eyes of the book's characters. This plot gave me an opportunity to let the reader know what an interested Navajo would know about the sorcery society and the Hopi beliefs about human evolution: that man progressed beyond the state of being an animal and lost the right to move back and forth between the world of animals and the world of humans. Instead of having two hearts, humans had finally only one, and only the sorcery society maintained two-heart characteristics, which allow this transition. The story reflects an unusual way in which the Hopi origin stories, unlike our own, seem to deal with human evolution from a lower state into a higher one.

The same book's plot requires that the reader know exactly when the murder victim was killed. It requires also that the policeman not know this. I knew where I wanted to set the story, and I knew I wanted to use the Hopi religion and ceremonials as much as I could. I arranged for the body to be found by a fellow known as a spruce-messenger. He is the man from one of the kivas who is responsible for the Niman-Kachina, the great ceremony when the Kachinas leave the Hopi village and go back to the other world through the San Francisco peaks. The Hopi have a very rigid liturgical year; so all of these dates are exactly the same. Everyone knows when the ceremony is held and when the spruce-messenger and his party go from the kiva to Kasigi Springs up on Black Mesa to bring back material to the kiva to be processed into prayer sticks and so forth. So, a knowledgeable person would know when the party went to the Springs and came back. They know when this person was killed, and the reader knows too, but they're on their way back to the kiva. It is crucial in the Hopi religion that while these ceremonies are being prepared, the participants' mental attitude be exactly right. No bad thoughts are tolerated. The spruce-messenger is an old man, and he explains this requirement to the people with him. "Be quiet about this," he says, "we can't have police coming in and bothering us about this. Keep your mouths shut until after the ceremony."

Once in a while, I can come up with a plot that I hope will turn on an important philosophical difference between the Navajo and the culture that surrounds them. In *The Dark Wind*, I thought I had such an idea. The Navajo put no value on revenge, and in this novel, a young Navajo is surprised when he first runs into the high value that is assigned to revenge by white people. My character has learned something about Christianity, in which revenge is explicitly ruled out, and he is especially surprised. He sees the clamor for capital punishment, he sees a white world that demands vengeance. He understands the hypocrisy; nevertheless, his own cultural background makes the notion of vengeance seem very peculiar indeed. If a Navajo does something antisocial, it means automatically that he is out of harmony and should be cured. He should go to a shaman and find out what is wrong, what taboos have been involved, and what rituals would put things straight, and he should have the cleansing ceremony done as soon as he can when the thunderstorm season is over. The idea of blaming the person who commits the antisocial act would be as wrong as if we wanted to blame and punish the rock we trip over. The fellow was not responsible for the misdeed. He is controlled by winds, which change color and affect the human in ways over which he has no control.

In general, the rules I play by are these: I'm writing mystery novels. While I know that some of my readers buy my books because they like descriptions of the Arizona landscape and are interested in the culture, I know also that most readers buy my books because they want to get caught up in a story. Therefore, my rule is that I can't use the cultural material unless it is necessary to move the plot along. For example, I have a subplot in a book in which boy meets girl. The boy is a Navajo policeman; the girl is a young woman from Minnesota who teaches second or third grade at Crownpoint School. They meet and have coffee and are sort of introducing themselves. She introduces herself as a school teacher, telling what she's done, what she wants to do, where she went to school. He introduces himself as the son of—he names his mother, his mother's clan, a couple of prominent people on his mother's side of the family; then he names his father's clan; he names his family. It's germane to the plot because they have to be introduced to one another, and it underlies a cultural difference. If I were to be introduced to Navajos in Navajo fashion, I would be introduced as the son of Lucy Grove, and then you would hear about my maternal aunts and my father and my father's family and no mention would be made of what I have done. It's a totally different notion of who we are. If I can get the reader interested at all in these cultural differences, perhaps he'll go to a librarian and be referred to the anthropologists who can explain all this better than I can.

Bibliography of Tony Hillerman's Works

MYSTERY NOVELS

The Blessing Way. New York: Harper and Row, 1970. Honorable mention as Best First Novel, Mystery Writers of America (MWA). American Library Association Best Books of the Year listing.

The Fly on the Wall. New York: Harper and Row, 1972. Honorable Mention for Best Novel, MWA.

The Dance Hall of the Dead. New York: Harper and Row, 1973. Winner of the Edgar Allen Poe Award of the MWA as the best mystery novel of 1973. New York Times Notable Books list.

Listening Woman. New York: Harper and Row, 1977. Book of the Month Club alternative selection. Finalist, MWA best novel competition. New York Times Notable Books list.

People of Darkness. New York: Harper and Row, 1980. New York Times Notable Books list.

The Dark Wind. New York: Harper and Row, 1983. American Library Association Best Books of the Year listing. Book of the Month Club alternate.

The Ghostway. New York: Harper and Row, 1986. Book of the Month Club alternate. New York Times Notable Books list.

Skinwalkers. New York: Harper and Row, 1987. Book of the Month Club alternate. New York Times Notable Books list.

A Thief of Time. New York: Harper and Row, 1988. Book of the Month Club alternate.

The Navajo Tribal Police mysteries have been published in Great Britain, France, Italy, Sweden, Denmark, Germany, Norway, Spain, The Netherlands, and Japan.

CHILDREN'S LITERATURE

The Boy Who Made Dragonfly. New York: Harper and Row, 1972, and the University of New Mexico Press, 1986. Honorable mention for children's literature, Western Writers of America. Junior Book Award, Border Regional Library Association.

NONFICTION

The Great Taos Bank Robbery Albuquerque: University of New Mexico Press, 1971.

New Mexico (with David Muench, photographer). Portland, OR: Graphic Arts Center Publishing Co., 1975.

Rio Grande (with Charles Reynolds, photographer). Portland, OR: Graphic Arts Center Publishing Co., 1976. Book of the Year Award, Border Regional Library Conference.

The Spell of New Mexico. Albuquerque: University of New Mexico Press, 1976.

Indian Country (with Bela Kalman, photographer). Flagstaff, AZ: Northland Press, 1987.

Canyon de Chelly (with Laura Gilpin, photographer). Austin: University of Texas Press, scheduled for publication in 1989.

MYSTERY LITERATURE AND ETHNOGRAPHY: FICTIONAL DETECTIVES AS ANTHROPOLOGISTS

James C. Pierson

ABSTRACT

Kenneth Millar, discussing the major character in the detective novels he wrote under the name Ross Macdonald, maintains that "a good private detective . . . likes to move through society both horizontally and vertically, studying people like an anthropologist. And like an anthropologist he tends to fall a little in love with his subjects" (Ross Macdonald in *Lew Archer, Private Investigator,* 1977, xii). Since Millar/Macdonald is discussing models for characters in his novels, he seems to imply that the activities of fictional detectives, private or not, may teach readers about "other" cultures in much the same way the ethnographer does. This paper examines that implication by discussing and comparing the cultures experienced by various fictional detectives. Some of Ross Macdonald's work is examined, as are novels set in Ireland, Holland, Japan, and South Africa. The emphasis is, however, on works by Tony Hillerman (among the Navajo and their neighbors) and Arthur Upfield (among Aboriginal and white Australians).

Mystery and spy literature make extensive use of a variety of geographic and cultural settings. In most novels of this type, however, the settings are primarily background; any cultural information is very general, almost stereotypic, and of little significance to the story's progress. It may therefore seem presumptuous even to suggest a relationship between ethnographic anthropology and some mystery literature. Nevertheless, there are a number of ambitious writers of detective fiction who include considerable cultural information in an attempt to do more than simply entertain the reader.

The activities of detectives, whether fictional or real, may be of interest to many readers because there is something at least vaguely familiar about their methods. Recognizing a problem, analyzing it, and determining and using methods of solving it are part of almost any occupation. Both Robin Winks (1986, 4, 5), a historian, and William B. Sanders (1974, xx), a sociologist, for example, discuss similarities between their professions' research methods and those of detectives. Mystery writer Ross Macdonald makes observations about detectives and the nature of their work that relate directly to anthropology. He contends that one of the most important qualities of good detectives is a

selfless chameleon aspect which allows them to move on various levels of
society, ranging from the campus to the slums, and fade in and out of the
woodwork on demand. They are able to submerge themselves in the
immediate milieu and behave according to its customs and talk the language:
a little Spanish in East Los Angeles, a little jive in Watts, a little Levi-Strauss
in Westwood. (v)

Although few anthropologists—and likely few detectives—would
claim to be selfless in their work, much of the statement is
consistent with general goals of ethnographic research. Macdonald also claims that "a good private detective . . . likes to
move through society both horizontally and vertically, studying
people like an anthropologist" (xii).

One implication is that fictional detectives who do their jobs
well, as almost all do, are successful at least partly because of
ethnographic knowledge and abilities. It seems logical, therefore,
that the works of fiction in which these detectives appear are
potentially useful sources of information about the various
groups of people dealt with by the detectives. A number of critics
are nevertheless reluctant to consider mystery literature as a
source of sociocultural information. The editors of two fifty-
volume series of classic crime fiction, for example, selected novels
by Tony Hillerman and Arthur Upfield, both of whom use
considerable cultural and geographic description. Hillerman's
novel is *The Fly on the Wall*, his only non-Navajo mystery; the
Upfield novel makes little use of his detective's part-Aboriginal
background. The editors' introduction to the former contends
that "reading about the American Southwest or the West Indies is
pleasant enough, but crime, character, clues, humor, and plot are
apt to be swamped in local color and factuality" (Barzun and
Taylor 1983, Introduction iv-v). Their introduction to Upfield's
work claims that his most admirable novels are his later ones that
"dispense with exotic scenery and native lore and concentrate on
character, mystery, and clues" (Barzum and Taylor 1976, i). It is
not just that ethnographic information is not considered
potentially significant; ethnographic references and contextual
descriptions seem to be considered distracting at best and
incompatible with the important qualities of a good mystery at
worst.

Some critics and novelists disagree with such limitations.
Margaret J. King (1980), for example, contends that whereas
considerable attention has been paid to detective stories as a part
of Western cultures, there has been little attention to what
detective stories can "teach readers about culture" (255). The

educational task of the authors is recognized as a difficult one: both the crime and the "foreign way of life" must be carefully described. John G. Cawelti (1977), on the other hand, maintains that although "the detective story situation works with many different cultural settings because the investigation of a puzzling crime casts light on the workings of a society by catching it at a moment of anomaly and disruption" (39), it is a Western cultural product, and its standard form is not adequate to portray most non-Western cultures. Even detective stories featuring cultural mediators or brokers are limited, claims Cawelti, because such characters fall into the Western tradition of mythical figures who perpetuate a fantasy that the inherent cultural conflicts between traditional and modern/colonial cultures can be "mediated and justly resolved" (40). Cawelti considers Arthur Upfield's fictional detective, Napoleon Bonaparte, to be one of the most successful examples of cultural conflict and ambiguity in detective fiction and a "major achievement" in the genre (41). The Bonaparte character, however, remains a fantasy to Cawelti for the reasons just discussed.

The potential in detective novels for cross-cultural education is obviously open to question. The rest of this paper is therefore concerned with examining the extent and realization of that potential in detective novels set in a variety of cultural and geographic settings. The discussion that follows is selective, emphasizing the work of writers whose books, all in series, are readily available in bookstores and libraries—these are the books likely to attract the general reader's attention. It begins with a very brief consideration of books that, whatever their appearances, tend to rely on quite general sociocultural information. It concludes with an examination of some works by Upfield and Hillerman.

LEW ARCHER AND OTHER DETECTIVES AS ETHNOGRAPHERS

A logical starting place would seem to be Ross Macdonald's novels. Ironically, however, the detective created by the author whose comments inspired this paper rarely gives readers specific ethnographic information. The problem, if that is what it is, is that Macdonald's novels are set in a complex society and that the characters in each are from quite diverse backgrounds. This not only tries the ethnographic abilities of his detective, Lew Archer, it also means that the reader is exposed to only a bit of the meaning of that diversity. The reader does not always share in the detective's specific knowledge about the people with whom he is dealing. Just as it would be impossible for even a team of ethnographers to provide a thorough overview of such settings and the people in them, it is impossible for Macdonald, through his detective, to do so. Thus Lew Archer may function like an anthropologist, but the nature of the society in which he works tends to keep his exploits from providing solid ethnographic examples.

The ethnographic potential of other detective novelists is similarly limited by the authors' broad perspectives. Some detective novels that initially seem to include numerous cultural details prove on further examination to provide only a bit of local color. A series of novels by Eric Wright featuring a Toronto police inspector and a series by Peter Corris about a private investigator in Sydney offer similarly impressionistic portraits of their specific urban, national, and cultural settings. There are few details that give a reader insight into the cultural traits of Canadians or Australians. The settings are used to make the novels appear different from other mystery novels, but are not utilized to make the stories themselves much different.

A series of novels by James Melville featuring Superintendent Tetsuo Otani and other detectives of the Hyogo Prefectural Police in Japan makes somewhat better use of its cultural settings. A few details of Japanese etiquette, religious practices, and other cultural traits appear in each book. A type of Japanese puppet plays a crucial role in *A Sort of Samurai*; ivory *netsuke* figures are central to *The Ninth Netsuke*, and traditional Japanese housing and living styles are important topics in *The Chrysanthemum Chain*. Although most elements of Japanese culture are discussed only generally, the detectives' tendencies to learn about both foreign and Japanese cultural traits as they work make them nevertheless similar to ethnographers attempting to piece together cultural information. The ethnographic picture is simply a fragmentary one that portrays only a small part of an immense national character and some of the changes and conflicts between that character and elements of Western life.

Irish Police Chief Inspector of Detectives Peter McGarr, the central character in a series of mysteries by Bartholomew Gill, encounters a variety of people and situations while solving crimes that take him to both rural and urban (especially Dublin) settings. There are generalized glimpses and insights into rural Irish life, sporting and leisure activities, and family and pub life.

Considerable attention is also given to the Irish Republican Army. The novels are not ethnographic, but they do provide some of the flavor of selected aspects of Irish culture.

Detective novels by Dutch author Janwillem van de Wetering have been praised for both their descriptions of Amsterdam and their originality, the result of the author's Zen-influenced orientation. Van de Wetering's novels and detectives deal with several topics that are of ethnographic interest. Most relevant here are Amsterdam's social and geographical components and cultural diversity.

Each novel contains characters and situations that take the detectives to different sections of Amsterdam or other parts of Holland. As a result the series has been noted as a useful introduction to Amsterdam (Shearer 1986). Non-Dutch visitors to or residents of Amsterdam provide van de Wetering's readers with general information about a number of different cultures. Although van de Wetering's first detective novel was titled *Outsider in Amsterdam*, each of his novels includes at least one character fitting that description. That first outsider is a Papuan with colonial ties to Holland; others are from Japan, Surinam, and Curaçao. Cultural diversity is further demonstrated through characters from a religious commune, or from a distant Dutch province, as well as others who are Jewish, Italian, American, and Arabic. Obviously, van de Wetering casts a broad net in all of his novels. This broad net does not allow extensive examination of Amsterdam or the cultural groups, but it does provide the basis for a generally informative and appealing series of books.

Another relevant series of detective stories, or "police procedurals," is by James McClure, a former South African journalist. The series features a white South African detective and his Zulu partner, who together are able to work in almost any cultural setting. The novels involve both black and white victims and/or suspects and illustrate a number of characteristics of apartheid, including white attitudes towards blacks and towards each other. Black adaptations to the South African situation surface frequently as the cases are investigated. In *Snake*, for example, the reader learns about black living conditions, such as the absence of electricity (1975, 46), and the scarcity of meat in blacks' diets (54). He learns also about whites' stereotyping of blacks as being a mixture of the worst characteristics of all races (116) and as believing that all whites are rich (126). Finally, he is presented with some alleged black superstitions or beliefs about

certain people being witch doctors or wizards (74). Subtle details
and local terms and ideas are scattered throughout the novels, but
most noticeable is a general sense of tensions and prejudice.

McClure is quite conscious of his presentation of South Africa
to outsiders. He notes that defining the fictional city of
Trekkersburg, based on his former home, was difficult. "It was, I
felt, not unlike writing science fiction, in that I had to get across
what amounted to a totally alien world, with its strange
languages, customs, scenery, and laws" (1986). This statement is
as applicable to anthropological ethnography as it is to science
fiction. It is therefore interesting that McClure has written
detailed nonfiction books about police departments in Liverpool
and San Diego on the basis of long-term first-hand research. It is
apparent that McClure's journalistic experiences give him
information and insights that are similar to those of more formal,
methodologically oriented researchers; he uses these data in works
of fiction as well as nonfiction.

ETHNOGRAPHIC MYSTERY NOVELS?

The authors of the works just discussed place their detectives in
complex sociocultural settings. Arthur Upfield and Tony Hillerman place their detectives, however, in much more specific
cultural units and settings, an Australian Aboriginal culture and
Navajo culture, respectively. The detectives are also at least
partially educated in the white cultures of their respective settings
and thus have the ability to interpret relatively subtle aspects of at
least two cultures. In fact, this ability is usually necessary for the
solution of their cases. The detectives subsequently provide the
reader with cultural information throughout a case rather than
only in isolated places. Because their socialization took place in
cultures that interact closely with the natural environment,
descriptions of the physical settings are also important and
detailed.

Despite the similarities just discussed, however, there are some
important contrasts between the two authors' detectives and
novels. Some of these are examined below.

ARTHUR W. UPFIELD AND NAPOLEON BONAPARTE

Arthur Upfield's novels featuring part-Aboriginal, part-white
Detective Inspector Napoleon Bonaparte may be even better
known now, more than twenty years after Upfield's death, than
they were when they were written. They are regularly available in

reprint, and it is almost certain that a knowledgeable librarian or bookstore clerk will suggest them if asked for mystery or detective novels with anthropological themes.

Napoleon Bonaparte is the main character in twenty-nine of Upfield's books, almost all of which take place in isolated areas of Australia. The detective's mixed ancestry directs at least some attention in each book to cultural and sometimes implied biological contrasts between Aboriginal and white Australians, especially as they affect Bonaparte's behavior or thinking. Bonaparte is an initiated Aboriginal male as a result of experiences and knowledge acquired late in life, which include tracking skills and religion; he was first formally educated in the "white world" (he even went through the university) after being found with his dead Aboriginal mother by whites when he was an infant. He is acquainted with both Aborigines who have been influenced by white cultural patterns, and with whites who have little formal education. Although some of his physical features demonstrate his part-Aboriginal ancestry, Bonaparte rarely fails to gain the respect of whites quickly when he chooses; when he does not choose to, he is able to play the subordinate role that most whites expect of persons of Aboriginal ancestry. As a Detective Inspector, Bonaparte is a representative of the government, but he has the freedom and the sometimes vague charge to stay with a case until it has been solved. These cases can apparently take him anywhere in Australia and do not always involve interaction with other Aborigines.

Upfield's accounts of outback cultures examine more than differences between Aborigines and whites. As has been discussed effectively by others (e.g., Cawelti 1977, 39-40; King 1980, 258), both groups have subdivisions. Bonaparte regularly contrasts the "wild" or traditional Aborigines and the less traditional ones who live near white stations and settlements. Another *very* small subgroup is represented by Bonaparte, the bicultural part Aborigine. There are several subdivisions among whites as well, including outback station owners and other people of property; station hands and other workers; and representatives of the government and other components of the distant, more "modern" national culture. Missionaries are noticeably absent from most Upfield books. Although it would be instructive to examine each of these groups, attention herein is limited to Aborigines.

A problem arises, immediately, however. It may seem that the multicultural Bonaparte presents an objective perspective of each group and a particularly instructive insider's view of the Aborigine cultures. Yet Upfield tends to send mixed ethnographic messages about Aborigines through Bonaparte, who makes some unfavorable observations about Aborigines despite the great pride that he seems to take in his part-Aboriginal ancestry. It is one thing to have white characters state derogatory attitudes about Aborigines, if that is part of the white world view, but it is quite another to have the hero, an apparently proud and well-adjusted part-Aboriginal, do the same. Upfield's novels are consequently sometimes confusing or misleading in an ethnographic sense because it is not always clear whether the perspective that is afforded is Upfield's or that of an "assimilated part-Aborigine," as interpreted by Upfield. In addition, readers can get conflicting messages about Aborigines from different Upfield books. Some specific examples help illustrate these points and the other types of ethnographic information the books contain.

Some of Upfield's plots center around elements of traditional Aboriginal cultures such as the importance of sacred stones and other objects and places (*The Will of the Tribe*), and the practice of causing the death of others through "pointing the bone." The tracking skills of many Aboriginal males, including Bonaparte, the knowledge and ability to influence events far beyond their own travels, the threats of punishment for breaking taboos, and the various spiritual beliefs are frequently part of Aboriginal behavior in Upfield's books. Upfield includes subtle but effective references to cultural traits such as the sitting postures of Aboriginal males, the etiquette of conversation that requires several casual topics to be discussed before getting to the reason for the conversation, and the "shutters" that are said to close in the eyes of an Aborigine when proper etiquette has not been followed or an inappropriate subject is pursued. If there is an ethnographic shortcoming in these and some other cultural references, it is that Upfield, through Bonaparte, tends to imply that there was much more uniformity among Aboriginal cultures than ethnographic records indicate.

A more serious shortcoming is that Upfield's Bonaparte often struggles to limit the influence of his Aboriginal heritage on his behavior as a detective. In one sense, such situations are ethnographically significant because they show the reader a conflict likely experienced by many people caught between two cultures. In another sense, they tend to demean the traditional culture because Bonaparte's "civilized" self eventually takes control. The struggle is not just implied but is one that Bonaparte recognizes. For example:

> Even the inherited influences of the two races warred for the soul of Napoleon Bonaparte, and it was the very continuity of his warfare which had created Detective Inspector Bonaparte, and which time and again prevented him from sinking back into the more primitive of the two races. (*Man of Two Tribes*, 57)

Although Upfield intends this passage to carry the idea that Bonaparte is a successful detective because he possesses knowledge and skills from two cultures, perhaps combining the best from both, it is phrased in a way that makes one culture appear quite inferior to the other.

In *Bony and the Black Virgin* (1959), Upfield sympathetically portrays a relationship between a white man and an Aboriginal woman, and Bonaparte notes the power of the woman's spirituality. These objective passages are undermined to some extent, however, by Bonaparte's thoughts about Aboriginal workers on white settlements as people who "invariably underdo it or overdo it" (117) and numerous "compliments" about the Aboriginal woman's appearance. These descriptions include "for an aborigine, she was pleasing to behold" (57), and Bonaparte's thoughts that "for an aborigine, she was good-looking" (123). The descriptions appear to be devices to convince readers why a white man would be attracted to an Aboriginal woman (i.e., she was not typical in appearance). The reader's ethnographic detective in this case provides distressingly subjective descriptions in the context of what appears to be an objective examination of a cross-cultural relationship.

In *The Bone is Pointed* (1947), however, Upfield not only examines the potential influence of traditional cultures on a "man of two tribes" like Bonaparte but also has the character make numerous observations that stress the strength and importance of Aboriginal cultures and the negative influence of white society on many Aborigines. Bonaparte, for example, explains that Aboriginal superiority in the bush is owing to the "apprenticeship" served by Aborigines while young rather than to natural abilities (105). He is described as "the man who had so often proved that aboriginal blood and brains were equal to those of the white man" (31). He points out that "in many things it is the aboriginal who is the highly developed civilized being and the white man who is the savage" (45), and he suggests that "in this country colour is no bar to a man's progress providing that he has twice the ability of his rivals" (53-54).

Bonaparte's attempts to solve a missing person case that becomes a murder case lead to his being "boned" (a form of sorcery) by local Aborigines. Although the murderer is white, his close relationships with the local Aborigines cause them, unsolicited, to try to help him. The Aborigines are aware that he killed the missing man, who was consistently cruel to them. Bonaparte recognizes that he is being followed and boned. He nearly dies, and he experiences another struggle between his Aboriginal and white selves. In this case, however, readers get a sense of the power of the Aboriginal beliefs. Most importantly, when Bonaparte does survive, it is because the boning is stopped, not because his white will triumphs. From the beginning, Bonaparte anticipates his struggle with the local Aborigines as a potentially difficult one because the Aborigines will not make the "stupid mistakes" whites usually do (92).

In general, *The Bone is Pointed* contains an objective and understanding picture of Aboriginal people and cultures and the potential problems of culture change. Many subsequent Upfield books offer less objective descriptions of Aboriginal cultures. Overall, however, Upfield's use of a part-Aboriginal hero and other Aboriginal characters at all is unusual for the time period during which his books were originally published (the twenties through the mid-sixties). At the same time, some of the situations Bonaparte encounters and his reactions to them may perpetuate stereotypes of Aborigines. Upfield's descriptions of Australian landscapes and the relationships of various cultural groups with the land and with each other are often vivid, but the perspective is that of a white with extensive outback experience, even though the protagonist is part-Aboriginal. Upfield does not often try to present an Aboriginal perspective, although Bonaparte's background makes him seem to be doing so. Bonaparte's main influences are white rather than Aboriginal, and these influences affect the ethnographic perspective.

TONY HILLERMAN, JOE LEAPHORN, AND JIM CHEE

Tony Hillerman's mysteries featuring Navajo policemen share several features with Upfield's novels. The mechanisms used by Hillerman to introduce cultural elements, however, contrast more with Upfield's than is initially apparent. For example, Hillerman consistently presents a Navajo perspective. His presentation of Navajo culture is a much more contextual, humanistic one than is Upfield's presentation of Aboriginal cultures, at least partly because of the differences in their detectives.

The first three of Hillerman's seven "Navajo" novels feature Navajo Tribal Police Lieutenant Joe Leaphorn, the next three feature Officer Jim Chee, and the latest features both. Certain characteristics that are the result of growing up in Navajo culture help make Chee and Leaphorn effective police detectives. Their familiarity with Navajo culture is obviously important, but their Navajo emphases on harmony and the interconnections of things and events make them discount coincidences and carefully consider all clues, including irregularities and inconsistencies. Both possess tracking skills and excellent memories that were developed through long, careful training. Chee at various times reflects on how these skills were developed, helping the reader see their significance in traditional settings and their cultural rather than biological basis.

Leaphorn is older and somewhat more comfortable (or familiar) with the ways of whites. Chee's connections to Navajo traditions, especially through his training to be a singer, or ritual leader, are strong. He finds certain Navajo beliefs, such as those in "skinwalkers" or practitioners of witchcraft, more credible and less harmful than does Leaphorn. Neither Chee nor Leaphorn has a thorough understanding of *both* white and Navajo cultures. Subsequently, neither is a so-called fantasy figure like Bonaparte, who is able to resolve cultural differences and misunderstandings. Chee, in fact, is sometimes surprised by whites' behavior and beliefs, which makes his character useful for illustrating Navajo culture and comparing it to that of non-Navajos. In some situations, the differences are subtle yet significant. Since revenge is not a motive for action among Navajos, for example, Chee is slow to realize in *The Dark Wind* that revenge is the cause of what seems to him to be unpredictable behavior. Both Chee and Leaphorn deal with whites in their jobs and often feel obliged to talk when it seems not only unnecessary but rude: "Chee was conscious that Bales was waiting for him to say something. This white man's custom of expecting a listener to do more than listen was contrary to Chee's courteous Navajo conditioning" (*The Ghostway*, 5). Chee has more of these thoughts not only because he is still learning about whites but also because he spends considerable time with or thinking about his white girlfriend. In one passage, Chee ponders her noticing his drinking the water with which he had just rinsed his coffee cup. To him, his behavior was so automatic that initially he couldn't understand her remark; hauling water most of his life made him so careful of using water that "it had seemed odd to Chee that not wasting water had seemed odd" to her (*Skinwalkers*, 146).

In other situations, the cultural differences are less subtle. In *People of Darkness*, for example, Chee reflects on what seems to him to be a strange inscription on a white woman's tombstone:

> Everything about the white man's burial customs seemed odd to Chee. The Navajo lacked this sentimentality about corpses. Death robbed the body of its value. Even its identity was lost with the departing *chindi*. What the ghost left behind was something to be disposed of with a minimum of risk of contamination to the living. The names of the dead were left unspoken, certainly not carved in stone. (11-12)

Some whites' stereotypes about Indians occasionally trouble Chee, and his reactions can also provide useful contexts for ethnographic information. In one situation, a white who generalized about Indians being good trackers receives an informative lesson from Chee about how and why some Navajos are good trackers while others aren't. The fact that the tracking of people, animals, and vehicles is important in Chee's (and Leaphorn's) work makes this explanation an important one; Chee's tracking abilities are subsequently considered by readers to be highly trained skills. Bonaparte's tracking abilities in Upfield's novels seem to be the result of a much more vague and consequently somewhat mysterious "apprenticeship."

In another case, the common conception among white visitors that many Indians look alike causes Chee to think about the obvious differences he sees not only among Navajo, Hopi, and Zuni individuals but also among Navajos from different areas. These differences, based not only on cultural and kinship differences but also on physical features, are often important to understanding the elements of a crime and its aftermath. It is a lesson on diversity *among* the Navajos, not just between them and their neighbors.

Chee, in *The Ghostway*, acquaints the reader with the Navajo death practices of preparing the body so the journey of the *chindi* will be completed. When death occurs in a hogan, Chee also describes the proper steps in removing the corpse, plugging the smoke hole, and abandoning the dwelling to the ghost. Knowledge of these procedures is important because their presence or absence can tell the policeman and reader a great deal about what has happened if other evidence is not available. In fact, knowing the importance of belongings or of behavior is often crucial to the Navajo policeman. Chee, for example, risks ghost contamination by entering a hogan with a corpse hole in it and finds a missing man's medicine bundle. This discovery immediately informs Chee that the man is dead because the bundle would have been "his most treasured belonging" and he would not have willingly left it (*The Ghostway*, 155). The significance of the bundle and the discovery is demonstrated in a passage in which Chee recalls collecting the contents for his own Four Mountains Bundle and considers the even greater difficulty the man would have had years earlier in getting to the four distant areas. It is an important clue for Chee and gives the reader information about several elements of Navajo culture.

Hillerman's detectives acquaint readers with such topics as the Navajo-Hopi land dispute, Navajo beliefs in ghosts and witchcraft (and those who oppose such beliefs and their consequences), Zuni Shalako ceremonies and preparations for them, and Hopi ceremonials. Readers learn also about the roles on the reservation of outsiders such as anthropologists, FBI and other federal agents, drug dealers, and trading post operators. There is considerable attention to Navajo rituals and those who lead or need them. Kin and clan relations are shown to be all-important in meeting and interviewing people and anticipating their behavior in a given situation. The detectives' actions, thoughts, and observations also bring out much more subtle elements of Navajo culture such as the etiquette of approaching another's dwelling, the rudeness of looking directly into someone else's eyes or pointing at them, and the actions that characterize a culture in which water is a scarce, valuable commodity.

It is difficult to separate the ethnographic information in Hillerman's novels from the rest of the text, not only because there is so much of it but also because it is well integrated. Hillerman's novels focus on Navajo culture much more than Upfield's focus on Aboriginal cultures largely because Hillerman's detectives are Navajos working for the Navajo Tribal Police. Despite the feelings of some Navajos, they are working for the Navajo; Bonaparte, whatever his own background and attitudes toward the local Aborigines in any given case, is a representative of the larger society. The Navajo police have been trained off the reservation and have been formally educated among whites in other contexts, such as the university, but their identities are those of Navajos with ties to specific regions and clans. When there is the possibility of a divided loyalty, as when

Chee has an opportunity to join the FBI and is romantically involved with a white teacher who does not want to remain forever on the reservation, his struggle does not involve the conflicting parts of his identity; instead, he must simply determine what will be the most appropriate decision. It is significant that Chee chooses to stay on the reservation for at least the time being. The decision is difficult, but Chee's Navajo enculturation and interest in continuing his training to be a singer give a meaning to his life that never really surfaces in Upfield's presentation of Aboriginal cultures.

Hillerman's novels are not ethnographic texts in disguise, but his detectives fulfill Ross Macdonald's aforementioned suggestions much better than do those of other writers largely because of the contexts in which he has them operating. Hillerman is commendably cautious about the use of ethnographic details, which he says must be "germane to the plot" ("Mystery, Country Boys, and the Big Reservation," 142). His concern for presenting the cultural traits and situations as objectively and realistically as possible is evident throughout the novels. It also is implied by the fact that the books are read with interest and pleasure by at least some Navajos (ibid. 147). It is unlikely that there has been similar interest in Upfield's books among any Australian Aborigines.

Ethnography Is Where You Find It

Detective literature has an apparent potential for extensive ethnographic content because of protagonists who regularly interact with representatives of different cultural settings. The potential is, however, rarely realized. Despite the apparent disapproval of some critics and a lack of interest or ambition among most mystery writers, a few authors of detective fiction do carefully integrate considerable ethnographic detail into their novels. Their detectives inform accurately as well as entertain.

Ross Macdonald's statement about detectives as anthropologists, quoted earlier, refers to detectives who provide ethnographic information about "other" groups. Yet, the most successful detective-ethnographers seem to be those who work primarily in their own cultures and provide ethnographic information to outsiders (readers). Their own and other cultures are clarified through comparisons and contrasts. The most successful integration of ethnographic materials into police or detective novels is found in novels by Tony Hillerman. Hillerman's policemen are credible, somewhat fallible, and, as participants in Navajo culture, unlikely to create or perpetuate ethnic stereotypes in readers' minds. Their behavior is consistent with their experiences and professional and cultural training. They do not become fantasy figures, as other ethnic detectives have been labeled, because their emphasis is on being Navajo within the larger society rather than on seeming to resolve conflicts between different ways of life. Most important in my opinion is the fact that the police detectives regularly provide information about Navajos, whites, Hopis, Zunis, FBI agents, anthropologists, and other groups of people. The information not only does not interfere with plot and characterization, as some commentators seem to fear, but is part of them. The novels can therefore increase cultural understanding, a worthwhile goal for ethnography in any format.

Note

Writing this paper involved anthropological research in the sense that it brought me into extensive contact with a "culture" of novels and literary criticism and analysis. The number of secondary sources is particularly impressive; a useful guide for sorting out the more relevant ones has been *Detective and Mystery Fiction: An International Bibliography of Secondary Sources* by Walter Albert (1985).

I wish to thank Linda Stockham for typing the manuscript and the symposium organizers for their patience and hospitality.

Works Cited

Albert, Walter. *Detective and Mystery Fiction: An International Bibliography of Secondary Sources.* Madison, IN: Brownstone, 1985.

Barzun, Jacques, and Wendell H. Taylor. Introduction to *The Fly on the Wall*, by Tony Hillerman. New York: Garland, 1983.

———. Preface to *The Bone is Pointed*, by Arthur W. Upfield. New York: Garland, 1976.

Cawelti, John G. "Murder in the Outback: Arthur W. Upfield." *The New Republic* 177, no. 5 (1977):39-44.

Corris, Peter. *The Dying Trade.* New York: Fawcett, 1980.

———. *White Meat.* New York: Fawcett, 1981.

———. *The Marvelous Boy.* New York: Fawcett, 1982.

Gill, Bartholomew. *McGarr on the Cliffs of Moher.* New York: Penguin, 1978.

———. *McGarr and the Politican's Wife.* New York: Penguin, 1977.

———. *McGarr at the Dublin Horse Show.* New York: Scribner's, 1979.

———. *McGarr and the Method of Descaries.* New York: Scribner's, 1984.

Hillerman, Tony. *The Blessing Way.* New York: Avon, 1970.

———. *The Dance Hall of the Dead.* New York: Avon, 1973.

———. *The Fly on the Wall.* New York: Avon, 1971.

———. *Listening Woman.* New York: Avon, 1978.

———. *People of Darkness.* New York: Avon, 1980.

———. *The Dark Wind.* New York: Avon, 1982.

———. *The Ghostway.* New York: Avon, 1984.

———. "Mystery, Country Boys, and the Big Reservation." In *Colloquium on Crime: Eleven Renowned Mystery Writers Discuss Their Work*, ed. Robin W. Winks, 124-47. New York: Scribner's, 1986.

———. *Skinwalkers.* New York: Harper, 1986.

King, Margaret J. "Binocular Eyes: Cross-Cultural Detectives." *The Armchair Detective* 13(1980): 253-60.

McClure, James. *Snake.* New York: Pantheon, 1975.

———. *Spike Island: Portrait of a British Police Division.* New York: Laurel, 1980.

———. *Cop World: Inside an American Police Force.* New York: Laurel, 1984.

———. "A Bright Grey." In *Colloquium on Crime: Eleven Renowned Mystery Writers Discuss Their Work*, ed. Robin W. Winks, 167-88. New York: Scribner's, 1986.

Macdonald, Ross. *Ross Macdonald's Lew Archer, Private Investigator.* New York: Mysterious, 1977.

Melville, James. *A Sort of Samurai.* New York: Fawcett, 1981.

———. *The Chrysanthemum Chain.* New York: Fawcett, 1982.

———. *The Ninth Netsuke.* New York: Fawcett, 1982.

Sanders. William B. *The Sociologist as Detective: An Introduction to Research Methods.* New York: Praeger, 1974.

Shearer, Derek. "Books Offer Clues to Solving the Mystery of a City." Los Angeles *Times* Travel Section, 5 October 1986.

Upfield, Arthur W. *The Bone is Pointed.* New York: Garland, 1947.

———. *Man of Two Tribes.* New York: Scribner's, 1956.

———. *Bony and the Black Virgin.* Sydney: Pan, 1959.

———. *Bony and the Mouse.* Sydney: Pan, 1959.

———. *The Will of the Tribe.* New York: Scribner's, 1962.

van de Wetering, Janwillem. *Outsider in Amsterdam.* New York: Ballantine, 1975.

———. *The Corpse on the Dike.* Boston: Houghton, 1976.

———. *Tumbleweed.* Boston: Houghton, 1976.

———. *Death of a Hawker.* Boston: Houghton, 1977.

———. *The Japanese Corpse.* Boston: Houghton, 1977.

———. *The Blond Baboon.* Boston: Houghton, 1978.

———. *The Maine Massacre.* New York: Pocket Books, 1979.

———. *The Streetbird.* New York: Pocket Books, 1983.

———. *The Rattle-Rat.* New York: Ballantine, 1985.

Winks, Robin W., ed., *Colloquium on Crime: Eleven Renowned Mystery Writers Discuss Their Work*, 1-6. New York: Scribner's, 1986.

Wright, Eric. *Death in the Old Country.* New York: Signet, 1985.

POINT OF VIEW IN
ANTHROPOLOGICAL DISCOURSE

Miles Richardson

ABSTRACT

It is a paradox that Story, the field of literature, can be seen as a behavioral act. Conversely, everyday life, the field of anthropology, can be reduced to a text. Point of view then becomes a strategic location from which the investigation of how being in a story is related to being human may be deepened. Point of view itself is composed of the knowledge the narrator possesses of the text, and the narrator's degree of participation in that textual world. The intersection of the two dimensions produces four distinct narrative selves which appear in four different texts: the "I" of the diary, the God of the Holy Writ, the "it" of the scientific report, and the "we" of everyday life. The ethnographer, as participant-observer, extracts the everyday from its matrix of ho hum facticity and reveals that the world taken for granted is, in fact, fictitious. It is a story. As teller of the human story, the ethnographer comes to resemble Gilgamesh, the Mesopotamian god-king, who, in 2000 B.C., wrote of how he came to know death, and in that knowledge, how he came to be human, that is, how he came to be you and I.

In the search to comprehend what it is to be human, anthropology pursues a multi-paradigmatic strategy. One part of anthropology suggests that the secret of being human lies in our biological makeup; another part of the discipline suggests that the secret resides in the material conditions of our living. In any assessment as to what is fundamental to our being, surely these strategies are correct: cut us and we bleed; deny us the fruits of our labor and we rebel. In addition to being both biological creatures and economic men, however, we are, in the same fundamental manner, storytellers.

There is a story told in anthropological circles (for example, by Gregory Reck [1986]) about Gregory Bateson, who supposedly said:

> There is a story which I have used before and shall use again: A man wanted to know about mind, not in nature, but in his private large computer. He asked it (no doubt in his best Fortran), "Do you compute that you will ever think like a human being?" The machine then set to work to analyze its own computational habits. Finally, the machine printed its answer on a piece of paper, as such machines do. The man ran to get the answer and found, neatly typed, the words:
>
> *That reminds me of a story.*
>
> (Bateson 1979, 13)

31

Storytelling is a fundamental quality of our everyday life. To be in a story is to be human; or better, the reverse, to be human is to be in a story.

A story is a narrative; everyday life is behavior. How might the two be related? I discuss herein the relation of different kinds of texts to life and then compare the ethnographer's text to the literary story of Gilgamesh.

THE NARRATIVE ACT

Until recently, literary criticism, inspired by the formalist methods of New Criticism or of structuralism, approached the text as a contained artifact, a thing in itself, detached from both author and reader. Narrative was art, and art was coolly cerebral. In her exploration of point of view in prose fiction, Susan Sniader Lanser has challenged this perspective of narrative as refined cognition. She writes,

> Because writing of literature is verbal activity, an inquiry into point of view at the level of the literary act might well begin by situating fictional writing within the framework of all language use. Though the writing of fiction is, of course, a particular type of linguistic act, it shares with all verbal production a conventional structure which is realized in a particular context. This means that literary communication is basically similar, rather than opposed, to other modes of verbal behavior. (1981, 64)

If intentionally we blur the distinction between literature and everyday life, then the literary text becomes simply another way of speaking. The text becomes an act, a speech act in which point of view becomes an important determinant in the shaping of the text.

Two of the various components Lanser discusses as composing point of view are especially appropriate to the task of relating narrative to behavior, story to everyday life (158-62). These are the privilege or knowledge the narrator has of the textual world and the representation or position of the narrator in the text. Let us continue to follow Lanser and treat these components as continuous variables. Knowledge the narrator has of the events he is recounting ranges from near total ignorance to God-like omniscience. The position of the narrator in the text moves from that of narrator as the principal participant (the protagonist) of his story toward that of the detached and objective observer who stands at the margins of the world he is relating.

To these two, continuous dimensions, I wish to insert a third component, a constant. Either as a participant or as an observer,

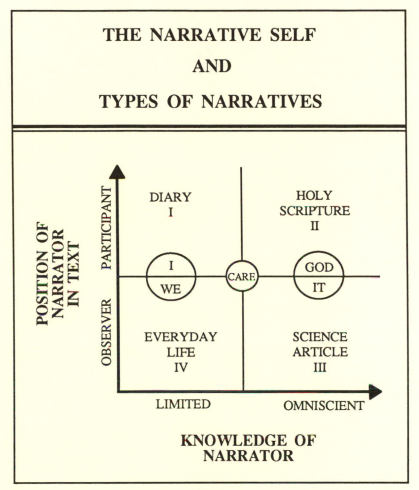

Fig. 1

as one who possesses limited or complete knowledge, the narrator cares. Even though he may know all and observe from the extreme edge of the text, the narrator remains focused on the textual world and is concerned about the outcome of the events occurring there.

The two continuous dimensions of textual knowledge and position in the text, as well as the constant, care, may all be displayed graphically as four distinct narrative selves whose speech results in four distinct narratives (figure 1).

Quadrant I is the intersection of limited knowledge and engaged participation. The narrator has only a circumscribed amount of information and is engaged in the text. The text is a diary and the narrator the presumed diarist, who writes, "Today, I ventured forth . . . ."

Quadrant II is the intersection of omniscience and participation. The narrator knows all, but is engaged in the text. The narrator appears as a character in the text, yet the narrator, at least according to the text, is the author of the text. The text is, of course, the Holy Scripture, and the narrator is God—he or she, but third person—as in "And God said, 'Let there be light. . . .'"

Quadrant III is the intersection of omniscience and detached observation. The narrator knows the material completely and stands at the margins of the textual world. The text produced is that of a scientific article. The narrator is the scientist-author who has complete control of the information appearing in the article. If he does not, the referees will reject it because the text seems unclear, or worse, ambiguous. Although scientific information is always subject to change as new theories arise and new hypotheses are confirmed, the individual scientist must appear in control in writing for scientific publication. One senses an illusion of omnipotence in the narrator, even though he or she may not be clearly positioned in the text. The author is at the textual margin in the role of observer, as indicated in the phrase "it has been observed."

Quadrant IV is a textual world seen from the view of a narrating observer who has only a limited comprehension of the story he is telling. Given the constant care, such a combination forms a strange and marvelous world. It is the world of everyday life that you and I, male and female, tell together.

THE BEHAVIORAL NARRATIVE

If a story is like life, then is not life like a story? If a narrative is an act, is not then behavior a narrative? How do the dimensions of quadrant IV constitute the narrative of everyday life? How does an observer who is participating in a world of which he has limited knowledge become the narrative self of everyday life? Where is the narrative text of everyday life?

Let's begin by repeating with Lanser, and for that matter with Ricouer (1979, 73-102), that text is discourse. Discourse is speaking, and speaking is what we are doing now. The text of everyday life is composed of my speaking and your speaking, my speaking out loud and your speaking silently. We, together in our speaking, are constituting the text of everyday life. Where is the text of everyday life? As we speak, it is here, right here, among us.

As circumscribed in quadrant IV, the world of everyday life appears to be a seemingly uniform text spoken in the bland verbs of conventionality. It is, in fact, diversified and even bewildering. At the extreme of near complete detachment and severely limited comprehension, the narrator of the everyday is alienated from his discourse. His text is either a scathing indictment of the insanity of the world or a passionate prayer for knowledge. At the lesser extreme of more engagement, our knowledge of what we speak remains limited. In comparison to the omniscient narrators of the Holy Scripture and of science, we are ignorant. We know not the outcome of everyday life; it is open-ended, and stochastic, and its "ultimate meaning [is] subject only to probability laws" (Perinbanayagan 1985, 12). Ignorant though we may be, nonetheless, we, you and I, speak. We care.

As we participate in our speaking, we also observe what we do. We are not only observers when we say to one another (or to ourselves, which is the same conversation), "Let's look." We are observers even as we participate without that heightened sense of observation. We are observers because we speak.

When we speak, we act, and when we act, as George Herbert Mead (1964) writes, we take the position of the other and act back toward ourselves. From the other's point of view, we become an object to ourselves. When I address you, I also address myself. As I observe you, I also observe myself. In this observational act, the inside of each of us, our subjective I's, become the outside of us, our objective me's. As I am a me to you, I become a me to myself. When I as a subject speak to you, I also speak to me as an object. As I distinguish you, I distinguish myself. In the same manner that the author and the reader come to be in the text, so you and I take shape in the dialogue of everyday.

In Meadian terms, the relationship between you and me is linguistic. Language itself is a vocal gesture that arouses in me the attitude it arouses in you. When a vocal gesture evokes the same response in a speaker that it evokes in the person spoken to, the gesture becomes a significant symbol. In other words, it becomes a name.

In everyday life, even as Adam in the Holy Writ, we name one another. As those who bestow names, we are creating observers even as we participate in the behavior of everyday, and in our naming we, you and I, create our textual world.

The narrative selves of the everyday text are positioned in a world in which they have limited knowledge. Where stands the ethnographer: in quadrant III, stating "It has been observed"? In quadrant II, announcing "Let there be light"? Or in quadrant I, muttering, "Today, I ventured forth"?

"What does an ethnographer do?" Clifford Geertz (1973, 19) asks. Along with Geertz, we can answer back "He writes." The task of the ethnographer is the inscription of everyday discourse, the extraction of "the said from the saying" (19-20). The ethnography is a type of everyday text, and the ethnographer stands in the text. As a participating observer, the ethnographer differs from the rest of us only in that he is more observant. After all, he gets paid for his work. His salary remains small, fortunately, and he cannot become a full-time observer, but must continue his participation.

What does the ethnographer do? He writes, and in his writing he heightens the sense of intersubjectivity of everyday life. He extracts the everyday from its matrix of ho-hum factualness and depicts its utter frailty. With Ernest Becker (1962, 109), he leads us to understand that the world we take for granted is "fundamentally fictitious." He searches among the fictitious text of everyday life for themes, plots, and characters. In this search, he tells a version of the human story.

What kind of story is the human story? Is it a western, a gun-totin', cattle-rustlin', hell-for-leather western, where the good guys face the bad guys at high noon on the dusty streets of life? Is it a Gothic novel, a creaking-door, musty-odored pale-figures-on-a-dark-moor Gothic novel, where the heroine discovers an unspeakable horror in her basement? Is it science fiction, an alien-threatened, mutant-riddled, green-oozing science fiction story, in which the special effects man puts the finishing touches to the nuclear holocaust as the last survivors lift off to the next universe?

Our story has elements of all of these, the Western, the Gothic, the science fiction extravaganza, but at times it supersedes these genres; it is more bizarre. As the smoke clears away from the Dallas street, it is the good guy who lies crumpled under the sun; the horrors behind the door of the basement at Auschwitz are truly unspeakable; and the neutron bomb, the bomb that kills people but protects property, has won congressional approval. Life *is* stranger than fiction.

THE EPIC OF GILGAMESH

Our story has not only these elements, but also much more. It has the sweep, the grandeur, the heroism, and the tragedy of an epic, such as the epic of Gilgamesh.[1] We ethnographers, anthropologists you and I, participant-observers with limited comprehension, seek to tell the human story, like Gilgamesh, who wrote his own story. This is the story of a man who was two-thirds god, and because of the god part that was upon him, wanted to do everything, learn everything, *understand* everything; but because he was one-third human, he was doomed to fail.

We know Gilgamesh, you and I, we know him by his name. From the day of his birth, he was called Gilgamesh, the place-builder. Look at Uruk, Gilgamesh's city. Climb upon its wall and examine well its masonry. Is it not of burnt brick, and did not seven sages lay its foundation? We know Gilgamesh, you and I, we know him by his name. From the day of his birth, he was called Gilgamesh, the secret-bringer. He went on a long journey, crossed the waters of death, and brought back a story of the days before the flood.

Even for those days, when men had hair like lions' manes and pride like that in stallions' eyes, Gilgamesh was extraordinary. He was two-thirds god and one-third man. He was restless, strong, and full of lust, leaving no virgin to her lover. He wanted to see everything, learn everything, understand everything. He was two-thirds god and one-third man and none could withstand him.

Then Gilgamesh, the great king, came to know death. In the agony of his knowledge, he cried out, "Oh Ninsun, Oh my mother, what is it to die?"

And Ninsun, his mother, made answer: "It is to go into the adobe out of which none ever return; it is to go into the dark abyss of the dread Goddess, Irkalla. They who dwell there are without light; the beings that live there eat of the dust and feed on the mud."

And Gilgamesh, the great king, groaned loudly, terribly, and tears flowed down his cheeks; no word that was said might comfort him. He groaned, he wept, even though he recalled his shout, still reverberating in the halls of the temple,

"Who is splendid among men?
"Who is glorious among heroes?"
And heard his own boastful reply return to him,
"Gilgamesh is splendid among men.
"Gilgamesh is glorious among heroes."

Gilgamesh, with the agony that comes from being two-thirds god and one-third man, set forth to find the secret of life. In his journey, Gilgamesh encountered one difficulty after another. Some wore away at his great strength; others sought to confuse his purpose, as did the woman of the wine: "Gilgamesh, where are you hurrying to? You will never find that life for which you are looking. So fill your belly with good things, dance and be merry, feast and rejoice. Make your wife happy in your embrace, and cherish the little child who holds your hand; for this too is the lot of man." But Gilgamesh's agony, the agony of a man who is two-thirds god, would not let him rest.

At journey's end Gilgamesh reached the waters of death. At the bottom of the waters of death grew the plant that granted eternal youth. In a feat that only he could achieve, he plucked the plant from the depths. Full of hope now that he had the secret of youth, Gilgamesh returned to Uruk. On the road back, he paused for a moment beside a spring of cool water. While he rested, a snake came out of the spring, snatched the plant, and ate it.

Gilgamesh wept, "Was it for this I toiled with my hands; was it for this I have wrung out my heart's blood? For myself I have gained nothing, but the beast of the earth has the joy of it now. I found a sign, and now I have lost it."

In his despair, Gilgamesh resumed the road that led to his city. As the city, his labor, his work, his acts, his *text* came into view, his despair lifted and he announced, "Climb up on the wall of Uruk, inspect its foundation, and examine well the brickwork; see if it is not of burnt brick, and did not seven wise men lay these foundations."

This too was the work of Gilgamesh, the king, who traveled the countries of the world. He was wise, he saw mysteries, and he knew secret things. He went on a long journey, was weary, worn out; but returning, he engraved on a stone the whole story.

To be human is to be in a story. That is, to speak is to act, to act is to observe, to observe is to inscribe, to inscribe is to tell a story.

Because we speak, because we symbolize, we conjure up worlds where hurts are healed, the hungry are fed, and people do not die; yet because we remain brother to the chimpanzee, cousin to the gorilla, we fail: wounds fester, the hungry starve, and people surely die. As with the Gilgamesh story, however, the human story is not a story of despair; it is a story of achievement. Two and a half million years ago, we walked across the African savanna with a rock in our hand, a dream in our eye, and a word on our lips. Today, we have planted our flag on the moon. Who can match our record? Who can best our deeds?

Our task, our lot, as it was Gilgamesh's, is to speak the text, to inscribe it through our acts, the acts of everyday life, so that those who come after us may read what we have done and marvel at our story. As anthropologists, our lot is to observe, to participate, and to write for others the many cultural variations of the human story, the story of Gilgamesh.

ACKNOWLEDGMENTS

I am grateful to Philip A. Dennis for his kind invitation to present an oral version of this article at the twentieth symposium on comparative literature at Texas Tech University, January 28-30, 1987. I am particularly grateful to Dr. Dennis for his assistance in revising the manuscript. I also thank Maudrie Monceaux for her expertise in preparing the manuscript and Clifford Duplechin for his skill in drafting Figure 1.

NOTE

[1]This account of the acts of Gilgamesh draws upon Miles Richardson (1972), "Gilgamesh and Christ: Two Contradictory Images of Man in Search of a Better World." which in turn is based on N. K. Sandars, *The Epic of Gilgamesh*. For a detailed, step-by-step tracing of the coming to be of the Gilgamesh story, see Jeffrey H. Tigay, *The Evolution of the Gilgamesh Epic*.

BIBLIOGRAPHY

Bateson, Gregory. *The Mind And Nature*. New York: E. P. Dutton, 1979.

Becker, Ernest. *The Birth and Death of Meaning*. New York: The Free Press, 1962.

Gardner, John, and John Maier. *Gilgamesh*. New York: Alfred A. Knopf, 1984.

Geertz, Clifford. *The Interpretation of Culture*. New York: Basic Books, 1973.

Lanser, Susan Sniader. *The Narrative Act*. Princeton, NJ: Princeton University Press, 1981.

Mead, George Herbert. *George Herbert Mead on Social Psychology*, ed. Anselm Strauss. Chicago: University of Chicago Press, 1964.

Perinbanayagam, R. S. *Signifying Acts*. Carbondale, IL: Southern Illinois University Press, 1985.

Reck, Gregory. "Narrative Anthropology." Paper presented at the American Anthropological Association meeting, Philadelphia, Pennsylvania, 1986.

Richardson, Miles. "Gilgamesh and Christ: Two Contradictory Images of Man in Search of a Better World." In *Aspects of Cultural Change*, ed. Joseph Aceves, 7-20. Athens, GA: University of Georgia Press, 1972.

Ricouer, Paul. "The Model of the Text: Meaningful Action Considered as a Text." In *Interpretive Social Science*, ed. Paul Rabinow and William M. Sullivan. Berkeley, CA: University of California Press, 1979.

Sandars, N. K. *The Epic of Gilgamesh*. London: Penguin Books, 1960.

Tigay, Jeffrey H. *The Evolution of the Gilgamesh Epic*. Philadelphia, PA: University of Pennsylvania, 1983.

LITERATURE AND THE STUDY OF MAN

A. Owen Aldridge

ABSTRACT

Literature as communication involving some degree of emotional or aesthetic response is both an independent discipline and one of the tools of anthropology. The latter is a description and explanation of social behavior in every possible environment—from the primitive to the sophisticated—in every part of the world. Exemplary models illustrate the two disciplines working together to reveal structural and ethnological relations. As physical and psychological characteristics of all nations and races are reflected in thought and behavior, these characteristics reveal universal patterns. Universal elements or invariables, as Etiemble calls them, may be perceived also in literature in its images of these same human characteristics and their incumbent emotional and aesthetic qualities. The search for these invariables is the closest link between literature and anthropology.

In a sense the title I have chosen for this discourse is an absurdity for it encompasses the whole of human experience, and I have a very limited amount of space. It took Will and Ariel Durant 6000 pages to write the *Story of Civilization*, a risky undertaking at that, and I seem to be trying to cover even more ground in less than half of one per cent of the space. Actually I propose merely to give a few examples of the collaboration of two academic disciplines, literature and anthropology. Both literature and anthropology record the activities of the human race as do history and philosophy. Man himself is the subject of anthropology, whereas literature is a body of writing about man and is the subject of literary history and literary criticism. Anthropology attempts a scientific portrayal of the human species, whereas literature presents human character and activities through the subjective perspective of other men. Literature exists as a residue of cultural activity, whereas anthropology is a methodology or process of investigation.

I have previously defined literature as "communication by written words or symbols when the purpose of communication involves some degree of emotional or aesthetic response as well as mere transference of information." In the most comprehensive sense, it "embraces not only the broad conventional genres such as poetry, fiction, and drama, but also ideological prose such as most works of history and philosophy, together with some textbooks and even some advertising" (Aldridge 1986, 37). I should emphasize that I am referring to communication by writing or ideograms, not by signs. The latter are the province of semiotics. Although contemporary literary theory is saturated with linguistic concepts and terminology, neither linguistics nor semiotics has the power to stimulate complex ideas or to arouse powerful emotions or states of mind in a reader. Roland Barthes and others have made the point that literature cannot escape from language and that writer and reader must submit themselves to the rules of grammar and usage. This is true enough. Barthes carries the argument further, however, and maintains that we can liberate ourselves from the confinement of language only by playing tricks with words and that this type of cheating is literature.

The notion of literature as a kind of word game parallels a widely known concept in the theory of mass communications that the medium is the message. The Italian novelist and authority on the Middle Ages, Umberto Eco, traces the notion that the code or structure of a language is the concept being conveyed to "the famous anthropological thesis of Benjamin Lee Whorf for whom the view of the world is determined by the structure of the language" (Eco 1986, 234). This is essentially another way of saying that form dominates content, a principle widespread in literary theory since the flourishing of the non-anthropological American New Criticism in the 1940s and 1950s. Linguistic structuralism and some forms of French New Criticism in the 1970s and 1980s perpetuate this dichotomy between form and content. Theoretical complexes such as these tend to reduce the importance of semantics or the communication of meaning in literature and to emphasize rhetorical devices, or the mechanical means by which ideas and feelings are transferred from one person to another. Traditionalists reject these theories and insist that language is subservient to ideas and feelings. There is little agreement at present, therefore, even on the definition of literature.

Defining anthropology is an even more hazardous process. Although its subject matter, man, is the same as that of literature, its approach to the subject is far more diverse. Indeed literature itself is one of the tools of anthropology. General anthropology is usually considered to have four subfields: archaeology, cultural anthropology, linguistics, and physical or biological anthropology. Archaeology consists in the discovery and analysis of the material remains of past human life and activities. Cultural anthropology considers the concepts of culture, sex and marriage patterns, family and kinship patterns, social control, and cultural developments, including religion, magic, science, and art. Linguistics concerns, of course, the structure of language, whereas physical anthropology deals with human evolution and race. Cultural anthropology is closely related to sociology. Indeed university courses in anthropology work with the language of sociology and investigate the basic areas of sociological inquiry, including the family, class, religion, and collective behavior. In general, anthropologists study these topics in primitive societies, and sociologists study them under contemporary conditions. This investigation of man's relationships to other men may also come under the heading of ethnography. When concerned with one's own culture, this form of inquiry is sociology; when it is focused upon a foreign exotic culture, it is ethnography. Umberto Eco has sardonically described cultural anthropology as "the bad conscience of the white man who thus pays his debt to the destroyed primitive culture" (39). Eco also observes that the anthropologist teaches "that even defecatory positions are part of a community's culture." (152). The methodology of anthropology has developed in two divergent directions. Its practical or pragmatic aspect consists of fieldwork, the gathering of specific information about clearly defined areas of investigation, for example, the wedding customs in a remote village in the Phillipines. Its organic or holistic aspect consists in the derivation of patterns or configurations over wide areas of investigation; for example, creation myths in ancient Greece and twentieth-century Brazil. Anthropology has also developed along cognitive and symbolic lines. In essence, anthropology is a study of how man lives; philosophy, a study of how man thinks; history, a study of what man has done; and literature, a written record combining all of the preceding topics and utilizing imagined characters and situations as well as real ones.

Because anthropology is in large measure a description and explanation of social behavior in every possible environment—from the primitive to the sophisticated—in every part of the world, it depends on day-to-day observation. This is the fieldwork already mentioned—the acquiring of firsthand knowledge through participation in the culture being observed, including use and understanding of its language. The material of anthropology—compared to the *Stoff* of the *Stoffgeschichte* of literature—respresents the sum total of all field investigations, but the aim of the anthropologist is not merely the gathering of information about particular areas and groups. He attempts to arrive at generalizations that will apply to most, if not all, of mankind. Only anthropologists themselves are ordinarily aware of these generalizations. The native African, for example, does not realize that he is going through a rite of passage when he undergoes customary physical testing any more than an American high school student realizes that he is participating in a similar ritual when he receives his diploma. This body of abstract theorizing represents one of the major links between anthropology and the study of literature; one of the reasons why anthropology has been defined as "a universal theory of society and history" (Clastres 1977, 17).

It can be argued that ethnography may be traced back to the ancient historians Herodotus and Tacitus. Another early example of anthropology in literature is a passage in *Prometheus Vinctus* of Aeschylus (442-506) in which the Greek dramatist through his protagonist proudly summarizes the origins, progress, and achievements of mankind. Among the triumphs of art and science that he describes are astronomy, mathematics, writing, navigation, the curing of disease through medicine, the interpretation of dreams and omens, and the discovery and use of precious metals.

A more familiar passage is that in which Shakespeare's Hamlet temporarily speaks in even more glowing terms: "What a piece of work is man! how noble in reason! how infinite in faculty! in form and moving how express and admirable! in action how like an angel! in apprehension how like a god!" (II. 2). Voltaire in the Enlightenment provides a completely contrary picture: "A stranger to himself, man is ignorant about mankind: what am I, where am I, where am I going, and from where did I come?" "Heaven in forming us, blended in our life desires, disgusts, reason, folly, moments of pleasure, days of torments; these are the elements of our imperfect being" (*Discours . . . sur l'homme*). It would be hard to generalize merely on the basis of these quotations, and the easy task of adding to them would only make generalization more difficult.

Hoping to be as up-to-date as possible in preparing this review, I ran a computer search under the joint headings of anthropology and literature, but the results were meager. One title that my computer produced was a collection of contemporary literary selections entitled *Anthropology Through Literature* (edited by Spradley and McDonough, 1973), designed, I presume, for undergraduate courses. The selections are predominantly fiction, but there is some autobiography and some narrative casework; for example, an extract from Oscar Lewis's *Five Families*. The selections are grouped under the headings of human nature and culture; subsistence and economic exchange; social organization—kinship and groups; politics, government, and law; religion and world view; language and communication; and cultural contact and change. It is hard to say whether the aim is to furnish literature as illustrative material for anthropological concepts or to use anthropological concepts as means of classifying literature and making it relevant to modern life.

My computer did not turn up what I consider the best general discussion to be found anywhere of the relations between literature and anthropology: Wayne Shumaker's (1960) *Literature and the Irrational: A Study in Anthropological Backgrounds.* Whether or not one accepts texts of presumed literary realism, treated here and in similar studies as reliable reflections of actual life, the authors deal with subject matter that is certainly similar to that treated by cultural anthropologists. At first glance, however, one would not assume much of a connection between literature and archaeology, the most concrete of all the branches of anthropology. But an example occurs to me that is both striking and significant. I am referring to the inspiration and information provided by Homer's *Iliad* that led German archaeologist Heinrich Schliemann to the discovery of the site of ancient Troy, which until his discovery was thought to be a mythological rather than a real city. Will Durant puts it, "Schliemann exhumed not only one Troy but seven after scientific historians had shown that there had been no Troy at all" (1926, 573). This notable contribution of literature to anthropology has been the subject of a recent television series on PBS, "In Search of the Trojan War." Few other examples as relevant as this may be adduced, but in the reverse direction, the nineteenth century developed a subgenre of the historical novel now known as the archaeological novel, in which the characters are not necessarily actual historical figures, but in which the dress, language, religion, manners and other aspects of the period are faithfully depicted. Flaubert's *Salammbo* is one example.

It is somewhat of an anomaly that contemporary anthropology—a methodology requiring fastidious study of the behavior of human beings in day-to-day situations in real life—should have accepted two theories affirming that the intellectual systems created by human beings have an autonomous existence independent of their creators. Both theories are presumed, moreover, to have universal application, describing the mental processes of all men at all times and places. One of these systems is based upon language. A Swiss linguist of the late nineteenth century expounded the theory that language is compounded of two elements, the signified and the signifier. The signified is a purely mental concept and the signifier is the actual word used to convey it. The notion of moving from one place to another, for example, is the signified; the phrase "I am going" is the signifier. The relationship between mental concept and verbal representation is completely arbitrary, an obvious conclusion from the multiplicity of languages and the continued introduction of new words. Contemporary linguistic structuralism is based on this dichotomy. In the structuralist scheme, all concrete words refer to a mental archetype; for example, a "fromage archetypal (archetypal cheese)," cited by Lévi-Strauss (1958, 107).

This notion of an independent universal language resembles Plato's theory of absolute ideas. But both systems may be given a positivist interpretation. Plato's theory may mean merely that observable constancies are not in things themselves, but have a reality and permanence of their own. The same could be said of linguistic similarities. Phonologists look for general laws, whether based on induction or logical deduction (Lévi-Strauss 1958, 41). Defenders of structuralism insist that they do not hypostatize an autonomous system of archetypes. They correctly observe that no single person invented the language he uses and that everyone has learned his native tongue from other people. In this sense, language is like the physical universe, pre-existing before the individual and independent of him. This may be an important truth in epistemology, but when we come to literature as distinguished from language, the relationship between the individual and his environment is not exactly parallel. The writer does not invent the language, but he uses it in a unique manner. His combination of words has never existed before. He is a creator as well as a user. He is not completely independent to the degree that he is influenced by his predecessors in theme, genre, and style, but he is, nevertheless, bringing into existence something that did not exist previously.

The other intellectual system considered by some anthropologists to have an independent existence is that of myth.

In an explanation of his method of "The Structural Study of Myth," Lévi-Strauss indicates that he breaks down the myth into its constituent elements and then rearranges them so that they may be perceived both diachronically—(in a chronological order of succession)—and synchronically—(in an order based entirely on content or concept) (Shumaker 1960, 120-21). When several versions of a myth are analyzed and collated in this way, the myth as a whole takes on a substantive character transcending any individual version. From this perspective, Lévi-Strauss affirms that "myths have no authors." A parallel exists with regard to literary themes such as that of Don Juan. The various metamorphoses that take place in this character type all belong to the theme as a whole even though many of them do not exist in the original version by Tirso de Molina. The notion of independent existence takes on an extreme form when every new character or relationship added to the literary empire is labeled an "archetype"; for example, Nabokov's Lolita, inhabiting the same world as Lévi-Strauss's archetypal cheese.

With the emergence of formalist criticism before World War I, a body of literary theorists then and since has sought to direct attention away from the author of a work to the written text itself, an effort leading eventually to the view that the author should be excluded altogether from consideration. Proponents of this view should consider that in the art world an anonymous painting has practically no monetary value in comparison with one by an acknowledged master. In literature, moreover, there are no anonymous masterpieces, and the only works without known authors to be widely studied are those whose eminence has been granted by their longevity.

If we were to go beyond anthropology and consider the latest excesses in what is generally called literary theory in the United States, we would encounter the opinion that not only language and myth, but all literature, belongs to a system of interconnecting units in the study of which semantic relationships may be disregarded. This at any rate is how I interpret the following quasi-definition by the late Paul de Man: "Literary theory can be said to come into being when the approach to literary texts is no longer based on nonlinguistic, that is to say historical and aesthetic, considerations or, to put it somewhat less crudely, when the object of discussion is no longer the meaning or the value but the modalities of production and of reception to meaning and of value prior to their establishment—the implication being that this establishment is problematic enough to require an autonomous discipline of critical investigation to consider its possibility and its status" (1986, 7). Rather than to proceed further with this speculation, which is an abstruse way of repeating that the medium is the message, I believe it wiser to remain with anthropologically related structuralism.

Most literary critics and historians trace the attachment between linguistics and anthropology to the French school of Lévi-Strauss, but it actually developed previously among a group of American ethnographers (Harris 1968, 103). Taking as departure the terms *etic* and *emic*, coined from *phonetic* and *phonemic* in linguistics, these theorists assumed that certain data, like those in phonetics, reveal no structural patterns, but that others, like those in phonemics, do exhibit structures that provide understanding of sociocultural systems (Harris 1968, 104-5). Other ethnographers, while accepting this terminology, argue that the parallel with linguistics does not extend to social organization. In the broad sense, *etic* refers to empirical evidence and *emic* to theories about this evidence. This dichotomy is similar to that between cultural materialism and cultural idealism. For example, "having children and feeding and housing them is an etic phenomenon, but doing it in a socially approved manner puts the whole matter in an eminently emic frame" (Harris 1968, 112). A parallel might be drawn in literary study, the etic activity referring to conventional literary history and the emic to literary criticism.

The essence of structuralism in both literary theory and anthropology is an effort to perceive a complete system in any intellectual discipline and to seek conclusions enveloping the whole (Lévi-Strauss 1958, 42). Anthropologists concerned with structures look for common properties in various national or tribal societies in such elements as kinship, codes of politeness and dress, and even cuisine (Lévi-Strauss 1958, 98). Recognizing that linguistics was the first humanistic system to approach a scientific level of knowledge, Lévi-Strauss and his disciples suggest that various aspects of social life, including art and religion, consist of "phenomena in which nature and language are conjoined" (1958, 7). The study of kinship seems to them to approach the degree of scientific rigor exhibited by linguistics. They notice that incest is nearly universally disapproved and place particular importance on avuncular relationships. In societies in which a large degree of familiarity exists between father and son (the matriarchate), the maternal uncle exhibits a stern control over the nephew, and conversely where the father is the austere and dominant force in the family (the patriarchate), the relationship between uncle and nephew is relaxed (1958, 50).

Although presumably ultra-scientific, structural anthropology contains a large metaphysical component. In the words of Lévi-Strauss, "If, as we believe to be the case, the unconscious activity of the mind consists in imposing forms upon content, and if these forms are fundamentally the same for all minds— ancient and modern, primitive and civilized (as the study of the symbolic function, expressed in language, so strikingly indicates)—it is necessary and sufficient to grasp the unconscious structure underlying each institution and each custom, in order to obtain a principle of interpretation valid for other institutions and other customs, provided of course that the analysis is carried far enough" (Lévi-Strauss 1963, 21-22). Lévi-Strauss affirms, moreover, that his theories of kinship, representing his paradigms of structure, are symbolic rather than empirical (1958, 62).

I have devoted this much attention to structuralism since it is the area in which the relations between anthropology and literature have been given most publicity. It should be noted, however, that many literary critics as well as many anthropologists have never accepted this approach to their respective disciplines. Also a great deal of what has passed for structuralism in recent writing about literature has little or nothing to do with anthropology. The vogue of structuralism in literary criticism illustrates a type of contemporary cultural lag. That is, it existed in American anthropology before being expounded independently in France by Lévi-Strauss. It then took a considerable length of time for his theories to pass from the world of social anthropology to that of literature. His seminal paper on structural analysis in linguistics and in anthropology was published originally in 1945; that is, to place it in chronological perspective, during World War II. His book *Les Structures élémentaires de parenté* appeared four years later and his *Anthropologie structurale* in 1958. Yet his influence in literary criticism did not surface until the late 1960s.

In my subsequent remarks, I shall give three examples or paradigms of the convergence of literature and anthropology; in two of the paradigms, literature and anthropology are conjoined, that is, in linguistics and ethnology. In the third paradigm, they are disjoined, that is, independently they pursue the same theme, in my example, primitivism.

The Linguistic Model

The generally recognized model for literary structuralism is that provided by Lévi-Strauss and Roman Jacobson in April 1962 in the French journal of anthropology *L'Homme*, edited at that time by Lévi-Strauss, an issue that contains also an article on myths in the Arab world. The model consists of a dissection of a sonnet by Baudelaire, "Les Chats." In an introductory note, Lévi-Strauss affirms that "the linguist discerns in poetical works structures revealing a striking analogy with those that the analysis of myths reveals to the ethnologist." In the reverse direction, myths arouse in the linguist "profound esthetic emotions." Lévi-Strauss admits, however, that myths and poems belong to different categories—that the structure of poems consists of superimposed layers of phonology, phonetics, syntax, prosody and semantics; whereas the myth must be interpreted on the semantic level alone.

The analysis of Baudelaire's sonnet consists of so many discrete details that a summary would require almost as many words as the article itself. As illustration, however, I shall show how the structural argument draws upon prosody in a consideration of the sonnet's rhyme scheme. It is divided into two quatrains and two tercets with a rhyme scheme abba cddc eef and gfg. Lines 1, 4, 6, 7, 9, 10, 12, and 14 are feminine and 2, 3, 5, 8, 11, and 13 are masculine. This arrangement of feminine and masculine rhymes conforms to the requirement that two "rimes plates" (that is, two couplets, one masculine and one feminine) must never follow each other, that contiguous lines with different rhymes cannot both be either masculine or feminine, and that in the last lines of contiguous strophes, masculine and feminine rhymes must alternate. Assuming that the two tercets form a unity, the authors point out an implied antinomy between the strophes with two rhymes and those with three, an antinomy counterbalanced, however, by a dichotomy produced by the two quatrains and the two tercets. While indicating that this balance conforms to a binary principle, the authors observe that it implies another antinomy between the first section with three rhymes and the second with two rhymes, and the first two strophes of four lines and the last two of three. In their words, "It is on the tension between these two modes of arrangement and between their symmetrical and asymmetrical elements that the composition of the whole piece is based." This reference to tension is a vestige of the even then old-fashioned American New Criticism.

The last paragraph of the article points to various binary relations in order to bring out the androgynous character of Baudelaire's cats. It is also indicated that all the personages of the sonnet belong to the masculine gender, that the cats participate in an androgynous nature, and that throughout the sonnet feminine substantives in grammar are used for masculine rhymes. A footnote draws attention to a contemporary dispute in French prosody over a theory that feminine and masculine rhymes have a sexual connotation and for that reason an alternation pattern was established in the seventeenth century.

One cannot very well question the view that many examples of the confrontation of masculine and feminine characteristics, both real and symbolic, are provided in nature, but this hardly amounts to a proof that the basis of all literature—even that of all French sonnets—partakes of this same balance of equals. As a kind of control experiment, I examined from the Lévi-Strauss-Jacobson perspective Rimbaud's "Les Voyelles," a sonnet even more famous than Baudelaire's and one that has been the subject of a book of more than 200 pages by Etiemble, the most eminent comparatist of this century. By the way, as early as 1968, Etiemble (1968) classed as parallel methods, "the alchemistic explication, the gnostic gloss, and the structuralist exegesis." In my cursory examination of "Les Voyelles," I discovered that this sonnet has a more complex rhyme scheme than "Les Chats," only five rhymes instead of seven (the fewer the rhymes, the more difficult the rhyming) and that an overwhelming twelve of the rhymes are feminine and only two masculine. There is no alternating scheme, and the other requirements concerning the rhyming of contiguous lines and the last lines of contiguous strophes are also violated. The sonnet is divided into two quatrains and two tercets—a convention ever since the sixteenth century—but there is no binary principle at work, merely a quintuple scheme to give equal treatment to each of the five vowels. The first quatrain introduces the subject and describes the vowel a; the second quatrain describes e and i; and the first tercet describes u, and the second o.

I have not entered into the syntactical and phonetical aspects of the article on "Les Chats," primarily for reasons of time and space. In my opinion, however, these aspects reveal even less evidence of universal patterns than does that of prosody. Moreover, Baudelaire himself was even less aware of these syntactical and phonetical relations than of those in the realm of poetic form. Although the authorship of the article illustrates the collaboration of an anthropologist and a linguist, its content owes considerably more to the academic structures of professional literary criticism than to those of anthropology. It is somewhat of an anomaly that the attention to structure in literature, which is attributed in some measure to anthropology or the study of man, has actually brought about a dehumanization of literature by drawing attention away from the creative aspects of the writer and the emotional reactions of the reader. As I have already indicated, structuralism in literary criticism is now passé after a life span of less than two decades, more or less contemporaneous with the vogue for the Afro hair style, but it still remains perhaps the most notable historical example of the convergence of literature and anthropology as academic disciplines.

The structural hypothesis as applied to the realm of myth and folklore has survived to the present day and is accepted guardedly by some major comparatists. There are almost as many different definitions of myth, however, as there are people who write about it. Some scholars insist that all myths are oral narratives, a principle that, if true, would automatically disqualify them as literature. Most authorities associate myth with sacred history, ordinarily with an event in the remote past associated with creation or the beginnings of some human institution. Myth is taken as sacred truth, legend as actual history adorned by fancy, and folklore as pure fiction intended primarily for entertainment. A distinction must be made, moreover, between literary myths; that is, between those that appear in writing and those that exist only in oral or pictorial form. The myths in Ovid, Shakespeare, and Milton reflect the mental processes of their authors, who usually do not consider them to be true, but those of primitive peoples illustrate the beliefs of an entire society and possibly of several generations. In ordinary nonliterary discourse, myth is something that a large number of people believe or would like to believe, but that others know is not true, for example, that the United States at present has the highest standard of living in the world or that its health care is better than that of any other nation.

An early and famous example of the use of anthropology in myth is a book by a Jesuit priest, Joseph François Lafitau, published in 1724. *Manners of the American Natives Compared with the Manners of Earliest Times* is a comparison of ancient Greek myths with those of American Indians. Lafiteau was a precursor of Lévi-Strauss in his argument that both groups had the concept of God and that it is etched in the heart of all men at the same time that it is depicted without by the beauty of his works.

THE ETHNOLOGICAL MODEL

To pass from structuralism to ethnography is to proceed from the highly theoretical and abstract to the particular and mundane, although obviously to the exotically mundane, a phrase that is not necessarily an oxymoron. For my example, I shall cite a combination of contemporary fiction and personal narratives derived from field interviews, the two sources brought together to illustrate and explain family relationships and the process of individual maturation in contemporary Japan. The method was devised by one of my colleagues at the University of Illinois, David Plath, an ethnographer, and explained in his book *Long Engagements*, a metaphor for the maturing process. The theme of the book is that each person in the process of maturing "must enter into long engagements with the cultural symbols that identify experience, and with others in society who guard the meaning of the symbols." Because the author assumes that "rhetoric is the social art of such identifications," he explores the rhetoric of maturity as it exists in modern Japan (1980, 3).

The substance of the book consists of the portrayal of four distinct character types in the urban area around Osaka, Japan. A separate section is devoted to each type. Each of these sections begins with the analysis of a Japanese novel concentrating on the life of the protagonist and revealing how it illustrates the "themes of human growth in the adult years." Next the author relates the novel to one or more "Of the dimensions of the rhetoric of maturity—pathways, convoys, self-images—as these are manifested in Japanese tradition." Subsequently, he provides a first-person narrative of an actual person living in the Osaka area, a narrative that he himself has composed after a series of field interviews. Finally, the author in his own person comments on the patterns that he sees as significant in the novel and in the actual life history that he has chosen as a parallel to it (37). He treats the novels as being themselves case histories rather than as works of literary craftsmanship because he has particularly "chosen them for their naturalism in depicting persons and events well within the bounds of ordinary human variation" (16).

The author uses the word *rhetoric* to refer to the vocabulary of sociology rather than to that of literary art. A rhetorical event in his analysis consists of three elements in a person's psychological development: identification, justification, and projection. In identification, a person is labeled as belonging to a specific time period in the course of the average human life span, such chronological types including an old maid, a grandfather, or a senior citizen. In justification, the person or members of his family vindicate the status that he occupies and offer reasons to maintain that it is a normal one, that it is conforming to the norms of society. In projection, the person looks ahead to the future and plans his behavior according to the conditions that he expects or hopes to encounter in later life (11-13). The operations of this sociological rhetoric are "conveyed by symbols and images that hold collective meaning," those that are found in both realistic novels and individual life experience (16). Plath's goal as an ethnographer is "to re-present the singularity and dignity of individual lives as he encounters them in alien settings" as well as "to convey the life-ordering powers, even the beauty, of the social institutions and cultural patterns found in those settings" (33).

Of the four character types illustrating a particular pattern or style of life that Plath offers in his book, I have chosen as an example of his method the one that he describes as "a spoiled daughter." The novel on which he bases his description is *Sasameyuki* by Jun'ichiro Tanizaki. In English translation, the title is rendered as *The Makioka Sisters*, perhaps, as Plath suggests, "to invite comparisons with landmarks of world literature such as *The Brothers Karamazov*". Apart from the theme of maturing, the novel provides a study of the anthropological topic of kinship in a middle-class family engaged in commerce. The spotlight is shared by the second and the third of four sisters, and Plath never declares which should be considered the protagonist. The two oldest sisters are already married, and the youngest has a fiancé ready to wed her when a suitable match has been arranged for their sister Yukiko. The latter has reached the age of 30, an alarmingly late age for marriage in their circle. Her name means *snow*, and the Japanese title of the novel refers to a "delicate snowfall." This phrase mirrors Yukiko's personality. Because of her delicate appearance and reserved manner, she has been passed over by potential suitors of the appropriate age. She is also physically attractive, but with the beauty of a bonsai tree, "carefully cultivated along traditional lines" (133). The family takes an ambivalent attitude toward her situation. Custom and propriety urge that she marry and assume the status of a wife and mother, but her unostentatious bearing and gracious demeanor exercise such charm that her family is reluctant to have her leave home. The second sister, Sachiko, is, however, the real protagonist, the one who holds the family together while the four sisters advance into the maturity of middle age. Even as she occupies the position of family pivot at the age of 35, "she retains traces of the spoiled daughter she had been," presumably having played the role of father's pet (129). The mother and father are deceased. The two youngest daughters prefer to live with Sachiko and her husband rather than with the oldest married sister, even though the latter would have been the more conventional arrangement. Placed by these circumstances in the role of mother or overseer of her younger siblings, Sachiko attempts to engineer their betrothals. The youngest sister, who already has a financé, declares that she will not marry before Yukiko, and then engages in a number of sexual affairs. Sachiko takes upon herself the resolving of these problems. She sees the younger sister through an unwanted pregnancy and a consequent abortion, and finally arranges a suitable marriage for Yukiko. In covering the failures of her younger sisters and salvaging their self respect, she reveals strong qualities of firmness, tact, and resourcefulness.

As a parallel from real life, Plath reports his interviews with a married woman of 43, mother and housewife, who rules over another middle-class domicile except when obliged by custom to defer to her mother-in-law, the senior wife in Japanese parlance, who according to the mores of the country is entitled to the respect and obedience of all younger females in the family. At the outset of the narrative, she declares, "I was the only daughter in my family, and people thought I was spoiled" (143). As a child she had resembled her mother's sister, with whom she had an easier relationship than with her mother—a curious feminine parallel to Lévi-Strauss's avuncular paradigm. Her major change in life during childhood came from the influence of a male teacher who inspired her to hard work, concentration, and acute consciousness of duty. From her earliest years, she had been reconciled to the custom of arranged marriages. After her marriage, she had like all good Japanese women taken the words of the senior wife or mother-in-law as gospel. Now in her middle age, one of her main tasks is working out an arrangement by which her mother-in-law seems to have power, but control remains actually in her own hands. With her husband, she enjoys a trusting, comfortable companionship, and she has a good-natured, tolerant relationship with her children, although conscious of a generation gap that she does not sense with regard to her mother-in-law. She has no difficulty in keeping on close terms with about ten women friends whom she sees every so often.

In bringing the fictional and real-life characters together, Plath emphasizes the dilemmas of maturity. Sachiko and the home-maker are forced to decide on their priorities in regard to the persons in their care—for the one it is playing the role of a junior wife, for the other, arranging the marriages of her younger sisters. Apart from this necessity of giving priority to a particular relationship, Plath does not elaborate many resemblances between the two women, not even in regard to their joint classification in "A Spoiled Daughter," the chapter in which they are discussed. They show none of the attributes accorded in Western fiction to the Jewish-American princess, a much more recognizable type. Indeed Plath's confrontation of the two Japanese women brings out contrasts rather than similarities. The homemaker's duties and demeanor toward her mother-in-law are closely defined by tradition and general acceptance. In becoming a pliant wife and maturing from absolute obedience to gracious cooperation as a daughter-in-law, she is merely fitting into a normal pattern. Sachiko, in looking after the welfare of her younger sisters, is playing, however, a role not expected of her and one that she has to learn through experience. The homemaker has achieved a certain fulfillment through maintaining ties with her friends, but in contrast, Sachiko has no friends to speak of and for that reason depends all the more on her sisters for affection. The two women are alike, however, in preserving their individuality. The homemaker, after initially subduing her personality in the shadow of her mother-in-law, matured into a competent domestic manager with personal interests outside the nuclear family, and Sachiko from the moment she took charge of the interests of her younger sisters occupied a position of responsibility and self-fulfillment.

The two women do not represent parallel lives, but are useful as a focus for ethnological explanations of the author. Both the novel and the composite interview provide pictures of the Japanese family that are interpreted for the reader by means of the author's specialized knowledge, which ensures authenticity.

A variant of the ethnological model may be seen in the work of one of Plath's colleagues, Cheiko Mulhern, a professor, not of anthropology, but of Japanese literature. Mulhern read a paper before the annual conference of the American Anthropological Association in December 1985, on the passage of a twentieth-century Japanese woman, Shizué Kato, from a feudal bride to a modern politician. This unpublished paper is in essence a book review of the latter's autobiography published in 1935 and brought out recently in a new edition. Mulhern presents a summary of Kato's career interlarded with commentaries based on socioanthropological principles. Ordinarily, anthropology focuses on the group, but this paper illustrates how the individual may also be studied in his relations with larger units.

Another variant of ethnological research that is of particular relevance to comparative literture is the study of ethnic writing, a new branch of literary investigation that has shown vigorous growth during recent months. Although there is a good deal of confusion concerning the nature of ethnic literature, that genre may be defined as comprising works by an author of one national or cultural heritage that reflect his contact by birth or immigration with a second cultural environment in which the members of his own heritage are in a minority. One of the best examples of the genre in American fiction is *The Woman Warrior* by Maxine Hong Kingston, a semi-autobiographical portrayal of the struggles of the author's Chinese mother to cope in a bicultural society. Tony Hillerman's detective novels, using as they do Navajo Indians as characters and revealing their cultural attitudes as background, present a problem of taxonomy. Should they be considered as belonging to the genre of ethnic literature? Although they describe a confrontation of cultures, the author himself is not bicultural. Hillerman is a Caucasian treating the reaction of Indians to European-American cultural patterns, not a native Indian portraying the problems of his own race in reacting to an alien culture. Hillerman represents ethnographic rather than ethnic literature.

THE DISJOINED MODEL: PRIMITIVISM

The theme of primitivism has been a feature of literature ever since ancient times, and primitive life has become one of the major topics of study for anthropology in nearly all of its branches. Indeed the development of the theory of evolution in natural science during the nineteenth century gave rise to anthropology as a parallel study in culture. Scientists assumed that people living in primitive conditions in contemporary times could furnish clues to the development of human life from early to intermediate stages. It was also believed that the evolution of physical life from lower forms to man was paralleled in man's cultural organization from primitive forms to those of civilization. Even in the theory of comparative literature, a pioneer in the discipline, Hutcheson Macaulay Posnett, published a book in 1886, affirming that the scientific foundations of literature may be perceived in the orderly historical changes in cultural organization. In his opinion, literature reveals "the gradual expansion of social life, from clan to city, from city to nation, [and] both of these to cosmopolitan humanity" (86).

In more recent literary studies, primitivism became a subject of investigation for two experts in the history of ideas, Arthur O. Lovejoy and George Boas, who planned a documentary history of the topic. Only one of several projected volumes has been published, however, *Primitivism and Related Ideas in Antiquity* (1965). This significant volume prints all the major texts in Greek and Latin expressing the view that life in primitive conditions is to be preferred vastly to that in civilization. The volume also contains supplementary essays on primitivism in western Asia and in India. It divides the concept into two forms: chronological primitivism affirms that a superior lifestyle existed in a previous period of time, usually the most remote; cultural primitivism maintains that vestiges of primitive life may be found in distant geographical areas in contemporary times. The basis of comparison is a norm, commonly referred to as *natural* or *according to nature*.

Lovejoy and Boas indicate that "the primitive condition of mankind, or the life of 'savage' peoples, has usually been extolled because it has been supposed to constitute 'the state of nature'" (12). They offer, therefore, a number of definitions of nature, nine in one section of their book and sixty-six in the appendix (12-13, 447-56). All of the material treated by Lovejoy and Boas is purely literary, but the two appendices written by other scholars contain a large number of footnotes referring to articles in archaeological and other anthropological journals. Their evidence, is however, provided almost exclusively by literary works.

In my own research, I have studied "the state of nature" in a political sense and the hypothetical portrayal in literature of the transition from life in the state of nature to that in civil society. In this sociopolitical sense, the state of nature refers to the status of human beings before entering into society, that is, prior to any kind of government. The problem does not concern man in his savage or brute state in the course of human evolution, but only in the period after he had acquired the physical and psychological characteristics that he possesses today. Two seventeenth-century philosophers, Spinosa and Hobbes, began the debate over the moral characteristics of man in the state of nature. At issue is whether man's basic patterns of conduct are innate or acquired through society, and if innate, whether they are fundamentally directed toward selfish ends or toward deriving pleasure from contact with one's fellow men. In the state of nature, according to Spinosa in his *Tractatus-Theologico-Politicus*, 1670, every man lives as he liked. He was pleased to have the company of his fellows, but not to the degree of accepting social organization. It was not that he preferred solitude to society. What he wanted was the freedom to do whatever was within his physical capability. Spinosa declared also that within the restrictions of civil society, man is still fundamentally selfish or unsocialized. Instinctively he seeks power and possessions, and he is more inclined toward oppression and exploitation than toward cooperation and mutual assistance.

Hobbes affirmed in Chapter 13 of his *Leviathan*, 1651, that the state of nature represents "the time men live without a common power to keep them all in awe," that is, a state of war, although not necessarily of actual combat. In this condition, there are "no arts; no letters; no society; and which is worst of all, continual fear, and danger of violent death; and the life of man, solitary, poor, nasty, brutish, and short." Hobbes admitted that this condition is hypothetical and may never have existed all over the world at any one time, but like early anthropologists he pointed to existing primitive races and earlier conditions in Europe to support his argument. He concluded that "so long as a man is in the condition of mere nature, which is a condition of war, his private appetite is the measure of good and evil."

Shaftesbury (1964, 2:79) in the next century objected that this "imperfect rude condition of mankind, if it ever were in nature, could never have been of the least continuance, or any way tolerable, or sufficient for the support of the human race. Such a condition cannot indeed so properly be called a state." He argued in addition that if generation and the care and nurture of the offspring be natural, it follows that society must also be natural to man and "that out of society and community he never did, nor

ever can subsist." Pope in his *Essay on Man* reverted to the
classical poets and looked upon the state of nature as a salutary
condition, a type of Golden Age:

> Nor think in *Nature's State* they blindly trod;
> The State of Nature was the reign of God.

(III, 147-8)

Another poet, Voltaire, in keeping with strong antiprimitivist
proclivities, ridiculed the state of pure nature as one of ignorance
and discomfort (*Le Mondain*), which no one is his right mind
would care to experience.

Although most eighteenth-century thinkers agreed that man
had basic social contacts in the state of nature, the fundamental
question was that of government—did any kind of political
control exist in the state of nature, and, if not, how did it come
about subsequently? This topic was widely discussed in connection with the doctrine of natural rights as expressed in the
Declaration of Independence, and it figured also in the debates
over the Constitution. Earlier in England, Mandeville in *The
Fable of the Bees*, 1714, suggested that "in the wild state of
nature" men were without government and incapable of agreeing
with one another. A number of wise or crafty men persuaded
their fellow men, therefore, to curb their appetites for the general
interest and in the process subjected them to labor, servitude and
misery. Rousseau in the opening sentence of his *Social Contract*,
1762, echoed this theory: "Man is born free; and yet is everywhere
enslaved." In his previous *Second Discourse*, 1755, he had
similarly declared, "The first Man who, after enclosing a Piece of
Ground, took it into his Head to say, *This is mine*, and found
People simple enough to believe him, was the true Founder of
civil Society."

In American literature, the most famous description of the
passage from the state of nature to civil society appears in
Thomas Paine's pamphlet of the American Revolution, *Common
Sense*. In the first paragraph Paine contrasts society which
"promotes our happiness *positively* by uniting our affections"
with governments which work *"negatively* by restraining our
vices." "Society in every state," he continues, "is a blessing but
government even in its best state is but a necessary evil" (Paine
1945, 1:4-9). To portray the origin of government, he asks his
readers to suppose "a small number of persons settled in some
sequestered part of the earth, unconnected with the rest, they will
then represent the first peopling of any country, or of the world"

(Paine 1945, 1:4-9). From this "state of natural liberty" they will come together in society, "the reciprocal blessings of which . . . would render the obligations of law and government unnecessary while they remained perfectly just to each other" (Paine 1945, 1:4-9). Only as they "relax in their duty and attachment to each other" will government be needed "to supply the defect of moral virtue." According to this imaginative portrayal of remote history, man in the state of nature and earliest stages of society was guided by his reason and virtuous instincts, but as his vicious and selfish impulses developed, he required the restraints of government. Paine's opponents—and indeed nearly all of his commentators—have treated this portrayal as an ingenious fabrication.

Modern anthropologists have approached this topic from both the emic, or empirical perspective, and the etic, or theoretical one. Morton H. Fried has taken the theoretical path in attempting to trace an evolution from simple social ranking to social stratification and finally to the complex state—an elaboration of the eighteenth-century dichotomy of society and government. He depends on theory alone, particularly in the definition of terms. A truly egalitarian society, which has never existed, has no members with more prestige than any others. A ranking society has positions of status or prestige, but these are devoid of power. A stratified society has differentiated levels conditioned by degrees of access to economic resources (Fried 1968, 569-70). The members of both ranking and stratified societies are related by some degree of kinship. When the state emerges from a stratified society, the organization of power takes place on a supra-kinship basis. Fried maintains that the various stages in this emergence or transformation are too complex to be traced, but he makes a distinction between a pristine state, one that has developed by itself out of local conditions, and a secondary state, one that has been pushed to a higher form of organization by some other state. In his opinion, a truly pristine state has not existed since the last one emerged in Mesoamerica, possibly two thousand years ago.

Another anthropologist who has followed the etic or empirical path, has produced evidence that societies without government such as Thomas Paine has described actually exist in the twentieth century. Presumably these are equivalent to those Fried has designated as ranking societies. A French ethnographer, Pierre Clastres (1977) in a study with the intriguing title *Society*

Against the State, posits the concept of power as the difference between the natural and the social condition. In the civil state, one or more individuals exert power and the others obey it; in the natural state, no such power exists. Clastres affirms that the concept of power does not arise from biological roots, that is, from nature, but derives entirely from culture (2). He then proceeds to demonstrate how tribes of South American Indians comprise a society without power. In so doing, he draws a parallel between western ethnocentrism and evolution, both states of mind assuming without warrant that the Western notions of the ideal man represent the best possible human being that the world could ever develop (10). The essence of his thesis has been summarized by Brian C. J. Singer:

> At the center of Pierre Clastres' political anthropology there lies the verification of a piece of evidence both banal and shocking: primitive societies do not have a state. That is to say, in these societies there is no division between ruler and ruled, no relation of authority and obedience, no monopoly of force by a separate body, no separate legal institutions with a power of punishment, no separate decision-making apparatus—in short, no domination. And in conjunction with the absence of a *political* division, there is an absence of any division into economic classes: that is, there is no appropriation of wealth by some at the expense of others, no alienated labour, no exploitation; indeed, in these societies it hardly makes sense to speak of rich and poor. These societies, in sum, present by virtue of their state of non-division a degree of egalitarianism and a freedom from external constraint that is without parallel in any other known society. (1986, 5)

If his fieldwork is valid, Clastres does seem to have demonstrated the truth of the assumption of Rousseau, Paine, and others that a state of nature—that is of society without government—has indeed existed in human experience.

I do not believe that in bringing these remarks to a close, I am justified in drawing general conclusions from the three models or examples that I have been presenting, other than that they show that literature and anthropology may sometimes support, complement, or corroborate each other.

All men have eyes for seeing, and the drives to appease human appetites such as hunger and sex are also universal. As these physical and psychological similarities are reflected in thought and behavior, they reveal universal patterns, but not necessarily the "unconscious structure" of Lévi-Strauss. Literature as an image of these human characteristics together with other emotional and aesthetic qualities may be said to exhibit identical universal elements, or *invariables,* as Etiemble calls them. The

search for these invariables is a close and undeniable link between
literature and anthropology.

Works Cited

Aldridge, A. Owen. *The Reemergence of World Literature: A Study of Asia and the West*. Newark, DE: University of Delaware Press, 1986.

Clastres, Pierre, *Society Against the State*. New York: Urizen Books, 1977.

Durant, Will. *Philosophy and the Social Problem*. New York: Macmillan, 1917.

———. *The Story of Philosophy*. New York: Simon and Schuster, 1926.

Eco, Umberto. *Travels in Hyper Reality*. New York: Harcourt Brace Jovanovich, 1986.

Elsbree, Langdon. *The Rituals of Life. Patterns in Narratives*. Port Washington, NY: Kennikat Press, 1982.

Etiemble. *Le Sonnet des Voyelles de Rimbaud*. Paris: Gallimard, 1968.

Fried, Morton H. "On the Evolution of Social Stratification and the State." In *Readings in Anthropology*. 2d ed. 2 vols. *Cultural Anthropology*, ed. Morton H. Fried. New York: Thomas Y. Crowell, 1968.

Harris, Marvin. "Emics, Etics, and the New Ethnography." In *Readings in Anthropology*. 2d ed. 2 vols. *Cultural Anthropology*, ed. Morton H. Fried. New York: Thomas Y. Crowell, 1968.

Lévi-Strauss, Claude. *Anthropologie structurale*. Paris: Plon, 1958.

———. *Structural Anthropology*. New York: Basic Books, 1963.

Lévi-Strass, Claude, and Roman Jacobson. "'Les Chats' de Charles Baudelaire." *L'Homme*. 2(1962):5-12.

Lovejoy, Arthur O., and George Boas. *Primitivism and Related Ideas in Antiquity*. New York: Octagon Books, 1965.

De Man, Paul. *The Resistance to Theory*. Minneapolis: University of Minnesota Press, 1986.

Paine, Thomas. *Complete Writings*. Ed. Phillip S. Foner. New York: Citadel Press, 1945.

Plath, David. *Long Engagements*. Stanford, CA: Stanford University, 1980.

Posnett, Hutcheson Macaulay. *Comparative Literature*. New York: D. Appleton, 1886.

Shaftesbury, Anthony Ashley Cooper. *Characteristics*. Ed. John M. Robertson. 2 vols. Indianapolis: Bobbs Merrill, 1964.

Shumaker, Wayne. *Literature and the Irrational. A Study in Anthropological Backgrounds*. Englewood Cliffs, NJ: Prentice-Hall, 1960.

Singer, Brian C. J. *Societies Against the State*. Minneapolis: University of Minnesota Press, 1986.

Spradley, James P., and George E. McDonough, eds. *Anthropology Through Literature*. Boston: Little, Brown, 1973.

SUCCESS IN SHAKESPEARE

Philip K. Bock

ABSTRACT

The upward mobility of families or individuals is certainly not an entirely modern phenomenon, despite the attention given to "yuppies" in the popular press. Americans have, for centuries, been preoccupied with equal access to the opportunity for advancement, and Roy D'Andrade (1984) has documented a distinctive set of concepts related to "success" in U.S. culture. This chapter explores the various meanings of *success* in Shakespeare's plays and sonnets, showing both differences from and similarities to the Baruya people of Papua.

The extraordinary creativity of the late Tudor age was accompanied by greatly increased individual mobility, both geographic and social. As D. C. Coleman has written recently,

> When Shakespeare left Stratford to seek his fortune in London, he was only doing what many others did. London's rate of growth was two or three times that of the population as a whole. As the center of government, the seat of the law, the focus of cultural life, and the commercial and financial capital of the realm, it attracted all sorts: the politically ambitious, the budding young lawyer, the merchant and the businessman, the courtier and the courtesan, the poet and the playwright. (1985, 68)

This chapter asks what constituted *success* in Elizabethan England? In particular, how did Shakespeare represent successful people and what were his attitudes toward Elizabethan "yuppies"? It then compares this historical situation with types of success in a rather exotic, far-off society to put our tentative conclusions into ethnographic perspective.

The forerunners of Renaissance *success stories* include tales of the classical heroes (especially Jason, Ulysses, and Aeneas), whose travels and adventures eventuated in a triumphant return home. Also important were the lives of the Christian apostles and saints whose triumphs were of a different order, resulting in their own salvation and the conversion or redemption of others. The books of Machiavelli, Castiglione, and similar guides to secular power or influence provided a third model of success.

In Tudor times, one could still evaluate one's life with reference to any or all of the standards mentioned above—honor, salvation, personal secular achievement—but concern with the last of these seems to have been increasing. Indeed, Alan

Macfarlane (1978, 63) has argued that individual mobility was possible and common in England as early as the thirteenth century. And Stephen Greenblatt has written that, early in the Tudor era, there appears "an increased self-consciousness about the fashioning of human identity as a manipulable, artful process" (1980, 12). By the time Shakespeare began to write (about 1590) there already existed a large body of middle-class literature and drama depicting the upward mobility of individuals and families who practiced the Protestant virtues or who managed to ingratiate themselves with the Court. But the goals of honor, salvation, or success imply quite different strategies and, most likely, different senses of the self that pursues them.

VARIETIES OF SUCCESS

In its modern sense of *attaining wealth, favor, or eminence*, the word *success* is just over five hundred years old. It is derived from Latin verbal forms meaning to come after, to follow, to succeed in time or in an office. As a noun, *success* was originally bivalent: it might designate good or ill success, but during the sixteenth century, it gradually narrowed to signify a good outcome. Let us turn to the plays to see if we can discern Shakespeare's attitude toward the different types of success.

Following the method of sampling used in my book, *Shakespeare and Elizabethan Culture*, I begin by examining the occurrences of the word *success* and related forms in the corpus of Shakespeare's works. The *Harvard Concordance* shows that, with few exceptions, *succeed* (plus various suffixes) carries the meaning *coming after in legitimate lineal or royal succession*, or *to be expected in a course of events*. For example, "Who should succeed the father but the son?" (3H6 2.2.94), or "What was past, what might succeed" (PER 1.2.83). In the poems, Shakespeare writes more generally of *succeeding times* (LUC 525) and even of *succeeding men* (SON 19.12). We need not consider these forms any further.[1]

The word *success* itself occurs (without suffixes) fifty-four times in twenty different plays and one poem; forty-seven of these occurrences are in verse lines, the rest in prose. We find also several suffixed forms: *successantly* (once), *successes* (three), *successful* (six), and *successfully* (three), but none of these enriches the meaning of the basic form. I limit myself for the present, therefore, to the fifty-four occurrences of *success*, examining each use in context to determine its range of meanings and to whom different kinds of success are attributed in various social and literary contexts.

Inspection of the fifty-four lines in context reveals a general meaning of *outcome* or *whatever follows*, for which the negative pole, *ill or bad success*, is always marked and the positive pole usually unmarked, though *good success* may be specified to enhance the contrast, or (more likely) for metrical purposes; for example, "Mistrust of good success hath done this deed" (JC 5.3.66). In the plays, one may occasionally anticipate good or bad success in one's travels, in appeals to higher authority, in intrigue, or in financial affairs; but the three most common categories of success are in love, in war (i.e., military victory of some kind), and in politics (where the related meaning of legitimate succession is often found). The word *win* is also used in these contexts.

These different types of success distribute across the genres as one would expect: the comedies deal largely with success in love, the histories with war and political succession. In several of the histories, the turning wheel of fortune is a dominant image: men are raised to heights of power only to be cast down again, perhaps because of specific evil deeds or a weakness of character (e.g., Richard II). King Henry VI moralizes "[t]hat things ill got had ever bad success" (3H6 2.2.46).

The tragedies show the greatest variety of types. Those with historical plots (JC, ANT, COR) contain many references to military success. In the tragedies, the characters' weaknesses are related more directly to their unhappy ends. The pride of Coriolanus and the ambition of Macbeth are familiar examples. Explicit references to secular success occur mainly in the comedies. For example, in *Two Gentlemen of Verona*, Valentine sets out to seek his fortune in the big city, is betrayed by his friend, Proteus, retreats into a Green World, and is finally redeemed by a Good Woman. In the romances, success usually requires incredible coincidences or supernatural intervention.

The notion of individual achievement is present throughout the plays, but we may ask just how strong achievement imagery is in the different genres. A convenient sample of genres can be constructed by using the nine comedies (excluding the three problem plays, TRO, AWW, and MM), the nine tragedies, and nine history plays (excluding the late collaboration, H8). If we chart the combined frequency of the words *success* and *win* by genre, we find the following pattern (Table 1):

Table 1. Frequency of *success* and *win* by genre.

	Comedies	Tragedies	Histories
Frequency	27	39	58
Average	3.0	4.3	6.4

Charting the occurrence of key words allows us also to ask whether *success* is ever an attribute of *women*. The answer is a qualified "yes." The only women to whom military success is attributed are the cross-dressing Joan of Arc (1H6) and Queen Margaret of Anjou, whose determination contrasts with the indecisiveness of her King. At one point, Clifford says to Henry: "I would your Highness would depart the field, / The Queen hath best success when you are absent" (3H6 2.2.74).

Two other women attempt kinds of success: Isabel (in *Measure for Measure*) hopes to succeed in convincing Angelo to release her brother, but her appeal to corrupt male authority fails. Helena (in *All's Well that Ends Well*) does succeed in curing the King of his affliction. But aside from *la Pucelle*, Queen Margaret, and Helena, no women in the plays are said to have success. For many male characters of high status, amorous, military, and political success are of a piece, though they may be achieved at the cost of salvation (e.g., Macbeth, Claudius, and Edmund).

Some Comparative Materials

In addition to systematic sampling and cross-tabulation by genders and genres, my approach to Shakespeare involves the use of selected ethnographic examples to give perspective on Elizabethan culture. For example, I have used materials on Apache sociolinguistics to compare with attitudes toward silence in the plays and materials on Ilongot concepts of body parts to illuminate many of Shakespeare's references to the heart (Bock 1984, chapters 8-11).

To highlight what is distinctive about Elizabethan concepts of success, I draw on a remarkable work by the French structural Marxist, Maurice Godelier: *The Making of Great Men* (1986). In this monograph, Godelier recounts the ways in which the Baruya of Papua identify promising boys, and "produce" great men of three kinds. He demonstrates also the relation of these means of production to the pervasive domination of women by men in Baruya society.

The Baruya are quite different from those neighboring peoples in Papua whose "big men" achieve temporary power by the manipulation of economic exchanges and relationships of obligation. There are no "big men" in this sense among the Baruya; rather, three kinds of successful individuals are recognized: *aoulatta* (the great warrior), *koulaka* (the great shaman), and *kayareumala* (the great cassowary hunter). Supporting the great warrior is *tannaka*, an outstanding farmer whose skill and industry enable him (by exploiting the labor of his wives) to stockpile the resources necessary for military victory. Finally, the *tsaimaye* produces the bars of potassium salt that serve as a medium of exchange in the southern Papuan highlands. But the warrior, shaman, and cassowary hunter occupy the highest positions in the Baruya social hierarchy. Future specialists are identified during the initiation process that reproduces that hierarchy.

Baruya male initiation lasts for more than ten years, a long period even by Melanesian standards. During this time, boys and young men are strictly segregated from the world of women and are subjected to long, painful ordeals, including several years when, as an aid to growth, they are required to ingest older boys' sperm. Young brides are also instructed to drink their husbands' sperm to aid in their growth and, after childbirth, their production of milk. Only after he has fathered several children is a man's initiation considered complete. By this time he is well on the way to one of the specialized careers or, by default, to a reputation as an ordinary "sweet-potato man." The specialized roles are not inherited, though sacred objects (*kwaimatnie*) that are passed through the male line may influence the selection process described below.

Godelier clearly explicates the system of oppositions that organize Baruya thought, especially the powerful symbols of sperm, human milk, and menstrual blood. He concludes that "male domination is . . . the outcome of distinct, complementary, and unequal powers, which ultimately place the men above the women, and . . . the great men above all others" (65). Male domination is also rationalized by reference to female anatomy which is regarded as inherently prone to leak dangerous sexual fluids (blood and sperm).

Godelier then describes the crucial transitional stages of male initiation when the owner of one of the sacred objects (a man who has previously used his powers to help all the boys to grow strong) divines the future of each initiate. He then informs the older men which of the initiates possesses the vocation of warrior, shaman, or hunter. The revelation of vocations comes near the middle of the initiation period when the boys are approximately fifteen years old and the adults have had many occasions to observe their conduct, including their reactions to ordeals and crises. The prophecies are confirmed by further behavioral signs and supernatural messages, but initial selection takes into account each boy's position in the lineage structure. Most of these predictions are fulfilled, though the Baruya do leave some room for uncertainty.

What kinds of *success stories* do Baruya tell about their great men? The great warrior "is described as being driven by a murderous force, by a magical power that goes before him and enables him to detect the presence of an enemy, to anticipate his moves, and . . . kill him" (108). The tales tell of single combat between warriors as their supporters (dogs) stand back awaiting the outcome and then helping the victor to drag the enemy's corpse behind their lines where it might be mutilated and, perhaps, eaten. These heroes gain fame and glory, but not wealth:

> An *aoulatta*, say the Baruya, is a man with few wives, few children, spending most of his time keeping watch over the enemy, laying ambushes for him, attacking him or escaping his clutches, and he usually leaves his descendants very little newly cleared land. [The warrior] derived his authority both from his bravery and from the fear that it inspired, and thus converted his prestige into social power. But there were limits to this power and it was dangerous to overstep them. (107, 109)

If he became a tyrant, it might be arranged for him to be killed in battle or murdered by treachery.

The great shaman played a more defensive role, protecting the community from illness or attack by enemy spirits. Women could become shamans but never truly great ones because they never performed war magic. A good shaman used his or her power in the service of the people, defending the social order. "Shamans are expected to behave with gravity, to maintain a calm, aloof bearing in public, and to speak little but wisely" (122). Villagers are glad to have a great shaman settle among them; a shaman may even be offered a spouse as an inducement. Though paid for their services, shamans never become wealthy.

Like the warrior, the cassowary hunter is always male; his chosen activity lies "midway between war and shamanism" (125). It differs from common forms of hunting because of the unusual nature of the animal, the techniques used, and the status that success confers on the lucky hunter. The cassowary is a powerful, swift, but flightless bird. It does not fit the usual categories of

Baruya thought and that consequently attracts ritual attention
(Douglas 1975, 27-46) Against empirical evidence, the natives
consider all cassowarys to be female and refer to them as "little
girls" or "old women." The bird can be trapped only with
difficulty, caught in a noose that strangles it to death or, once
trapped, clubbed to death without actually shedding its blood.
Special precautions must be taken by the hunters, especially
sexual abstinence. They also consume hallucinogenic mushrooms
so that they will be possessed by the cassowary spirit and receive
visions of success, after which imitative masked dances are
performed. Godelier interprets this complex as expressing the
superiority of men over women. Although not as prestigious as
the great warrior or shaman, the cassowary hunter will be lifted
above the ordinary men so long as his luck lasts.

Elizabethan Analogs

What does my summary account of Baruya great men enable us
to see that we might previously have overlooked? Beginning with
the great warrior, we might look for parallels in the plays of
Shakespeare. We seek a hero of superhuman ability who defends
his community against human enemies. He may achieve high
prestige but little wealth, and should he overstep the limits of his
power, he is betrayed, murdered, and mutilated. Of the dozen or
so soldiers to whom Shakespeare attributes military success, three
match closely the Baruya concept of a great warrior in their
displays of personal valor.

In Shakespeare's very first history play (1H6), Lord Talbot
shows these characteristics in his "rare success in arms," his
fearful ability to surprise and defeat the French, often in single
combat. His very name becomes a rallying cry to the English
forces. Lord Lucy likens him to Hercules, "the great Alcides of
the field" (4.7.77). Like the Baruya warrior, Talbot has no
opportunity to profit from his success because he already lies
dead clasping his dead son in his arms, and the French King has
to overrule the Bastard's suggestion that Talbot's body be
mutilated: "O no, forbear! for that which we have fled / During
the life, let us not wrong it dead" (4.7.49-50).

Another fearless soldier who refuses any reward is Coriolanus,
but the pride of this Roman hero leads to his downfall. The
tribune, Sicinius, says of him: "Such a nature / Tickled with
good success, disdains the shadow / Which he treads on at noon"
(1.1.259-61). Coriolanus considers only the great enemy warrior,

Aufidius, to be a worthy adversary. Finally, turned against Rome, he is betrayed and murdered by his new allies, meeting the same fate as a proud and tyrannical Baruya warrior.

Our last successful soldier does profit for a time from his victories. Ross delivers the good news:

> The King hath happily receiv'd, Macbeth,
> The news of thy success . . .
> And for an earnest of a greater honor
> He bade me, from him, call thee Thane of Cawdor. . . .
>
> (1.3.89-90,104-5)

The witches had predicted this honor, and Macbeth reflects that their "supernatural soliciting / Cannot be ill, cannot be good. If ill / Why hath it given me earnest of success" (1.3.130-32), with a play here on the older meaning, *succession*. He writes to his wife that the witches "met me in the day of success" (1.5.2), and, with her encouragement, his ambition grows. Yet when he is about to murder Duncan, Macbeth's soliloquy indicates his uncertainty about the outcome of their plot:

> If th' assassination
> Could trammel up the consequence, and catch,
> With his surcease, success . . . [again, both meanings]
> We'ld jump [risk] the life to come.
>
> (1.7.2-3; 7)

There are no further references to *success* in this play. Deceived by the spirits, Macbeth ultimately meets the fate of a tyrannical Baruya warrior: he is betrayed by his supporters, his body mutilated and dishonored.

The term *shaman* refers to any curer who uses spirits to diagnose, or to heal or harm. Even in this general sense, it would be difficult to find a great shaman in Shakespeare's plays. Helena, as we have noted, asks for "leave to try success" with her remedy for the King's affliction (AWW 1.3.247), and she is rewarded with a spouse (the reluctant Bertram).

The rest of Shakespeare's curers are male, and they limit themselves to treatments of physical ailments. In *Macbeth*, for instance, when the Doctor of Physic is asked, "Canst thou not minister to a mind diseas'd?" he replies: "Therein the patient / Must minister to himself" (5.3.40; 45-46). One human figure in the plays does have, however, many characteristics of a great shaman. Prospero, in *The Tempest*, commands invisible spirits and uses them to confound his enemies and please his friend. Having settled in the enchanted island with his daughter, Miranda, he uses his magic to dominate Caliban and Ariel. With his sacred objects (staff and book), he foresees the approach of his enemies, produces the great storm, divines Ferdinand's true character and future greatness, and drives the traitors to madness! Yet, like the good Baruya shaman, he seeks no lasting power and seems content to uphold the social order.

With some effort, Prospero can be made to fit the pattern of great shaman, but what in the Elizabethan world corresponds, even roughly, to the role of cassowary hunter? I can produce a few rather unlikely candidates. For example, Caliban, in a highly altered state of consciousness (his first drunk), promises to teach Stephano how "to snare the nimble marmazet" (TMP 2.2.170). The *marmoset*, a small New World monkey that fell outside the usual categories of English animals, is one possible analog for the cassowary, especially if we recall that Caliban also plans to steal Miranda for Stephano; dominance over women should be symbolically established by our hunter to fill out the parallelism with Baruya shamanism.

I next considered, but set aside as an unworthy symbol, the proverbially stupid woodcock that is easily trapped in *springes* or *gins* (HAM 1.3.115, 5.2.306; 3H6 1.4.61; TN 2.5.83). I then discarded the pathetic but unspecified birds that are caught in sticky lime spread on twigs or perches, although as Caroline Spurgeon wrote, Shakespeare's "bird images are remarkable for the intense feeling they reveal for the trapped, limed, or snared bird" (1958, 27).

It then struck me that one of the lines in my original sample of success stories contained a better analog to the cassowary hunter. In Act 3 of *The Merchant of Venice*, after Bassanio has won Portia and Gratiano claims Nerissa's hand, Gratiano says: "I know he [Antonio] will be glad of our success; / We are the Jasons, we have won the fleece" (3.2.240-1); earlier Bassanio likened Portia's "sunny locks" to the fleece, and her home at Belmont to Colchis, where "many Jasons come in quest of her" (1.1.170f).

This passage recalls the exploits of the Argonauts (who subdued the independent women of Lemnos), and especially Jason, who, with the aid of the barbarian princess and shaman, Medea, captured the golden fleece of the magical ram. Shakespeare seems to have drawn on Ovid rather than the Greek sources (Homer, Hesiod, and Apollonios Rhodios) for this story. The emphasis in Book VII of *Metamorphoses* is on Medea's divinely caused love and her willingness to abandon her home and

(paternal) kin to help the stranger, even against her better
judgment (Innes 1955, 155).[2]

The reference to the golden fleece in *The Merchant of Venice*
suggests that the men's domination of the women and their
wealth is, like Jason's, the result of supernatural intervention.
With the aid of Medea's magical herbs, Jason overcame the
dragon guarding the fleece just as Bassanio solved the riddle of
the three caskets, and just as the great cassowary hunter traps and
kills his "female" quarry with a combination of skill and magic.
All of these acts express male domination for, as Godelier writes,
the cassowary is "a savage woman familiar with the forest spirits
and supernatural powers, but she is defeated by the power of a
man, who captures her spirit and bends it to his law (Godelier,
129)."

CONCLUSIONS

What have we learned from this survey of Shakespearean
success stories and the comparison between Elizabethan and
Baruya modes of success? I hope that the perspective provided by
the Papuan material enables us to see similarities and differences
between the kinds of success available in both societies, one
obviously more complex and hierarchical than the other, but
built on the same principle of male domination. The kind of boy
who might be singled out in Baruya initiation rites as a
prospective great warrior, shaman, or hunter would have been
sent, in Elizabethan England, "in service" to the royal court or a
noble household, and later to University, the Church, or the Inns
of Court. In Shakespeare's plays, the possibility of greatness was
still viewed as regulated by noble birth and male gender. The
limited *success* of Joan of Arc, Queen Margaret, and Helena are
exceptions that prove the rule.

I would not want to press the analogies between Baruya and
Elizabethan warriors or curers too far, and the parallels between
cassowary hunters and the Argonauts is quite fanciful. As for the
Baruya concern with semen, milk, and menstrual blood, I find
little explicit concern in the plays with any of these substances,
aside from a few passages in *Macbeth* and Gonzalo's surprising
reference to menstruation in the midst of the tempest ("The
ship . . . as leaky as an unstanch'd wench" 1.1.46-48), although
the flow of a man's *tears* is often feared as feminizing him.

Yet, in a recent article, Thomas Laquer (1986, 8) has suggested
that the Renaissance received from antiquity a medical doctrine

stating the equivalence and mutual convertibility of semen, maternal milk, and blood! Perhaps we should look more closely at Shakespeare's references to milk and blood and investigate more carefully the Elizabethan ideas about hereditary substance, nobility, and masculinity before we dismiss these topics as irrelevant to success in Shakespeare.

NOTES

[1] All Shakespeare quotations are from *The Riverside Shakespeare* edited by G. B. Evans. Abbreviations are those used in that source and in Spevak.

[2] On Shakespeare's use of Ovid, see also P. K. Bock's "'Neither Two Nor One': Dual Unity in *The Phoenix and Turtle*," *The Journal of Psychoanalytic Anthropology* 10 (1987): 251-67.

WORKS CITED

Bock, P. K. *Shakespeare and Elizabethan Culture*. New York: Schocken, 1984.

Coleman, D. C. "Economic Life in Shakespeare's England." In *William Shakespeare, Vol. I: His World*, ed. J. F. Andrews. New York: Scribner, 1985.

D'Andrade, R. G. "Cultural Meaning Systems." In *Culture Theory*, ed. R. A. Shweder and R. A. LeVine. Cambridge: Cambridge University Press, 1984.

Douglas, M. D. *Implicit Meanings*. London: Routledge and Kegan Paul, 1975.

Evans, G. B., ed. *The Riverside Shakespeare*. Boston: Houghton Mifflin Co., 1974.

Godelier, M. *The Making of Great Men*. Translated by R. Swyer. Cambridge: Cambridge University Press, 1986.

Greenblatt, S. *Renaissance Self-Fashioning*. Chicago: University of Chicago Press, 1980.

Innes, M. M., trans. *The Metamorphoses of Ovid*. New York: Penguin, 1955.

Laquer, T. "Orgasm, Generation, and the Politics of Reproductive Biology." *Representations* 14 (1986): 1-41.

Macfarlane, A. *The Origins of English Individualism*. New York: Cambridge University Press, 1978.

Spevak, M., ed. *The Harvard Concordance to Shakespeare*. Cambridge, MA: Belknap Press, 1973.

Spurgeon, C. E. *Shakespeare's Imagery and What It Tells Us*. Boston: Beacon Press, 1958.

VONNEGUT'S ANTHROPOLOGY THESIS

James S. Whitlark

ABSTRACT

Not only Kurt Vonnegut's novel *Cat's Cradle* (which the University of Chicago accepted as an M.A. thesis) but all of his books have grown from his graduate work in anthropology, particularly from the concepts of *cultural relativism* and the *Folk Society*. By examining the synthesis of these ideas in "Fluctuations Between Good and Evil in Simple Tales" (an unaccepted attempt at a thesis, c. 1947), in *Cat's Cradle* (1963), and in *Galapagos* (1985), one may survey his developing theory of how anthropology and literature interrelate. Despite its roots in anthropology, this theory is not anthropocentric but *biocentric*, to use Margot Norris's term (although she has written that the biocentric tradition ended in the first few decades of the twentieth century).

In 1971, the University of Chicago accepted the novel *Cat's Cradle* by Kurt Vonnegut, Jr., as a thesis and awarded him a master's degree in anthropology.[1] Considering that universities seldom bestow less than a doctorate on famous authors, this was a decidedly small honor, yet it did not come easily. More than 25 years earlier (in 1945), on what Vonnegut calls the "happiest day of [his] life" (1976, 175) he became a graduate student at that institution. Subsequently switching from one anthropological specialization to another, he settled finally on the cultural variety. As he remarked in a self-interview, cultural anthropology was what he was seeking because it is a "science that is mostly poetry" (1981, 100), or as his graduate adviser, Sydney Slotkin, reportedly termed it, "poetry which *pretends* to be scientific" (Vonnegut 1971, 176). After two years of measuring skulls with rice, examining Indian pottery, and listening to sometimes stimulating lectures, he tried more than once to submit a master's thesis. Among these attempts was a project to which he has often since alluded, "Fluctuations between Good and Evil in Simple Tales."[2]

Its title suggests accurately that it was a pioneer effort in the relationship of literature and anthropology, and, like most pioneer efforts, it had problems. According to Vonnegut, "It was rejected because it was so simple and looked like too much fun. One must not be too playful" (1981, 312). The comment about playfulness registers an understandable bitterness about academia, but since the University of Chicago accepted the whimsical novel *Cat's Cradle*, the weightier ground for rejection seems more likely to have been oversimplification—a charge critics sometimes still make about his work but with less justification. Although the thesis itself is lost, he includes an abstract of it in his book *Palm Sunday: An Autobiographical Collage* (1981, 312-16). By his own testimony, the rejected manuscript contained little more than curved lines on graph paper charting stories from many cultures according to characters' variations from good to ill fortune. He was hesitant even to note that the graph for the Judeo-Christian notion of fall and redemption resembled the graph for Cinderella, but, realizing that both plots have widely influenced Western culture, he finally mentioned the parallel. Unfortunately, when he was asked to explain the significance of his findings, he argued merely that his "graphs were at least as suggestive as [archaeological] pots and spearheads" (314). The Anthropology Department was not amused—and Vonnegut was not yet ready to say what his results suggested.

In the prefatory first chapter of *Slaughterhouse-Five* (1966, 5), he describes his graphing the novel preliminary to writing it, but such application of his 1947 methods to later writings is less interesting than the fact that he has continued to think about the link between anthropology and literature. At Texas Tech University in November 1983, Vonnegut gave a chalk talk including a summary of his rejected thesis, but in a significantly more developed form than the version published only two years before. The addition arose from his new ability to treat precisely those stories that did not fit within the scope of the original manuscript, because the events in them could not be classified as either clear-cut good or evil. His examples consisted of Shakespeare's *Hamlet* (which has defied definitive explication for centuries) and an American Indian tale narrating a seemingly pointless journey.[3] He argued that life resembles such stories more precisely, yet writers have misled us disastrously by giving simpler shapes to narratives. The probable source for this observation is his own novel *Deadeye Dick* (1982), the publication of which fell between the 1981 abstract and the 1983 speech. In Chapter 26 of that novel, the narrator argues for three pages that people and nations may even become suicidal if they try to turn life into a shapely tale with a clear-cut end (208-10).

This argument is, however, merely the most extensive treatment of a notion that appears again and again in his works, most notably in *Mother Night*, where the narrator talks repeatedly of suicide, seriously contemplating it at the book's conclusion. He regrets not having killed himself at the climax of his life, for, as he explains, "I admire form....I admire things with a beginning, a middle, an end" (1961, 136)—an Aristotelian literary pattern often discussed at that most Aristotelian of schools, the University of Chicago. Also in *Mother Night*, Vonnegut writes, "Aristotle is said to have been the last man to understand the whole of his culture" (49)—a two-pronged observation suggesting both the greatness of Aristotle and the pathetic case of modern intellectuals, who must ignore what they cannot understand in order to organize what they do. Vonnegut's thesis adviser once told an anthropology class that the common denominator of all the arts was the artist's belief, "I can do very little about the chaos around me, but at least I can reduce to perfect order this square of canvas, this piece of paper, this chunk of stone." Vonnegut (1981, 321) comments:

> Everybody knows that.
> Most of my adult life has been spent in bringing to some kind of order sheets of paper....This severely limited activity has allowed me to ignore many a storm. It has also caused many of the worst storms I ignored.

In *Mother Night*, the form-loving narrator is a writer, whom a fellow artist describes as "a political idiot, an artist who could not distinguish between reality and dreams" (189).
Vonnegut sees two sides to art. On the one hand, he says:

> I guarantee you that no modern story scheme, even plotlessness, will give a reader genuine satisfaction unless one of those old fashioned plots is smuggled in somewhere. (1981, 110)

In other words, a writer must be aware of and use those simple patterns charted in Vonnegut's 1947 thesis because, by reinforcing the culture's values, they genuinely satisfy. Nonetheless, on the other hand, he argues that writers "should be—and biologically have to be—agents of change" (1976, 215). He believes that they ought to further human evolution. Indeed, if they employ the old plots in a facile manner, they do much damage. The ease of ending with a shoot-out may reinforce violence. The aesthetic simplicity of stressing major characters and treating minor ones like "disposable...Kleenex tissues" may reinforce social stratification (1973, 215). Consequently, an author should begin with anthropological understanding sufficient to hold a reader's attention with old patterns, yet reshape them into those forms necessary to speed social development.

Vonnegut relies particularly on two anthropological principles in this mission. The first of these is cultural relativism. He comments:

> A first grader should understand that his culture isn't a rational invention; that there are thousands of other cultures and they all work pretty well; that all cultures function on faith rather than truth; that there are lots of alternatives to our own society. I didn't find that out for sure until I was in the graduate school of the University of Chicago....Of course, now cultural relativity is fashionable—and that probably has something to do with my popularity among young people. (276)

Cultural relativism underlies the basic idea of his 1947 thesis: comparison of patterns from different societies. His relativism explains also one of the paradoxes in his work, his agnosticism yet preoccupation with religion, for he believes "all cultures function on faith." He says that anthropology itself is the only religion for him (1981, 101). Most importantly, cultural relativism allows a way out of the dilemma: how can a writer use the old plots without injuring social evolution? The answer is simple: juxtapose patterns from many societies against science-fiction "alternatives to our society." This he does throughout all his fiction, particularly his accepted thesis, *Cat's Cradle*.

The second fundamental idea that he grasped at the University of Chicago was what his teacher Robert Redfield (head of the Anthropology Department) called *The Folk Society*—a concept stressed in many of the latter's lectures and, eventually, constituting an article published (ironically) the very year Vonnegut left Chicago (Redfield 1947, 293-308).[4] Vonnegut went to the University of Chicago because he thought its anthropology department "was a small, like-minded society which [he] was being allowed to join," that is what he learned to call a *folk society*. He was wrong and has been pursuing a sense of community ever since. He writes, "the First Law of Life...is this: 'Human beings become increasingly contented as they approach the simpleminded, brotherly conditions of a folk society'" (1976, 179-80).[5] In his 1947 thesis, his focus on simple tales, many from folk societies, reflects his early fascination with this theme. Later, Vonnegut repeatedly advocated the creation of extended families. In his novel *Slapstick* (1976), for example, it is one of the major themes. Unfortunately, a *folk society* is one in which "there [is] little change" (1976, 177); thus it cannot serve as a model for social evolution, unless it is the goal of such evolution—a notion he toys with in his most recent novel, *Galapagos*. There is no more striking way of surveying his anthropological development than by briefly comparing that novel with his thesis one, *Cat's Cradle*.

Published in 1963 (only eight years before the University of Chicago recognized it as a work of anthropology), *Cat's Cradle* combines cultural relativism with the folk society through a strange invention of Vonnegut's: the religion of Bokononism. Previously, at the University of Chicago, "Religions were exhibited and studied as the Rube Goldberg inventions [Vonnegut had] always thought they were (1981, 101). Therein lay the temptation to invent a Rube Goldberg religion of his own—one that would embody the community and personally meaningful universe of folk societies, but with irony to furnish the liberating detachment of cultural relativism. Bokonon, the prophet of the faith, admits openly that all his revelations are lies, like Plato's teaching through self-declared myths. Bokonon arranges to have himself and his followers persecuted, to add drama to the faith. "So life became a work of art. . . ." (1963, 119). Unfortunately, as is invariably the conclusion of Vonnegut's literary anthropology, art does not fit the complexity of life. Bokonon suffers from having to suppress his own "piratical" side in order to play persecuted saint while one of his former friends, chosen as his persecutor, finds the role of tyrant so uncongenial that he kills himself. The tyrant is succeeded by another suicide, who manages to destroy virtually the whole world. Such destruction occurs partly because of a dramatic display of his air force. It leads to a freak accident that ruins the government's pageantry—its venture into artistry. Life always eludes artistic control, so (according to Vonnegut) the attempt to produce artistic order is self-destructive for individuals and nations, even though it may allow one to ignore one's sufferings temporarily. The novel has as its epigraph a quotation from the fictional Book of Bokonon: "Live by the foma [harmless untruths] that make you brave and kind and healthy and happy." Above the quotation he writes, "Nothing in this book is true." In this novel, his attitude *seems* to be that one can distinguish harmless fabrications (such as the novel itself) from harmful ones; but Bokonon is the author both of comforting prevarications and of the lie-sustained dictatorship, so the distinction is already problematic[6] and becomes more decisively so in Vonnegut's later fiction.

For the moment, though, Vonnegut keeps his own fictionalizing from being harmful (that is, serious) through his anthropological relativism, his juxtaposing radically different cultures in quick succession until none seems to have any special claim to truth. He begins with a jumble of three American worlds: that of conscienceless absent-minded scientists; that of earthy, ordinary citizens; and that of the conscience-ridden narrator, who seeks to write a truly Christian book. Then the story moves to an island modeled loosely on Haiti, but with Bokononism instead of voodoo and a bizarre Christianity extemporized by mail-order ministers instead of Roman Catholicism. Each world is moored in a different faith while Vonnegut gleefully undercuts them all.[7] Slightly more than half-way through the novel, its title inspires him to provide a little ethnographic digression on the wide diffusion of the cat's-cradle game throughout the world, even though, as one character explains there is *"no damn cat and no damn cradle"* (1963, 114); ten pages later that character finally identifies the cat's cradle with "Religion!" (124).

At the heart of that novel is Vonnegut's play with the old, simple plots, especially the two that his attempted thesis on "Fluctuations . . ." identified with one another: Cinderella and the Judeo-Christian doctrine of fall and redemption. In *Palm Sunday*, Vonnegut writes of the Cinderella *Märchen*, "A lot of people think the story is trash, and on graph paper it certainly looks like trash" (315). His objection is to the happy ending, which complicates the graph and, Vonnegut seems to imply, strains his credulity. Thus, he prefers to truncate the graph: God creates mankind, presents him with Eden, and then drives him forth/the fairy godmother clothes Cinderella, transports her to the ball, then strips her to rags at midnight—end of story. This shortened version is a favorite pattern of Vonnegut.[8] In *Cat's Cradle*, the narrator is suddenly raised to a modern equivalent of royalty, the Presidency of San Lorenzo, and given the modern equivalent of its princess, the most beautiful woman on the island and ward of the previous dictator. Then that domain (and the rest of the world) are destroyed almost completely, so that the narrator has nothing to rule and his beloved, out of Bokononist convictions, refuses either to have sex with him or to confine her chaste affections to him alone. With the annihilation of Bokonon's pseudo-paradise, he concludes the novel and his lying Book by writing what may be a blasphemous suicide note. Novel after novel thereafter Vonnegut continued to worry about the relationship of literature to humanity. In *Breakfast of Champions* (1973), for example, one character becomes a homicidal maniac partly because of reading a novel by Kilgore Trout, Vonnegut's persona.

Galapagos foregrounds, however, the dangers of fiction-making, because its narrator is the embittered ghost of Leon Trotsky Trout, the son of Kilgore. According to the son, his father was "an insult to life itself . . . when he went on doing nothing with it but writing and smoking all the time—and I mean all the time" (1985, 256). (Vonnegut, by the way, has frequently described his own existence as consisting largely of the same two actions). Leon Trotsky Trout finds himself, nonetheless, in the even more pointless task of writing *Galapagos* in the year A.D. 1,001,986, when no one is capable of reading it. The human race as we know it had died out "in the nick of time" (167) and been succeeded by mutated descendants—seal-like creatures saved from evil by their small brains and lack of hands. For a time during the transition to that future, a computer called the "Apple of Knowledge" preserved some "Immortals" of literature while a woman tempted the "new Adam" with it (62, 70); but he finally threw it into the sea because he couldn't stand the buzzing it made when she pressed the buttons. The term "Immortals" is doubly ironic. First, so many of the cited examples of immortal literature are such old chestnuts that they seem well lost. Second, literature's often-heard promise to bestow immortality turns out to be a hoax, since no one is left to appreciate it. In the earlier novel, *Slaughterhouse-Five* (1969), the protagonist delivers a revelation from outer space on a radio program devoted to the question: "Is the novel dead?" *Galapagos* is a ghost novel, seemingly persisting after the death of its genre. Narrated by a phantom, it deliberately sets a worldwide catastrophe in the very next year after its hardbound publication, so that virtually by the time of its mass-market distribution it will be dated, in a sense, obsolete.

Why does Vonnegut write about the extinction of *Homo sapiens* and of literature itself? A suggestion of an answer rests perhaps as far back as his 1947 attempted thesis "Fluctuations between Good and Evil in Simple Tales." His treating literary patterns as objectively as spearheads or pots constituted a proto-structuralism—not a surprising orientation at the University of Chicago, where the seeds of structuralism had been laid, later to flourish as translations of continental structuralist anthropology stimulated the discipline. As Nathan Scott, Jr. (1984, 75-76) remarks well, structuralism has come to represent a spirit of *anti-humanism*, preaching the death of man. Even before such extreme developments, Vonnegut's anthropology courses taught him to treat cultures like broken crockery in the kitchen middens of the world.

More significantly, Charles Darwin's biology had incalculable impact on nineteenth-century anthropology, virtually bringing the discipline into existence and shaping its course. Vonnegut's anthropological education included inevitably the theory of evolution, a doctrine he has subsequently discussed from time to time, most extensively in *Galapagos*, devoted to evolution on islands closely associated with Darwin. According to Margot Norris (1985), Darwin's influence generated what she calls a *biocentric* tradition in literature, characterized by being "hostile to art," critical of man's anthropocentrism, and sympathetic to all animals, particularly to man's own animal nature. She presumes that this tradition largely vanished in the 1930s because "its writings [were] at war with themselves" (1-3). *Galapagos*, however, fits her criteria better than any of the examples she cites. In addition to its pervasive connection to Darwin and its hostility to literature, it also criticizes man's cruel treatment of the "so-called lower animals" (39) and his destructive anthropocentrism.

Even before *Galapagos*, Vonnegut's anthropological speculations grew progressively biological. In 1971, for example, Vonnegut expanded Redfield's idea of the *folk society* into what Vonnegut calls his own *biochemical-anthropological theory*: "we are full of chemicals which require us to belong to folk societies, or failing that, to feel lousy all the time (1976, 178-80). In *Galapagos*, our seal-like descendents have regained that folk innocence and feel relatively content, except when they are being eaten by sharks. Their activities have become largely instinctual, though Vonnegut hints that ours already are. The Trouts continue their pointless writing, like trout beating themselves against the current, or like the repeatedly described, compulsive mating rituals of the Galapagos fauna. The latter inspire the following poem (attributed to a fictional biology student):

> Of course I love you,
> So let's have a kid
> Who will say exactly
> What its parents did;
> "Of course I love you,
> So let's have a kid
> . . ."
> *Et cetera*

Thus the old, simple plot boy meets girl appears as biochemical anthropology, just as writing itself is presented as a hereditary ritual ended only by biological mutation.

How seriously should one take the narrator's praise of mankind's reversion to thoughtless animals? Vonnegut has frequently expressed a longing for the relative mindlessness of folk societies, but evolving into seals certainly does not solve all of humanity's problems. After all, there are the sharks. Furthermore, except for the ghostly narrator, this new world lacks the joy of appreciating that humor found by Vonnegut in his tales of good and evil. Does mankind have a chance at a better fate? The narrator describes the 1980s as a period when humans experimented with personalities as nature later did with "body type" (83). Conceivably, experiments with personality, involving culture as well as the kind of ideas and attitudes that a novel may convey, could have brought people to a less dismal future; however, Vonnegut neither points the way to utopia nor reassures the reader that culture could produce real progress. He continues his anthropological fiction-making, but without faith that either literature or anthropology will be of lasting value. Not just his 1947 manuscripts and *Cat's Cradle* but all of Vonnegut's works are anthropology theses—or more precisely, drafts of a single one, which has not yet reached a hopeful conclusion.

NOTES

[1]According to University of Chicago policy, publications in a discipline subsequent to the rejection of a thesis or dissertation in that field may be considered in place of that rejected work if the University deems the new work to make a significant contribution to the discipline.

[2]Another of Vonnegut's attempts at a thesis (a comparison of the American Indian Ghost Dance with Cubist painting) inspired reference to the Ghost Dance in *Player Piano*, according to Jerome Klinkowitz (1982, 38).

[3]Vonnegut used the same example of an Indian tale in a 1986 speech at Northlake Community College: "We crossed the river. We went to the mountain. We saw a bird. One of the beavers died. That sort of stuff." Brad Bailey (1986), a Dallas reporter, however, alleges that Vonnegut spoke of having left anthropology out of boredom at folktales. Even if Vonnegut made such a joke, it does not erase the fact that not boredom but his repeatedly submitting unaccepted theses caused him to abandon academia. (I thank Dr. Wendell Aycock of Texas Tech University for bringing this newspaper article to my attention.)

[4]For Redfield the "folk society" is an "ideal type" in the sociological sense, "an imagined entity, created [in the mind of the sociologist] only because through it we may hope to understand [the] reality [of actual non-literate societies]" (1947, 295). For Vonnegut, the folk society is an ideal type in the religious sense, an edenic condition now lost.

[5]Related to his longing for brotherhood are other liberal attitudes that Vonnegut (1966, 8) says he learned in the anthropology department, notably his conviction that people are essentially the same and deserve respect—reasons why (according to him) his books lack villains.

[6]Since his statement (that nothing in the book is true) is itself in the book, truth and fiction are inextricably intermingled by a version of the ancient Cretan

paradox. Comparably, the narrator mentions "the cruel paradox of Bokononist thought, the heartbreaking necessity of lying about reality, and the heartbreaking impossibility of lying about it" (189).

[7]He is not, though, anti-Christian but a "Christ-worshipping agnostic" as he revealed in a sermon that he delivered at St. Clement's Episcopal Church, New York, on Palm Sunday, 1980. He preached that Jesus was at least sometimes joking (1981, 325-30). This contention that the gospels (like Vonnegut's novels) should be read as irony is common in modern biblical hermeneutics; for example, Tinsley's (1974, 51) statement:

> The method of Jesus was cryptic (*en krupto* in John), indirect and allusive. His parabolic and ironic method was central to his purpose because, to use Blake's phrase, it 'roused the faculties to act.' This 'indirect' method of Jesus did not impose on others but submitted itself to their free judgment.

[8]For his use of the fall of man, see Steven Marc Gerson (1977). Unfortunately, Gerson finished his research too soon to make use of information (published in 1981) that links his two authors: Vonnegut's comparison of himself with Bellow in their both being "Products of the Anthropology Department of the University of Chicago" (1981, 103). Thus Gerson lost the opportunity to see that both authors' treatments of edens may partly derive from exposure to the notion of a "folk society."

WORKS CITED

Bailey, Brad. "Northlake College Students Get Lesson in Life from Author." *Dallas Morning News*, 10 April 1986.

Gerson, Steven Marc. "Paradise Sought: Adamic Imagery in Selected Novels by Saul Bellow and Kurt Vonnegut, Jr." Diss., Texas Tech University, Lubbock, Texas, 1977.

Klinkowitz, Jerome. *Kurt Vonnegut.* London: Methuen, 1982.

Norris, Margot. *Beasts of the Modern Imagination: Darwin, Nietzsche, Kafka, Ernst, & Lawrence.* London: The Johns Hopkins University Press, 1985.

Redfield, Robert. "The Folk Society." *The American Journal of Sociology* 52 (1947):293-308.

Scott, Nathan A., Jr. "Santayana's Poetics of Belief." In *American Critics at Work: Examinations of Contemporary Literary Theories*, ed. Victor A. Kramer. Troy, NY: Whitson, 1984.

Tinsley, E. J. "The Incarnation, Art and the Communication of the Gospel." In *Art and Religion as Communications*, ed. James Waddell and F. W. Dillistone. Atlanta, GA: John Knox Press, 1974.

Vonnegut, Kurt, Jr. *Mother Night.* New York: Dell, 1961.

——. *Cat's Cradle.* New York: Dell, 1963.

——. *Slaughterhouse-Five: Or the Children's Crusade, A Duty Dance with Death.* New York: Dell, 1966.

——. "Address to the National Institute of Arts and Letters, 1971." In *Wampeters, Foma, and Granfalloons (Opinions)*, 175. New York: Dell, 1976.

——. "Address at the Rededication of Wheaton College Library, 1973." In *Wampeters, Foma and Granfalloons (Opinions)*, 215. New York: Dell, 1976.

——. "Playboy Interview." In *Wampeters, Foma and Granfalloons (Opinions)*, 237. New York: Dell, 1976.

——. "Self-Interview." In *Palm Sunday: An Autobiographical Collage*, 100. New York: Dell, 1981.

——. *Galapagos.* New York: Delacorte Press/Seymour Lawrence, 1985.

FROM STENDHAL TO MALINOWSKI: DIARY AND ETHNOGRAPHIC DISCOURSE

Bernadette Bucher

ABSTRACT

Since Malinowski set the rules of ethnographic fieldwork, diaries and fieldnotes have been the anthropologist's trademark. This paper discusses the poetics of private diary writing and its relevance to the epistemology of ethnographic worktools. The sources analyzed are Malinowski's *A Diary in the Strict Sense of the Term* and Stendhal's own diary.

> I undertake the task to write the story of my life day by day, I don't know if I will have the strength to fullfill this project, already started in Paris. Here is already a grammar mistake. There will be more to come, as my principle is not to be bothered, and never to erase.[1] (Stendhal, Journal, 10 April 1801).

> Resolution: calmly, without clinching my teeth, write the retr[ospective] diary, as a preliminary work. The essence of it is a look into the past, a deeper conception of life . . . But for this purpose you must write diary, and recall facts in a somewhat formal way.
>
> Malinowski, 1967.

When Malinowski's *A Diary in the Strict Sense of the Term* appeared in 1967, twenty-five years after his death, the anthropology community was shocked. Here was the self-proclaimed pioneer of the fieldwork method, the master of intercultural communication, the advocate of tribal societies, caught, so to speak, with his hair (if not his pants) down: subject to alternate bouts of ambitious daydreaming and self-doubt, fits of anger against the natives or the missionaries, both of whom he abuses in the most offensive, even racist terms; working somewhat haphazardly, with a sporadic urge to escape in "trashy" novels and Romantic French poetry; obsessively longing for his fiancee and the delights of "Civilization"; rapt in erotic fantasies about native girls or missionaries' wives; overly heedful of his body to the point of noting down doses of arsenic, calomel, quinine, or enema he administers to himself; complaining of mental confusion, irritability, laziness, blamed on either character flaw or constipation; terrified of the dark; and finally, after the news of his mother's death, collapsing in sobs, self-pity, and moral disintegration. In a way, it was a death blow to the ethnographer as hero-scientist, as if the exposure of Malinowski's intimate weaknesses and one could say too human nature cast a shadow not only on his work but on ethnography itself.

The same shock may occur to Stendhal's fans, followers of Beylisme, if they read his unexpurgated diaries. Who would imagine the creator of Mathilde de la Motte, Julien Sorel, and Armance, interspersing reflections on art, music, and high-strung emotions with an account of his sexual prowess or fiascoes, as well as those of others, described in the crudest possible terms? This morning, for instance, he masturbated before dressing; last night he accomplished the big feat of fondling Mlle d'Oehnhausen's, his host's daughter's, most intimate parts under the table, or of *fucking* (spelled out in the text) so-and-so in such a position at such a time and place. He bought a cane or a new jacket for so many francs and spent time in front of a mirror watching the impression that he could make with them. Like Malinowski, he too is preoccupied with his own body to the point of sketching a "nosographic diary" with onset of symptoms, physician's diagnosis, fee, and prescription. Material life in its most trivial or even sordid aspects and the pettiness of everyday life strewn with washer-woman gossip unfold the behind-the-scenes of the Romantic stage in even more graphic and detailed ways than Malinowski's diary did in dispelling the ethnographic mystique.

The demystification that posthumous publication of such work created in their respective fields emphasizes the issue of the construction of reality in both the novel and ethnographic writing. But my concern here is not with the fictionality of ethnographic discourse, which has already been deftly documented (see Clifford 1986; Clifford and Marcus 1986). It is rather with the production and poetics of the private diary and its continuity with the ethnographic project as observation and description of the culturally distant other. My point is that the reader's negative response to these two diaries comes from measuring them by the aesthetic, moral, or scientific standards of their authors' published works. These standards are not only inapplicable but also precisely the opposite of those on which the diaries are based. My argument is that the motivations for writing a diary (quite explicit in both of these cases), are the key to its epistemology and to its poetics. Diary writing converges with and does not contradict some of the premises of ethnographic fieldwork.

In this respect, I would like to reassess Malinowski's own private diary and its relevance to ethnographic method in the context of a twofold tradition: (a) a secular, agnostic legacy, already found at the crux of Stendhal's diary writing, under the influence of the so-called French Ideologues and (b) a religious tradition that urges the individual to practice self-analysis in the form of written spiritual exercises, as a means of achieving mastery of the self and salvation of the soul.

DIARY-WRITING AS THE ROAD TO HAPPINESS

Behind the young Henri Beyle's (alias Stendhal) project to record the most trivial details of his everyday life, as well as the thoughts, emotions, and sensations that surround them, as they come to him, there is a consistent plan or strategy. Beyle is quite aware of the external constraints that motivate it. He names his masters: Destutt de Tracy and Cabanis, members of the influential "Societé des Observateurs de l'Homme" in Paris and also referred to as the Ideologues after Destutt de Tracy's book *Eléments d'Idéologie* (1825-27). The main lesson Stendhal drew from them is that man's happiness is the supreme goal in life. The *hunt* for happiness, as Stendhal calls it, can be led successfully only through a true knowledge of man's needs. Thus the Delphic and Socratic injunction, "know thyself," remains the prerequisite of this new hedonism: "NOSCE TE IPSUM. I believe with Tracy and Greece that this is the way to happiness. My own means is this diary" (1053).

Thus defined, diary writing is a means to an end. Far from being a narcissistic exercise bringing about its own pleasure, it becomes a cognitive tool, an instrument of self-discovery, itself a prerequisite to achieving happiness. The logic of this double quest (happiness and self-knowledge) entails a dialectic rooted in the tenets of the "Observers of Man." For Destutt de Tracy, the science he calls *ideology* deals with the understanding of man's cognitive processes. As heirs to the eighteenth-century Sensationalists, the Ideologues equate thinking with feeling. There is no break between man's physiology, his sensations, desires, instincts, ideas, and thoughts. This continuity is why, for Tracy, Ideology, the science of cognition, is part of zoology. Likewise, Cabanis, a physician, sees the development of a new science geared at understanding the relationship between physiology (*le physique*), that is "the totality of organic phenomena that, as they are not associated with an idea, occur without our knowledge" and what he calls *le moral*, defined as "the totality of organic phenomena, associated with an idea and accessible to consciousness" (Cabanis 1843, xxviii). This moral science must be independent of any dogma and based, as in the physical sciences, on the understanding of man's "true" internal needs. Thus, for both Tracy and Cabanis, ethics does not consist in rules to follow, but in the discovery of the origin of our desires. Ethics is thus subordinated to psychology; and psychology itself, to man's deepest, organic, unconscious needs.

As it emphasizes the continuity between body and mind, physiology and psychology, this theory of needs is also the key to a dialectic between the self and the other. As the individual explores himself, he discovers, through empirical observation, the interrelationship between what is social and physiological, "home socialis," as Malinowski will say later, and "homo sexualis." The pursuit of individual happiness is thus inseparable from the common good, introspection leads to the observation of the other, and diary writing becomes a tool of apprenticeship toward a dialectic and ethic of alterity, whereby the self, made aware of its true needs, can only reach happiness through a surrender of the ego, a dissolution of subjectivity through empathy or love.

From Private to Ethnographic Diary and Fieldnotes

As I have shown elsewhere (forthcoming), this dialectic has a practical implication. It leads Stendhal to pay minute attention to every down-to-earth detail of not only his own material, social, emotional, and sexual life but also others'. As love with "the best of women" is the only way to find happiness, one must succeed in the social world where these elite women exist. One must not only meet them, but be loved by them. Worldly success requires a knowledge of the tacit rules that govern society, and the diary becomes a tool to master them. As such, it records what Stendhal calls "small true facts," observations of everyday social life that bear a striking resemblance to either what Malinowski calls the "imponderabilia of actual life," such as,

> the routine of a man's working day, the details of his care of the body, of the manner of taking food and preparing it; the tone of conversational and social life around the village fires . . . , the subtle yet unmistakable manner in which personal vanities and ambitions are reflected in the behaviour of the individual and in the emotional reactions of those who surround him (1961, 18-19)

or to the *corpus inscriptionum*, that is "the natives' views, opinions and utterances" (ibid. 22), the former to be recorded in an ethnographic diary, the latter in fieldnotes.

Long before the bard of the Argonauts, de Gérando, another "Observer of Man," made similar recommendations in his "Considérations sur les Diverses Méthodes à suivre dans l'Observation des peuples sauvages." However, fieldnotes must also contain other aspects of the society studied, which Stendhal ignores: the description of institutions, kinship genealogies, charts, and diagrams. The filiation between the French Ideologues and the epistemology of Malinowski's ethnographic fieldwork has been recognized by a few historians of anthropology (see Stocking 1964, 134-50; Copans and Jamin 1978). What I want to stress is how intertwined is the practice of writing a personal diary with the elaboration of methodological tools in ethnographic fieldwork. Both are rooted in a continuum that relates two domains traditionally opposed: epistemology, as history of theories and methods, and the history of sensibility, especially literary Romanticism.

The search for man's biological and psychological needs is at the base of biocultural functionalism as propounded by the Anglo-Polish anthropologist. The notion of happiness, as justification for the study of man, also pervades his work. As he put it in *Argonauts of the Western Pacific,*

> To study the institutions, customs, and codes or to study the behavior and mentality without the subjective desire and feeling by what these people live, of *realising the substance of their happiness* [my emphasis]—is, in my opinion, to miss the greatest reward which we can hope to obtain from the study of man. (25)

Likewise, in his diary, "utilitarian hedonism" is, in his own terms, "the only rational system: the happiness of the individual with the collectivity (that this must be the *Grundton* [keynote] of instinct can be deduced a priori, from the fact 'homo animal socialis')" (186). The "yearning for happiness, pure as gold, pure as crystal" (18), as he lyrically describes it, is as ever present in his diary as in Stendhal's. For both, this goal can be achieved only by ultimately renouncing the self in a fusion of body and soul with the other, either through passionate love with a fiancee (a recurrent theme), or in a Rousseauist fusion with nature, which, curiously enough, is more developed by the Victorian anthropologist than by the Romantic novelist: "nirvana-like contentment with existence" (186), or "feeling of a dull pleasure in soullessly letting myself dissolve in the landscape" (73).

The paradox, then, is that Stendhal's diary is, to a certain extent, more ethnographic than Malinowski's and the latter more Romantic than the former. What happens in fact is that the French novelist's text is more inclusive than the British. For one thing, it is much longer. It covers more than two decades (1801-1823), as opposed to hardly nineteen months (1914-1918) for the Trobriands diary. But, more to the point, it includes material that Malinowski deliberately reserved to other writing tools: fieldnotes and the ethnographic diary. These are meant to help the fieldworker traverse what he calls the enormous distance "between the moment he sets foot upon the native beach . . . and the time he writes down the final version of his results" (*Argonauts*, 4). Why, over and above these two writing media, he felt the need to use a third tool of a more personal type is a moot point. Taking a closer look at the poetics of personal diary, one can better grasp the relationship among the three distinctive tools of ethnographic research devised by Malinowski in the Trobriands.

POETICS OF PRIVATE DIARIES AND ETHNOLOGY

Let us see first the writing codes of the two diaries. They can now be deduced from their epistemology. For the cognitive/hedonist quest to succeed, the reader must be eliminated and with him, the writing codes of "good" literature, be it novels or finished ethnographic text.[1] The sensationalist, anti-cartesian stand with its emphasis on the continuity between body and mind, the search for the smallest impression, as it emerges, without trying to control it, commands the broken, impressionistic, irreverent style, and the lack of hierarchy among the topics evoked. If Bakhtin's work on the Grotesque (1968) has made the crudeness of Rabelais and Jarry respectable as reversal of the high and the low, there is no such reversal in our two intimate diaries. What makes them shocking is precisely the fact that they ignore all hierarchy of topics or vocabulary. Everything has equal value. Anything can be said at any time (having had "a violent shit" for excess of cathartics, or longing for one's fiancé, a heroic life or scientific headway in one's work). The point is to search for one's "true" needs, whatever they are; to really know how one actually feels, thinks, and reacts, and to state it regardless of any selective criteria (propriety, timeliness, taste), or attempt to reconstruct, erase, or rationalize. Hence, there is the abundance of four-letter words, the emphasis on body functions (urination, defecation, copulation, disease), the uninhibited expression of taboo feelings (hatred, scorn, depression, vindictiveness), and irrational thoughts, as found in accounts of dreams. In this respect, the two diaries with their matter-of-fact approach are perhaps closer to a genuine self-analysis than Freud's, whose results are presented as a "model" to the public.

It is easy to see how these cognitive, quasi-psychoanalytic goals also entail a nonaristotelian poetics—a loose, fragmented structure with no justified beginning or end. The disintegration of the self follows from these premises. (What is the self, but a construction, a fiction?) The quest for a "moral personality" implies a dialectic often overlooked or seen by the reader as contradiction. Let us see it at work in Malinowski's diary. The *I* of the solitary anthropologist, while seeking to "deepen himself," does not take the self for granted, as an entity, an essence. The diary is a heuristic tool to discover it, but in the process, it reveals itself as otherness. The discovery of how the self actually behaved yesterday leads the diarist to self-criticism—"I am incapable of bringing myself in my work, of accepting my voluntary captivity" (16), or "I clearly realized the stupidity of getting angry and insisting on point of honor" (193)—and to self admonitions and moral resolutions:

> The total lack of moral personality is disastrous. For instance, my behavior at George's; my pawing of Jab . . . is caused mainly by a desire to impress the other fellows: . . . I must have a system of specific formal prohibitions: I must not smoke, I must not touch a woman with sub-erotic intentions . . . Preserve the essential inner personality through all difficulties and vicissitudes: I must never sacrifice moral principles or essential work to 'posing' . . . My main task now, must be: work. Ergo: work! (268).

Following the topoi and paths of "spiritual exercises" in the Christian tradition,[2] the diary is here an instrument of apprenticeship that leads ultimately to the dissolution of subjectivity for the benefit of alterity. As such, it should be viewed indeed as another methodological tool for the anthropologist. As Stocking pointed out, it has a purgative function. It is the place where Malinowski vents his frustrations, curses the natives,[3] hates his work, feels disgust toward himself, and, by the same token, trains himself to be an ethnographer:

> . . . finishing the wagas in Roge á; comparative studies of canoes; but I felt that my ideas were getting muddled. I also thought that I should take a deeper view of things when writing diary. Principle: along with external events, record feelings and instinctual manifestations; moreover have a clear idea of the metaphysical nature of existence. Of course *training* [my emphasis] myself to keep a diary affects my way of living. (130)

This constant effort to take distance toward himself and the others as object of study is indeed part of the training of the anthropologist. Seeing this distancing as a contradiction to the empathy and closeness that the fieldworker's position as participant-observer presupposes is missing the dialectic of the self and the other that is inherent to ethnology. This dialectic, which we have seen elaborated in these two private diaries, implies a theory of alterity (and not of identity) based upon a dialogical principle. As Bakhtin puts it:

> In what way will the event be enriched if I succeed in fusing with the other? If instead of two, there is just one? What do I gain by having the other fuse with me? He will know and see but what I know and see.[4] (quoted in Todorov, 1984, 108)

This observation echoes Malinowski's own concern with controlling his movement toward fusion and empathy:

> Summary reflections: since Thursday, I have been in a state of utter distraction. I must absolutely stop this. It is caused by too violent and too passionate contact with people, by an unnecessary communion of souls. (264)

The diary indeed deals with the fundamental ambivalence of the fieldwork method: the necessity for the participant-observer to maintain, within the closeness of his situation, an exotopic position for the benefit of knowledge of otherness. In this light, discovering one's otherness seems a rather appropriate, not futile, exercise, as commendable as self-analysis is to a psychoanalyst.

NOTES

Quotations from Stendhal's journal are my translation from the La Pléiade edition of *Oeuvres Intimes*.

[1]In other words there is no "autobiographical contract" (Lejeune 1982) with the reader, for it was the editor who imposed one on the posthumus work: Casimir Stryenski & F. de Nion for Stendhal's *Journal*, first published in 1888 (Paris: G. Charpentier), and Malinowski's widow, Valetta Malinowska, for *A Diary in the Strict Sense of the Term*. The same is true for Kafka's *Diaries*, published against his expressed wish by Max Brod.

[2]On the role of the Christian tradition of diaries as spiritual exercises, see Delauny's excellent study, *British Autobiography in the Seventeenth Century* (1969).

[3]For a further discussion of the use of the term "nigger" in Malinowski's diary, see Stocking (1973). My reading of the diary will also, I hope, place his fits of anger and disgust about the Trobrianders in perspective.

[4]Many of the texts cited by Todorov are not available in English translation. The reference given for this particular passage is Bakhtin (1979).

Works Cited

Bakhtin, M. *Rabelais and His World.* Cambridge, MA: MIT Press, 1968.

Bakhtin, M. "Autor i geroj v estet--cheskoj dejatel' nosti." In *Estetik slovesnogo tvorchestva.* Moscow: Baocharov, 1979.

Bucher, Bernadette. "Littérature intime et anthropologie des sexes." *L'Homme* 29(3-4, 1989, numéro spécial "Anthropologie et Littérature"). Forthcoming.

Cabanis, J. G. *Rapports du Physique et du Moral de l'Homme.* 1st ed. 1802. Paris: Charpentier, 1843.

Clifford, James. "On Ethnographic Self-Fashioning: Conrad and Malinowski." In *Reconstructing Individualism*, ed. Thomas Heller, David Welburg, et al. Stanford: Stanford University Press, 1986.

Clifford, James, and Marcus, eds. *Writing Culture: The Poetics and Politics of Ethnography.* Berkeley: University of California Press, 1986.

Copans, J., and J. Jamin, eds. *Aux Origins de l'Anthropologie Française.* Les Mémoires de la Sociétié des Observateurs de l'Homme en l'An VIII. Paris: Le Sycomore, 1978.

Delauny, P. *British Autobiography in the Seventeenth Century.* London: Routledge and Kegan Paul, 1969.

Lejeune, P. "The Autobiographical Contract." In *French Literary Theory*, ed. S. Todorov, pp. 192-222. Cambridge: Cambridge University Press, 1982.

Malinowski, Bronislaw. *Argonauts of the Western Pacific.* [1922] New York: E. P. Dutton. 1961.

———. *A Diary in the Strict Sense of the Term.* New York: Harcourt, Brace & World, 1967.

Stendhal, Henri Beyle. *Oeuvres Intimes.* La Pléiade edition. Paris: Gallimard, 1966.

Stocking, George. "Empathy and Antipathy in the Heart of Darkness." In *Readings in the History of Anthropology*, ed. Regna Darnell. New York: Harper and Row, 1973.

———. *French Anthropology in 1800.* 55:2, 180. 1964.

de Tracy, Destutt. *Eléments d'Idéologie.* Vol. 3. 1st ed. 1802. Paris: Nizet, 1970.

Todorov, Svetan. *Mikhail Bakhtin: The Dialogical Principle.* Minneapolis, MN: University of Minnesota Press, 1984.

THE LITERARY WORK AS CULTURAL
DOCUMENT: A CARIBBEAN CASE

John Stewart

ABSTRACT

Before the formal social science monograph achieved ascendancy as the form best suited to documenting society and culture, such documentation was generally the province of storytellers. In Third World societies, which face the task of re-shaping themselves in the postcolonial world, and where social science (except for economics) is not a well-developed tradition, the literary text still carries much of the responsibility for presenting reliable examinations of society. A scrutiny of two works by Trinidadian authors published more than forty years apart shows that as the problems of social, racial, and cultural distinctions survive, so too has the dramatically structured social narrative. In this fiction, social, racial, and cultural relationships present critical commentary on existing structures. They also present images of the liberating possibilities that inhere in the historical situation. This literary method of presentation achieves the revelatory profile of Victor Turner's "social drama," in which the dialectic between persistence and change in social life is highlighted.

The written text is one of the most common ways in which we store and transmit information. In modern industrial society, it has superseded both professional and folk memory as the device on which we rely for information of every sort. Along with this development, there has been a continued refinement of the various categories into which written texts are divided, and a reliance on such categorization for direction as to what may or may not be usefully retrieved from particular texts. Whereas formerly texts might have been often composed with mixed intentions (myth in some traditional societies is aesthetically pleasing, informative, entertaining, and instructive, simultane-ously), we have come increasingly to expect of the modern text that it be "single-minded," with an established logic linking form, intention, and subject matter. For purposes of storage and retrieval, form, among the major characteristics of the written text, is perhaps of primary significance. Through form we infer initially what the true intention and subject matter of a text might be. Form is the basis upon which our textual categories and sense of genres are founded.

When we go to the modern library and approach the shelves labeled *social science*, we do not expect the texts stacked there to be entertaining or heavily concerned with aesthetics or humor, except, perhaps, as topics for analysis. Instead, we expect them to be dull but direct, dependable reading, in which we encounter reliable fact, precise thought, and well-founded conclusions based on carefully reasoned analysis. We expect interpretation of the phenomena represented by social science texts to be theoretically limited and straightforward. When we approach literary texts, our expectations are somewhat different. We expect them to constitute something of an emotional experience that is entertaining, possibly enlightening, and elevating, too. We expect their serious meanings, if they have any, to be hidden or indirect, and to require great skill in interpretation if we are to uncover them.

Unlike the conventions that limit scientific and documentary texts to observed, observable, or measureable detail, and clear distinctions between replicable situations and speculation, literary conventions license the (apparently) arbitrary invention of details and their arrangement. The critical purpose in the literary text may be not to record and pass on historically correct information, but to generate an effect that might be both correct and timeless. This "open" feature of the literary text reduces for many anthropologists its reliability as an ethnographic resource.

The literature that anthropologists have adopted traditionally for disciplinary purposes is folkloric—myths, tales, legends, etc.—and is usually collected by individual researchers themselves. Two characteristics that make folklore attractive to anthropologists are its orality and its presentation as dramatic performance, usually associated with some ritual. Orality signals that composition is a social affair, and dramatic presentation usually indicates some direct relation between the story and other elements of a cultural complex:

> The drama in nonliterate societies affirms some of the deepest sanctions of living. The myths declaimed and acted, the choreography of the dances, the rhythms of the drums, the verses sung and spoken, call forth responses from participants and onlookers that bear profoundly on the value system of the individuals who compose the group, and their adjustment within the system. They give assurance that the rains will come, that crops will be abundant, that calamity will not befall, that the group will continue (Herskovits 1970, 427).

The folkloric story assumes significance not as a discrete cultural performance in its own right, but as part of a broader enactment that links the social group to its spiritual and environmental provenience through ritual.

The close association between drama and ritual is widely recognized. Literary scholars tend to emphasize the evolutionary or syncretic relations between these two forms of cultural performance. Anthropologists, on the other hand, tend to regard them as functions through which culture itself is, to some extent, realized. In this view, ritual and drama are not primarily species of artifice but enactments in which people together carry out various aspects of their culture (Becker 1979). Given this pattern of perception, we understand that the written imaginative work, which stands apart from those who perform it and assumes no clearly distinguished role in a particular group ritual, poses its own anthropological difficulties.

In the past, such difficulties were avoided, because imaginative literature was treated as peripheral to the ethnographic documentation of cultures. Lately, however, as the significance in culture of the imagination—or what Armstrong calls "the universe of man's interiority" (1971, 43) is being realized, the written imaginative work is being included increasingly in anthropological reading lists, and concepts such as *textuality, social drama,* and *narrativity* are being adopted as useful analytical devices in the study of society and culture. The metaphorical application of these literary concepts takes into account that, in some fundamental way, the imaginative work can be a reflection of deep social and cultural processes: "The artist who uses words as his medium, no less than the artist who works with paints or in wood or stone, acts as a creature of his culture; his responses are always relative to its formal patterns, and his values reflect its underlying values" (Herskovits 1970, 419).

Among the literary metaphors applied in sociocultural analysis by Victor Turner and others who followed him is the *social drama.* On the basis of his field research, Turner, who was trained as a British social anthropologist, came to understand the social world as "a world in becoming, not a world in being" (Turner 1974, 24). "There is no such thing as static action," he wrote, and "such a view violates the actual flux and changefulness of the human social scene" (24). Yet, if flux and mutability were unremitting conditions of social life, so too was persistence. Indeed, he found persistence to be "a striking aspect of change" (32). To account for the simultaneity of change and persistence, Turner conceptualized social existence as "a sequence of processual units of different types" (43), among which he located the social drama. Analysis of these units, and especially of the social drama, Turner posited, would reveal micro-units of flow, schism, and resolution, which in their unending repetition constitute what could be experienced as the apparently contiguous or paradoxical level of social life.

The social drama as defined by Turner is a public episode "of tensional irruption" (33), during which social process is unmasked sufficiently to reveal its tendrils and the stresses under which they function. "Social dramas . . . are units of aharmonic or disharmonic process, arising in conflict situations" (37). They punctuate an otherwise ongoing and ostensibly harmonic flow. In this essay, Turner does not elaborate on what constitutes a harmonic phase, other than to imply that it is marked merely by the absence of irruption. It follows from his argument, however, that harmony—like structure—is a transitory state that is constantly achieved and lost in a continual alternation with its opposite. Harmony may in fact be a desirable state toward which social process leads, and for which such process needs to be constantly adjusted.

Irruptions, or social dramas, then, may be understood as occasions of intensified adjustment, in which the potential for change in the direction and magnitude of social process is revealed and appropriated. Irruptions do not lead necessarily to dramatic change in social ideas and activities. What is to be emphasized is that irruptions expose certain elements of both change and persistence, and the enactment of strategies by which both are achieved.

If irruptions and their resolutions are a constant and necessary aspect of social existence, so too must be their anticipation and the preparation for their enactment. Social irruptions tend to release both creative and debilitating powers. To protect against excessive debilitation, certain cultural forms, such as ritual and ceremony, permit the imitation of disruptive performances and their resolution in controlled contexts. The conservative nature of these forms and their reconstitutive and redressive properties have been long recognized, and are well documented. Less well recognized—among social scientists, anyway—is the contribution of the written imaginative work. Yet, beyond and before its role in the analytical strategies of social scientists, the imaginative text functions precisely to simulate incidences of irruption and resolution in a controlled context. It permits a certain experiencing of and preparation for process, without the risk of penalty that may result otherwise.

Prose fiction, especially that fiction classified as *social realism*, is a source of repeatable experiences that simulates Turner's social drama. In so doing, it reconstructs how disruptive tensions emerge and are resolved in the posited social existence of identifiable characters. Once written, such fiction encloses dramatic situations that remain fixed and dated, but the experiences simulated are vicariously available for as long as the fiction itself survives. Thus, fiction documents and stores repertoires of social strategies and values that are integral to the nature of social process. Further, fiction makes this repertoire available to each individual, under individually selected circumstances. One does not have to be a collaborating member of any group to encounter the experiences stored in the written text, except in cases in which censorship of one kind or another applies. That encounter is generally a private one, and therefore subject to being colored by the quality of our private lives. The written text, therefore, makes a wide variety of reactions to stored social experiences possible and in so doing enhances the factors on which change and persistence are simultaneously sustained.

To summarize, (a) social process is an integrated system of persistence and change, harmony and disharmony, with each of these opposite categories necessarily containing strategies for its own permanence; (b) the nondisruptive experience—or accommodation—of dissonance is an aspect of strategy in the harmonic phase of social process; (c) one of the ways in which such experience occurs is its affective presentation and storage in repeatable texts that simulate Turner's *social drama* (d) such texts are cultural performances that communicate cultural patterns and values; (e) the subgenre in imaginative writing known as *social realism* constitutes a category of repeatable texts that is based on the presentation of social conflict; and (f) in this subgenre, the presentation of conflict is balanced invariably by models for its accommodation, and the text contributes therefore to the harmonic phase in processual flow.

To demonstrate these last propositions in particular, I draw attention in the rest of this paper to two novels in the tradition of social realism, that treat incidences of social conflict that have also been studied by anthropologists.

THE SOCIAL CULTURAL CONTEXT—TRINIDAD

A frequent theme in Trinidadian prose fiction is the class oriented encounter with an aggressively debilitating social structure. Debilitation threatens in various ways. But, in general, it underlies the suppression of initiative and is expressed in a cultural incapacity that makes dependency a preferred choice. Resistance against the forces of debilitation is, in a grand sense, the central drama in Trindadian culture, and in this regard the fictional world corresponds closely with the historical.

Social organization in Trinidad has its roots in the society's genesis as an extension of British nineteenth-century imperial colonialism. Among the factors that dominated colonial Trinidad were a plantation economy owned and controlled by absentee metropolitan interests; an imported labor force segmented on the bases of race, color, language, and national origin; and a cultural system in which all local forms and expressions were subordinated to those of expatriate origin.

Toward the end of the eighteenth century, Trinidad was still an underdeveloped Spanish colony, populated by a few officials, some African slaves, and American Indians. To accelerate development, the Spanish opened the colony to other Catholic immigrants. This led to a significant influx of French and Creoles from other parts of the West Indies. Under British control in the nineteenth century, the official recruitment of identured laborers and others continued. Additional European groups— Protestant in this instance—and fresh numbers of West Africans, Chinese, and especially East Indians came in as workers in the plantation economy.

Social structure as crystallized, then, tended toward a rigid castelike hierarchy based on race, color, ethnicity, social status, and occupation. This rigidity was balanced somewhat by a minimal pattern of ceremonial practices—including the annual carnival for which Trinidad is now justly famous—and informal accommodation in respect to mating along the color spectrum. In this arrangement, the superordinate colonists not only established themselves as an exclusive and dominant group, they also pursued a policy of aggressive acculturation for other segments of the population. This policy led to the development of two opposing cultural postures: one thoroughly assimilationist, holding as ideal the monocultural assumptions expressed in dominant expatriate norms; the other, ingeniously adaptive, integrating elements from African, American Indian, Asiatic, and European traditions into a new complex that at the same time honored ethnic differences.

The conflict between these two postures and the tension between competing subordinated traditions continues to have a major influence on social processes in Trinidadian society. The new independent political leadership of almost thirty years has accelerated the establishment of a central set of traditions around which a core culture and tempered social system might crystallize. But there remains some overlapping of postures, and the development of a fully indigenous core culture and social system continues to face serious challenge. The impulse to assimilation through cultural borrowing and dependency and the impulse to independence and creativity continue to coexist.

A hierarchial class system based on color, lineage, ethnicity, and occupation survives, though distinctions are not as deep and enclaves not as secure as they were during the colonial period. The elite is now a local monied elite with control over a significant portion of the domestic economy. Personal privilege and defiance remain markers of social success. Yet to the extent that categorical subordination is no longer deeply enforced, this system makes for a socially combative atmosphere in which independence, personal dignity and indignation are useful techniques for negotiating social space and legitimizing cultural ambiguity. All of these conditions reduce the potential for any rapid achievement of social and cultural solidarity. They are also the factors that underlie debilitation as a major characteristic of the overall system.

Social scientists have developed various models—the plural and consensual among them—to describe and account for the arresting complexities in Trinidadian society and culture, and they have done so, by and large, without any particular attention to the creative literature by Trinidadians.[1] Yet, the very conditions that they assume to analyze have been poignantly present in Trinidadian letters for over fifty years. One could go back to a group of writers who in the 1930s took it upon themselves to perform as the social conscience of the society. Mostly of middle- and upper-class backgrounds, this small group recognized in their own alienation as enlightened intellectuals a link with the "common man."

They wrote polemic, poetry, and fiction that criticized the Philistinism of their own classes. They were the intellectual humanists of that period who strove to awaken the society to the ill effects of its social caste system. The work of two significant writers, C. L. R. James and Alfred Mendes, demonstrated ably that adaptive indigenous culture—mostly a folk enterprise—was circumscribed and subverted by surviving caste pretensions and assimilationist proclivities. James and Mendes did so by adopting social realism as their literary method (Ramchand 1970, 65). They focused attention on everyday life among the lower classes and presented the struggle against established order in a sympathetic light. This practice has since become established among Trinidadian writers, and is evident in the works of Samuel Selvon, Merle Hodge, Earl Lovelace, and others.

SOCIAL REALISM—TWO NOVELS

MINTY ALLEY

Of all the texts produced by the significant writers of the 1930s, C. L. R. James's *Minty Alley* (1936) remains the most widely read. It is a groundbreaking example of regional social realism. The central character in the novel is a young black man of the genteel middle class. His claim to status is not based on lineage, color, or wealth, but on education and his occupation as a white collar clerk. When his fortunes change, and he abruptly finds himself among the lower class residents of an urban *yard*, he is inexorably initiated into an unfamiliar world. By the end of the work he is a changed person, and the reader has shared emotionally and intellectually in the cultural and social experiences which bring about this change.

The yard in *Minty Alley* is fenced off from neighboring properties. Within the walls are a main dwelling house, a separate barracklike structure for tenants, and a third building, which houses a common kitchen and a bakery. This arrangement, fairly common in Port-of-Spain during the 1930s, was based upon the estate model of the plantation period. On the traditional estate, the big house was occupied by the seigneur and his family; the barracks, by workers; and a third building served, as in the novel, as a work venue. But Minty Alley is on the decline. It is now a mortgaged property in the hands of an ambitious but struggling member of the working class. It is subject to demanding and penalizing forces centered somewhere on the outside and consequently quite vulnerable to extreme dissension on the inside. Under constant tension, the yard is a forging ground where the elements of social affiliation are laid bare and tested.

The chief resident, who is also responsible for the mortage, is Mrs. Rouse—a faded mulatress. She is the owner of the small bakery, the source of income for herself and most of the others. She has three young women helpers. One is a relation who is mulatto herself. She see her future in the cleverness with which she attracts and manipulates men; she intends to escape the yard. The second helper is an Indian who is a sincere and reliable worker. She has no will to escape. Her satisfaction comes from doing her work well, exercising thrift, and knowing that others can depend on her. The third young woman is thoroughly black. She is a servant girl without alternative prospects. Two older females are tenants. One is of the proprietor's age. She is retired and quite cynical. The other is somewhat younger, and is blessed with color and a respectable profession. She is a still attractive mulatto, who could on occasion be mistaken for white. A private nurse, she works exclusively for "the white people." She has a son from a dissolved union and is only temporarily in the yard awaiting the restoration of her fortunes.

The males in the yard are for the most part peripheral. The oldest and senior of them all is the dugla common-law mate of Mrs. Rouse. He is a master baker, whose ambitions transcend those normally fulfilled by someone in his trade. He is at his peak both as a tradesman and as a virile male and must do something to satisfy his urge to achieve and ensure his future. Two other younger black males come and go as occasional laborers. When not in prison, they do some of the heavy work at the bakery and make deliveries, but they do not live in the yard. The other males come into the yard as visitors and informal mates to the females. Within the walls, the yard is an impoverished and open place. The dwellers have no escape from the awareness of each other. Feelings ramify easily. When they are good, the yard is a pleasant place. When they go sour, it becomes vicious. It is into this context that James places the innocent protagonist. The complex social processes in the yard are presented from his point of view.

James does not present a direct confrontation between the classes. Instead, the novel reveals both the power and frangible character of those factors that hold people together in such a milieu. James juxtaposes two lines of action: (a) the decline of Mrs. Rouse and (b) the awakening of the central character. Kinship, work, and affection are the three main factors that hold the people of the yard together as a social unit. Of the three, kinship is presented as the most trying, the most fragile. Kin relationships are involuntary and a source of extreme tension. When they rupture, they tend to generate profound and lasting alienation.

Work relationships fare somewhat better. The residents of the yard are closely bonded through their work. What work provides, more than income, is opportunity and rationale for people to relate to each other in a way that expresses voluntary commitment to mutual survival, especially in a crisis. The need to be needed is satisfied. In the responsibility that the characters assume for each other in their work, their being motivated by awareness of a common plight, their sharing of both effort and reward, the novel posits that social relationships are better and more reliably grounded in awareness of a common class status than in genealogy.

Work by itself is not, however, the main integrative tissue. It provides the viable context in which love and morality may be fully acted out. The successful expression of morality and affection involves careful balancing between personal needs and social requirements, as well as a firm commitment to honorable and moral behavior. External pressures and the very nature of the social and cultural mix in the yard produce obstacles to such balancing and commitment. These obstacles lead finally to an insecurity in the central relationship between Mrs. Rouse and her common-law mate.

As the relationship deteriorates, Mrs. Rouse suffers one loss after another. She loses the respect of her relative; she loses her lover, her self-confidence, and in the end, her property. The central character who struggles to remain an aloof observer is nevertheless caught in the raw and tangled process. He is forced to recognize that, alongside the genteel world of form and manners, another world exists, one without the obscuring safety of abstractions. The yard also teaches him his own capacities for honesty and integrity, and he acquires a lasting appreciation of the palpitant tragicomedy which underlies upper-class posturing.

THE DRAGON CAN'T DANCE

In the 1970s, the contradictions between indigenizing and assimilationist norms continued to be a debilitating factor in Trinidadian society. Earl Lovelace illustrates this condition well in his novel *The Dragon Can't Dance* (1979). Although there are some differences in detail, this novel shares certain structural features with *Minty Alley*. Instead of a single *yard* the setting is a *hill*—which is a complex of small yards and the public spaces that link them. The occupational range among hill inhabitants is greater, and the survival of the *community* is not immediately threatened. A significant difference is that males are prominent residents of the hill, and violence is an inescapable context in which masculine integrity is forged. This hill is, however, a lower-class neighborhood.

Here live the laborers who do menial and "dirty" work elsewhere in the city. Here are the women struggling to raise their children in circumstances that breed irresponsible mating and serial companionship as norms. Here are the young men who will have extremely limited opportunity for expressing their creative abilities, the young women who are likely to be mothers before they are ready. Above all, here is a community that has been driven to expect so little of itself and the society of which it is a part that residents submit to blackmail by hooligans and suffer feelings of spontaneous hostility when one among them assumes to claim a higher station. The hill is an isolated enclave, quarantined by its inabilities and discontents, as well as by the active vigilance of an oppressive order, evoked constantly in the presence of the police.

The cast of characters is more numerous than that of *Minty Alley*, but certain types recur. There is the faded mullato woman of some minor means, the nubile black girl whose gift and problem is her sexuality. There are the middle-aged women whose penchant for fostering is tempered by a certain cynicism. There is the middle-aged calypsonian who debases himself to capture the woman of color and thereby acquire status. Finally, there is the young Indian couple. They begin in the roles of laborer and loyal neighbor, but become neighborhood entrepreneurs when they are rejected.

The young black males here are not all as passive as those of the 1930s. Alienation is a badge some wear militantly. For them, the hill is both a trap and a domain that they try to protect against outside forces. They are aware of the corrupt nature of the new political regime, and of the spiritual loss that is a consequence of alignment with it. Each must choose whether to fight for an essential self and come up against the system, or compromise the quest for honor and integrity in joining with the authorities. Some choose not to fight. They have already invented the steelband—the most radical contribution of the lower classes to modern Trinidadian culture—and would now compromise to protect this evidence of the legitimacy of their creative powers.

Others have confidence enough to stand up against the police on occasion, and among them the very "bad-john" who had decades earlier led the battle for the steelband, is a leader and hero. He is an anachronism, though, a throwback to simpler

times, and ill-equipped to deal with the subtleties of the new
system. He is doomed to fail. In fact, he will be tricked into
constructing his own failure. On the other hand, there is the
choice of cultivated isolation, expressed in the cult of carnival.
For two days each year, all of the rage and frustration, the
hostility and rejection felt towards the outside community can be
mobilized and spewed in the playing of the carnival. For the
remainder of the year, one may ignore or avoid dealing with the
pressures overtly while waiting for the next carnival season.

The character that commands our greatest sympathy opts for
this third choice. He is satisfied with masquerading as a dragon
during carnival—until he is swept up in the eruption of open
conflict between dissenting forces on the hill, and between the
culture of the hill and the social power of the outside world.
Internally, conflict centers on neighborhood hostility against the
Indians, and the sexual exploitation of the young girl. "The
dragon" is not party to either. Both pain him, but he steels
himself against interfering. When, however, he is forced with the
other young toughs into a confrontation with the police, he falls
into a series of bizarre incidents that replicates the ritual carnival
and reveals its inadequacies. Ritual release, he comes to
understand, does no more than fortify the system with which it is
associated, and he sees his commitment to the metaphor of release
as merely a gross compromise itself. He has time in prison to
absorb this lesson. And, after release, he who once masqueraded
as a dragon now drops the mask to pursue a more substantive
liberation through the gift of himself as a man to others.

As the novel comes to an end, other individual resolutions
occur also. The bad-john declines into a total imbecile, overtaken
finally by the acceptance of his own impotence. The calypsonian
realizes his talent for composing self-denigrating songs. Finally
acclaimed, he wins the hand of the aging mulatress and so assists
her in sustaining her self-flattery. The young black girl has
survived early exploitation, and the Indian couple has accepted
that their neighbors are not ready for the affection and loyalty
that they wanted to contribute to the community. It is clear that
the factors that make life on the hill tense have been neither
eliminated nor subdued. They survive. And those who will
transcend them must do so out of personal fortitude, and a
clearer understanding of the hill's dilemma.

LITERATURE AS A PERFORMANCE OF CULTURE

As cultural performers, writers must undertake the task of converting experience into symbolic action. The successful completion of this task requires an allocation of meaning to individual and social experience. Such allocation involves selection of a central point of view and a controlling sensibility. It must take into account also the authorial question—what exactly is going on here? An answer to that question must be simultaneously moral and practical. In the novels by James and Lovelace, the answer is not a balanced one. Practicality, it seems, supersedes by far the moral in influence, and the culture that results is that of a people being defeated by the social patterns that govern their lives. The characters in both novels are dominated by a social system more esurient and hostile than they generally comprehend. It is not a benign system. In shaping their lives, it shrivels their historical imagination and trivializes their creative efforts. To salvage their moral—and ultimate—selves they must confront the system and stand against it. And even then, rebellion might be converted to the advantage of the system.

Minty Alley and *The Dragon Can't Dance* are both recognized as significant literary achievements among Trinidadians. Both works are lauded for the accuracy, fullness, and poignancy with which they dramatize not only the deficits of class and cultural conflict, but also the survival of problematic sentiments that beset the society. Both works have been adapted recently to the stage. Their popularity is grounded not only in the success with which their dramatic moments are achieved, but also in the sense that they are in fact legitimate pieces of social history. They simulate situations, characters, and incidents that are for the most part credibly analogous with widespread experience.

Although the *yard* as an important social context may not be as common as it once was, neither has it wholly disappeared. Many adult Trinidadians are familiar with the yard, and some are given to lamenting its passing. The *hill* is a current and vibrant context to be found in enclaves surrounding the city of Port of Spain. Hills are not the only locations in which the urban under-class is clustered, but they are favored by the most rebellious and intransigent of that class. The ethnographic authenticity of the social relationships posited in the novels can be readily confirmed, as can the paradoxical patterns of progress and loss, change and constancy, which characterize individual and social experience.

As has been shown, Trinidad is culturally and socially a highly complex society. In such a situation, mechanisms of accommodation become paramount. What is revealed by the two novels is, however, that although such mechanisms are extant and being developed, they are as yet poorly institutionalized. Thus, until forced into service, they remain inchoate, or are invoked in quite arbitrary, sometimes contradictory, manners. Their use can lead to elaboration in the fields of dissonance as much as it may contribute to a transcendence of cultural and social difference.

From the national carnival to personal exchanges of food and favors, the manipulative objectives of accommodation are often thinly concealed. One must be constantly on guard. Without an aggressive personal vigilance, one can be easily exploited. Yet, personal vigilance by itself does not assure social success. This is best pursued in keeping with the interests of some group, such as the family, age group, work group, neighborhood, or otherwise. In this case individuals are very much like groups. They can be neither isolated nor static. They are responsive to the contexts within which they occur, and their interests are therefore not secure from contradiction. Individuals are called upon to be flexible, to be ready to transcend, absorb, or otherwise negate contradictions that inevitably form part of their experience.

These novels, then, present examples of myriad individual actions that simultaneously carry forward routine, express contradiction and rupture, and restore routine. Whereas the standard ethnographic text usually emphasizes routine, the dramatic novel emphasizes the emergence of contradiction, the rupture and restoration of routine. Such emphasis locates the sentiments of significance in a social system, and shows how they may be managed in the interest of integrity and harmony.

Harmony is constructed around symbolic actions and the metaphors they precipitate. Because social dramas present instances in which breakdown in the symbolic system occurs, and misunderstanding or inappropriate performance intrudes, they are also instances in which the possibilities for new meanings and recognitions are opened up. As the novels of James and Lovelace illustrate, social dramas allow a close, personal experiencing of their details—from the recognition of breach to the moment of resolution. In this way, social dramas occur as liminal instances in which new meanings may be given to existing metaphors, or old ones confirmed. In any case, after the moment of contradiction and rupture some mediation leading to the strengthening of structure takes place, even if structure then takes on a different shape or direction.

Where real life social drama functions as the model for fiction, the resulting texts preserve both routine and contradiction (conflict), and demonstrate the engagement with process and structure from one era to another. They themselves become metaphors capable of catalyzing the experience of social drama. This they accomplish by positing the superiority of intangible states (Armstrong's *interior universe*) and displaying how intangibles play a significant role in impelling the social process. In their metaphorical assertion, novels can present tangible actions as fictions through which intangibles are expressed. Satisfying, as they do, an internal need, novels play their role in the maintenance of structure.

It has often been observed that the novel in its early stages was as concerned with an understanding of social life as social science later came to be. Both the novel and social science, we are reminded, "sought to explain life on the basis of institutions created by men and women rather than by appealing to immutable absolutes and divine powers. Both also widened the scope of inquiry to include social classes and processes formerly ignored or seldom given major consideration in poetry and drama or in history and philosophy" (Berger 1977, 215-16). These similarities between the novel and social science have been ignored excessively in recent years. As late as the mid-nineteenth century, novelists such as George Eliot were clear that systematic social inquiry and the "exercise of a veracious imagination" (Berger 1977, 217) were very much a part of the novelist's work. In the twentieth century, however, creative experimentation and literary scholarship have focused primarily on aesthetics and philosophy in the novel, whereas in the social sciences emphasis has been on emulating the natural sciences in the application of positivist principles.

Nevertheless, in at least one of the several categories into which the fiction may be subdivided—social realism—the novel remains focused on problems of social class and process. Here, the details of character, action, and setting are organized in a manner analogous to the case study. Significant relationships between a selected number of individuals are focused, as are relationships between them and the social environment to which, and for which, they are responsible. Analysis takes form in the manner in which relationships are conducted, and the degree to which they are, or are not, successful. In this way, the social principles applied in individual relationships are revealed. Because all action in the novel occurs in a moral atmosphere, readers are directed to an asserted judgment on the quality and desirability of social life as presented in the text. Perhaps the most telling difference between social science and the novel is, after all, the moral dimension.

In social science, moral categories tend to be implicit, and the reader is given minimal directions as to how they might be invoked. In the novel, on the other hand, moral categories are foregrounded. The moral life is always at least as important as, and often more important than the practical life, and serves as vantage point for sustained criticism of the latter. In this way, the novel mirrors a salient characteristic of social process—a tension between moral and practical systems, and their constant adjustment, evoked by constraints levied from time to time by one against the other. Tension between systems is displaced as culture occurs. Between the moral and the practical lies, therefore, a significant space in which culture continually originates and undergoes adjustment. In the simulated enactment of this process, the novel reveals culture and makes it available as a subject of discourse.

NOTE

[1]The work of V. S. Naipaul is exceptional in this regard. His novel *A House for Mr. Biswas* (1961) is increasingly being cited by social scientists as an exemplary presentation of East Indian life in Trinidad. See the following chapter by Michael V. Angrosino.

WORKS CITED

Armstrong, Robert Plant. *The Affecting Presence.* Urbana: University of Illinois Press, 1971.

Becker, A. L. "Text-Building, Epistemology, and Aesthetics in Javanese Shadow Theatre." In *The Imagination of Reality*, ed. A. L. Becker and Aram A. Yengoyan. Norwood: ABLEX Publishing Corporation, 1979.

Berger, Morroe. *Real and Imagined Worlds: The Novel and Social Science.* Cambridge: Harvard University Press, 1977.

Herskovits, Melville. *Man and His Works.* New York: Alfred A. Knopf, 1970.

James, C. L. R. *Minty Alley.* London: New Beacon Books, 1971.

Lovelace, Earl. *The Dragon Can't Dance.* London: Audre Deutsch, 1971.

Naipaul, V. S. *A House for Mr. Biswas.* London: Andre Deutsch, 1961.

Ramchand, Kenneth. *The West Indian Novel and its Background.* London: Faber and Faber, 1970.

Turner, Victor. *Dramas, Fields, and Metaphors: Symbolic Action in Human Society.* Ithaca: Cornell University Press, 1974.

IDENTITY AND ESCAPE IN CARIBBEAN LITERATURE

Michael V. Angrosino

ABSTRACT

In common with other colonial areas, the Caribbean has developed an extensive literature (both prose and poetry) devoted to the exploration of national identity. The Caribbean is unique, however, in that its native population was virtually eliminated within one hundred years of contact, so that its people came to the area or were brought from somewhere else. This paper uses Caribbean poetry and prose to analyze the evolution of consciousness of a cultural identity. It contrasts the colonial and immediate postcolonial era, when writers and other intellectuals defined their identity in terms of escape (*back to Africa*, Indian awareness, identification with the culture of the European *metropole*), with the current period, a generation after independence. The paper's general thesis is that in colonial and postcolonial society, culture is organized around the theme of identity: How does a person define himself in a world of conflicting, or even alien, value systems? The author argues further that consciously created art, which is the product of the intellectuals most affected by this identity crisis, is especially useful to anthropologists in understanding the nature of that culture.

> When I was in the fourth form I wrote a vow on the endpaper of my Kennedy's *Revised Latin Primer* to leave [Trinidad] within five years. I left after six; and for many years afterwards in England falling asleep in bedsitters with the electric fire on, I had been awakened by the nightmare that I was back in tropical Trinidad.
>
> Naipaul, *The Middle Passage*

INTRODUCTION

IDENTITY AND SOCIAL CHANGE

The development of individual personality pivots on one's quest for an integrated identity. According to the anthropologically influenced psychoanalyst Erik Erikson (1963), the crisis of identity is most characteristically a feature of adolescence. Adolescents, insecure in their social status, like to identify with sweeping ideologies that explain everything, and which often have a "revolutionary" ring that satisfies their need to pull down the institutions into which they do not yet fit, so as to "start fresh." The healthy maturation process ultimately enables individuals to define their identities in terms of strengths of character intrinsic to themselves. The need to adhere to external rhetoric and the ready-made answers of the mass movement falls away.

In the life of societies, there is an analogous developmental process. It is most clearly seen in those societies emerging from colonialism or other forms of political-economic domination. Emergent nations are unsure of their identities, and so tend to rely on slogans promising solidarity with forces that are powerful in the great, wide world. But once the experience of independence has settled in, a people can begin to think of, and take heart in, a national identity drawn from local tradition. *Modernization* has, indeed, been defined as a process that originates "when a culture embodies an attitude of inquiry and questioning about how [people] make choices" (Apter 1965, 7-10).

The quest for identity, both in the personal and in the sociocultural sense, is often clarified by popular art forms that create recognizable images of identity conflict.[1] People participate symbolically in the resolution of those conflicts as they enter into the dramatic world conjured up by the creative artist. Art may thus be a means by which the innermost psychological blocks to identity development are purged. We are not here speaking of "salon art," created for purely aesthetic reasons, but rather of art created by writers keenly aware of identity conflicts which they have personally experienced. Such writers can consciously present their personal conflicts in such a way as to make them paradigmatic of the experiences of their less creative or articulate brethren. Members of the audience can thus fight their own identity battles on a symbolic stage shared by many others, and hence overcome their sense of aloneness, even if they cannot immediately resolve their more specific problems.

CARIBBEAN CULTURE AND IDENTITY

Of all the areas that emerged from the colonial shadow in the decades after World War II, the Caribbean has undergone perhaps the most dramatic crisis of identity.[2] The problem stems from the peculiar history of the region. The natives of the Antilles were exterminated within one hundred years of Columbus's first voyages. Since European settlers were, on the whole, not as interested in relocating to the tropical West Indies as they were to the North American colonies, the mercantile enterprise of the plantation economy had to be fueled by the importation of labor—first African slaves, and later indentured laborers from India, China, and Java, as well as by free migrant laborers from Portuguese Madeira and Syria. As a result, no "natives" of the

West Indies can trace their roots back more than four hundred years in the Caribbean. Moreover, the circumstances that brought people to the region were unhappy ones, as even those who came "freely" did so to escape dire privation at home. Unlike the settlers in temperate colonies, those laborers who came to the Caribbean had little hope of ever acquiring either the land they worked, or any of the other recognized accoutrements of wealth and power.

For all these reasons, West Indians have historically seen the Caribbean as a place of sojourn. An extreme version of that view, current among the radical Rastafarians of Jamaica, for example, sees the West Indies as Babylon, and the people as wanderers in exile. The place where they lived and worked has not been seen as "home." Unlike colonial Africans, who lived in their native land surrounded by all the artifacts and symbols of their traditional cultures, West Indians could think of a cultural identity only as something from the long ago or far away. The "mother country," the "metropole," was the source of oppression, of course, but it was also the source of the only immediately identifiable, coherent standards of culture. West Indians were thus rarely "nationalist" in the sense that African or Indian leaders of the postwar generation could be so described, because they had learned to despise their "little islands in the sun" as worthless places of exile. Attempts at thinking in terms of larger units such as the whole region were usually frustrating. The nature of the plantation political-economic system was such that people tended to develop loyalties to the local district, and only rarely to a unit as large as the island, let alone the whole region—which, after all, was divided for centuries among Spanish, English, French, and Dutch sovereignty. The culture of Europe held a powerful allure for Caribbean intellectuals, but they were always conscious of the trap into which they could fall. By identifying too much with the metropole, they would lose their sense of solidarity with their own people. That solidarity might not replace an identity rooted in a "real" culture, but on the other hand, no matter how much they had assimilated the metropolitan culture, they knew that in Europe they would be treated simply as "niggers from the colonies."

LITERATURE AND IDENTITY IN THE CARIBBEAN

Caribbean nationalism therefore underwent what Erikson might describe as a prolonged adolescence because there was no easy way for West Indians to take their identity *as* West Indians seriously enough to be able to commit their emotional energies to it. But this extended quest for identity had one very positive benefit—a strong and vibrant literary tradition. Poetry, prose, and drama had long flourished in the English, French, Dutch, and Spanish Caribbean, but Caribbean literature came into its own in the twentieth century, as artists and intellectuals tried to come to grips with the glamorous allure of other cultures and identities as a necessary prelude to coming to terms with what it might mean to be a West Indian.

The Guyanese novelist Jan Carew has characterized Caribbean writing of the late colonial period as a matter of "exile." However, the Caribbean writer has often sought to escape the place of exile that was the West Indies in favor of some place with richer possibilities for identity (1979, 111). This paper is an elaboration of Carew's thesis.

It would be fair to characterize twentieth-century Caribbean literature as a "literature of escape" on both the literal and symbolic levels. It was literally a matter of escape because so many of the key writers who came of age in the late colonial period ended up by settling in the metropole. They did so partly because of the opportunities for a larger readership, but mostly because they could no longer deal with the ambiguities of their statuses at home. Whether they literally left or stayed, these writers were still able to make themselves and their fictional characters into models of struggle. In their grand conflicts people of humbler means could find validation of their own experiences, and perhaps purgation of their own doubts. These writers, who used various means to escape what they felt to be the unacceptable reality of the Caribbean, kept in touch with the people in a very direct way. Their writing was almost always accessible to the general reader, even as it appealed to the sophisticated critic. They were, in effect, inviting a public response.

But we must also keep in mind that Caribbean literature has been a literature of symbolic escape as well as of literal departure. That is, it has sought to create idealized images of cultural identity that might seem to be more satisfying than the "little island" anomie of the "real" West Indies. Hence the evocation of "negritude," the image of the universal black soul; or the obsessive attraction of a romanticized, glamorized past; or the endless fascination with the innocence of childhood. These three symbolic realms of escape have dominated much of the literature of the Caribbean. Until the 1950s, relatively little of this literature dealt head-on with the realities of the here and now. The literature, by avoiding "social problems," may be criticized as escapist in the negative sense. However, I contend that in constructing what amounted to archetypal fantasies of what might have been, West Indian writers affected a particular kind of catharsis in their readers that enabled them to have their fill of unfulfillable romance, and then turn their attention to the real Caribbean with clearer eyes and wiser hearts.

In this paper, then, we will look at Caribbean literature not primarily as a series of texts for critical study, but anthropologically as a process of dialogue between artists and their public whereby a people come to evolve a new definition of their personal and cultural identities. It is impossible to do justice to the full sweep of Caribbean literature in a brief survey paper, and so the interplay between escape and identity will be viewed through the careers of just a few selected writers, whose literary lives seem best to express the important role Caribbean literature has played in helping transform West Indian society.

THE LITERATURE OF ESCAPE

NAIPAUL AND THE CULTURE OF THE METROPOLE

The most internationally honored of all West Indian writers is the Trinidad-born V. S. Naipaul. This perennial Nobel candidate is also in many ways the classic Caribbean escape artist. The schoolboy vow cited at the head of this paper is probably the most straightforward statement of the need to escape ever to appear in the published writings of a Caribbean author. Except for the long nonfiction essay, "Michael X and the Black Power Killings in Trinidad," Naipaul has not written directly about the Caribbean for more than a decade. But his writing revolves almost exclusively around the theme of the failure and defeat of the colonial society and of the inability of the colonial-bred intellectual to fit in anywhere—a world view nurtured by his Trinidadian childhood. In a recent autobiographical essay (1984, 72), Naipaul has spoken of the source of his inspiration as a writer. It was, from the beginning of his career, a need to "go back"—at first, in the literal sense of creating characters in situations like those of his childhood, but later in a more general sense of trying to understand the specific forces which drove him to leave Trinidad for England.

When one looks at photos of this elegantly garbed man of letters and sees pictures of his ever-so-English country manor, one might conclude that Naipaul himself gives the lie to these downbeat images. He is an acknowledged master of the English language, a major literary figure on both sides of the Atlantic. But the essence of Naipaul's style is his ironic perception that while the clever intellectual may take up the protective coloration of whatever culture happens to be dominant in his world, that pose is still a sham.

Naipaul's literary output has over the years deepened from a comic to a tragic view of this deception. His earliest novels and short stories dealt with people of relatively petty ambition who either gave in to the futility of the "little island," like the several hapless politicians contesting a local election in *The Suffrage of Elvira*, or who left it, like the "mystic masseur" Ganesh Ramsumair, who ended his days in England as Mr. G. Ramsay Muir in *The Mystic Masseur*. In either case, their lives were seen as essentially wasted. But this process was treated with light irony. The failures of these would-be heroes were rarely serious, and their downfalls were more ridiculous than heartbreaking.

Naipaul's more recent heroes, however, have edged closer to tragedy, for their failures have implications for the fate of their entire societies. These characters, in novels like *Guerillas* and *Bend in the River*, are not simply pathetic victims of the colonial order; they are, by their stubborn blindness to the limitations of their societies, accomplices in its further degradation.

Naipaul himself was born into the Indian community on Trinidad. The descendants of the Indian indentured laborers have maintained a very strong sense of communal identity by enforcing an endogamous marital pattern and by keeping to the land. But the enclave mentality has prevented Indians from becoming full participants in the political life of Trinidad. They have consistently been unwilling to make common cause with other communities. More thoroughly than any of the other major population groups of the Caribbean, the Indians have denied the very existence of the West Indies. So secure were they in the glories of their ancient culture that they declined to take notice of the place where an accident of history had physically marooned them.

Naipaul clearly limns the root conflict of Caribbean identity in his writings: the reality that sits right outside one's window is irrelevant or worthless, while the fantasy one creates of an idealized ancestral culture is treated as if it alone were real. This conflict may be exaggerated by the particular circumstances of the

Indian community, but it is one that tears at the psyche of all West Indians, at least of those who grew up in the pre-independence period.

The early Naipaul was able to see the humor in this stubborn refusal to come to terms with reality. There was even a sort of cockeyed, perverse nobility in some creative eccentrics who lived out their fantasies. The apotheosis of this early viewpoint is *A House for Mr. Biswas*, arguably the finest of all Caribbean novels. Although it deals in specific, intimate detail with the Indian community in Trinidad as Naipaul knew it in the 1930s (the protagonist was based on his own father), its dramatization of the inability of even an intelligent man to escape the dead hand of a stagnant, traditional society makes it a landmark in the literature of Caribbean identity. Indeed, the black Trinidadian writer and politician C. L. R. James (1962, 150) has noted that "after reading *A House for Mr. Biswas* many of our people have a deeper understanding of the West Indies than they did before."

Mohun Biswas is a man who has been imperfectly assimilated. Too sophisticated in the ways of the world to be truly comfortable in the stifling extended family household into which he has married, he is still too much a product of his upbringing to be able to stand on his own two feet as an individual. The household of his wife's rich and numerous clan, the Tulsis, is, to be sure, a specifically Indian institution. But it can surely stand as a symbol of the stultifying old order in general. Mr. Biswas kicks against it, but his rebellion is futile because he has no sense of how to achieve his goal. He has many vague ambitions, but does not know how to set long-range plans. And so he mostly ends up slinking back to the family, despising it all the more as the forces of time erode its solidarity, and yet still unable to break free of its bonds.

Mr. Biswas eventually builds his own house, his symbol of independence. It is described in gently romantic terms that contrast sharply with the hard-edged descriptions of the Tulsis house. But Naipaul (1961, 8) had already told us in the Prologue the less romantic truth: Mr. Biswas "thought of the house as his own, though for years it had been irretrievably mortgaged." Moreover, the house is a ramshackle affair, and its construction costs Mr. Biswas the support of his family. He drifts off into sickness and disillusionment, loses his job, and finally dies, accounted a fool and a failure even by his friends. Yet even "during these months of illness and despair he was struck again and again by the wonder of being in his own house, the audacity of it: to walk in through his own front gate, to bar entry to whoever he wished, to close his doors and windows every night," (ibid). It is a small, but a deeply felt triumph.

The story is a sad one, but it is told in a spirit of brave good cheer. Much of the novel details the low-level guerrilla war between Mr. Biswas and his awful in-laws. Mr. Biswas often acts the clown—to disguise his pain, to be sure, but also because humor is the one weapon against which the ridiculously haughty Tulsis have no defense. The greatest irony in Naipaul's portrait of Mr. Biswas lies in the fact that the hero is a failed writer. Although he finds employment as a petty journalist, his real ambition, to publish stories, is never realized. He starts scores of them, but is never able to finish them. And the title of each of these abortive efforts includes the word "Escape." But as Ramchand (1983, 204) has pointed out, Mr. Biswas's life does not so much *create* order as "confirm its possibility."

Mr. Biswas dies with his faith intact "that below it all there was an excitement which was hidden but waiting to be grasped" (Naipaul 1961, 341). The essence of Caribbean culture, for Naipaul, was that it derived from a "picaroon" society, enamored of the romance of the "camp," where one made one's fortune, lost it, shrugged, and moved on to brighter horizons. That insouciance soured, however, when Naipaul returned to the West Indies after his first spell in London as a professional writer in the early 1960s. He came back to an independent West Indies, and he shocked himself by knowing it intimately as an insider and yet evaluating it with the clinical objectivity of an outsider. And his evaluation, recorded in the remarkable, bitterly painful travel memoir *The Middle Passage*, was not a happy one.

Shortly after that disappointing trip, he went to India to explore his own roots. The title of the resulting book, *An Area of Darkness*, tells the emotional story. Not only did he realize that *he* did not fit into the real India of the 1960s, but, even worse, that India was simply a bigger, more spectacular version of Trinidad—a squalid colonial mess full of self-deluding politicians, pretentious and irrelevant intellectuals, and a populace that, despite all hopes to the contrary, could never rise to reclaim its ancient and glorious heritage.

The trip to India marked a turning point in Naipaul's career, convincing him as it did that the Third World was doomed to wallow in its hopeless fantasies and be the perpetual victim of the uncaring "metropole." Such a conclusion might have made Naipaul a revolutionary. But, put off by the emptiness of revolutionary rhetoric which he saw as simply more of the same self-deluding fantasy, be became instead a cynic, spinning out a steady stream of elegant, mordant satires and despairing essays.

This new phase in Naipaul's career was signalled by the publication of *The Mimic Men*, his most controversial novel. The St. Lucia-born poet and dramatist Derek Walcott, in a famous review of this novel, expressed his amazement at the way in which Naipaul's love of his people had begun to "choke on abhorrence." Abhorrence may be too strong a word, but certainly the novel's protagonist, Ralph Singh, is presented in a far more pitiless light than was Mr. Biswas. Singh is a kind of colonial golden boy. The son of a noted labor leader during colonial times, he receives the finest education abroad, pursues both artistic and political ambitions, and plays an important role in the independence movement in his homeland. He rises to heights far headier than those ever envisioned by poor Mr. Biswas, but his fall is all the more painful. Singh's defeat is not simply a personal one—it is quite explicitly the symbol of all the colonial "mimic men" who are so absorbed in taking on the trappings of everyone else's culture that they neglect to nurture their own selves. Singh, like his whole island society, is all mask, all sham, with no interior, and he falls with pathetic ease into corruption and the betrayal of his followers. He is still alive at the end of the novel, but he is more truly dead in the near-catatonia of his defeat than Mr. Biswas.

Singh's tragedy lies in the fact that, unlike Biswas, he *does* escape—and finds out how empty are the images of escape that once nurtured his hopes. In one telling passage, Singh describes his first experience of snow, the very symbol of the nontropical metropole. It is beautiful, enchanting—but in the end it cannot disguise the startling and disquieting shabbiness of London. It might strike the North American reader as odd that something as mundane as a dreary rooming house could crush the spirit of a brilliant and talented young man. But the point is that the West Indian lives on dreams and fantasies of escape. When unvarnished reality obtrudes on those dreams and renders the fantasies just as squalid as the "unreal" tropics, there is disillusionment aplenty.

Fantasy and disillusionment are the themes of this acerbic and disturbing novel, and they were to become the hallmarks of

Naipaul's later style. As Bruce MacDonald (1982, 23) has pointed out, Naipaul's view of postcolonial society is that it is marked by "taint and despair." It is no wonder that nationalist intellectuals like Walcott were upset by Naipaul's vision. But even more to the point is the way this vision nagged at the consciousness of ordinary readers. I first arrived in Trinidad nearly three years after the publication of *The Mimic Men*, but it was still a topic of heated—and anguished—discussion, even among people far from the literary circles of the capital. Almost every literate person had read it, and felt shocked and depressed. Many of them told me that they could understand Naipaul himself wanting to escape, and they wished him well in England. But why, oh why did he have to be so cruel to the people he left behind? Worse still, they sometimes whispered, could he have been right after all?

AIMÉ CÉSAIRE AND THE CULTURE OF THE SOUL

If Naipaul's response to the perceived ambivalence of West Indian identity was to leave it behind and abhor it from afar, the response of the great Martinique-born poet and philosopher Aimé Césaire was to create a world in which his "little island" became part of a greater universe, not so much of the mind, but of the soul. Césaire became the major West Indian prophet of the movement called "Négritude" in French.

Césaire's Martinique background is just as germane to an understanding of his approach to escape as Naipaul's Indian affiliation is to his. The remnants of the once extensive French Caribbean empire have, in the twentieth century, been officially drawn into the political structure of the French republic. Martinique is an "overseas department" of France, and theoretically is on equal footing with other administrative regions of metropolitan France. Martinique is represented in the French National Assembly, and Césaire himself has served as a deputy. Again in theory, there is no racial discrimination in Martiniquan society, since all Martiniquans are citizens of France. Indeed, ever since the heyday of colonialism, the French have held to the ideal of their "mission civilisatrice," a movement to bring the "natives" the benefits of French culture. In the thinking of the French colonialist, even the blackest African could be considered French—and claim all the rights of a Frenchman—as long as he adopted French culture. Such a person was called an "évolué" as if to emphasize that, in assuming the mantle of Frenchness, he had become truly human.

On one level, this philosophy, and the political integration it spawned, were beacons of enlightenment. People in the British and Dutch West Indies could only look longingly at those in the French Antilles who seemed to have arrived at a plateau of metropolitan acceptance undreamed of in their own territories. But on the other hand, this policy, well intentioned though it may have been, had the vicious effect of relegating local culture ever further to the shadows. For the French West Indian, there *was* no culture but that of France. An English-island intellectual like Naipaul could *choose* to try to adopt English culture; a French-island intellectual was either French, or he was a savage.

For a self-aware Martiniquan of the late colonial period, this situation was intolerable. Césaire, for example, saw perfectly well that while he might be accorded an official status of Frenchman, he was certainly *not* French in the truest sense. His Frenchness was but a mask of culture. It is no accident that Martinique also produced the radical philosophy of Frantz Fanon. While Césaire, unlike Fanon, was able to play along with the system for most of his long and productive career, he was never unaware that the mask of the *évolué* was a betrayal of his deepest self.

At first, however, Césaire could not think of Martinique, per se, as the locus of this truest identity. Martinique was, after all, nothing but the creation of French colonialism. Césaire found his place of escape from this dilemma in negritude. By this term, we must remember, he did *not* mean "back to Africa" in the literal, political sense. He was speaking of a spiritual connection with the soul of black culture. That soul followed exiled Africans wherever they went and it bound all black people together into a spiritual union more potent than any temporary political or economic accommodation.

Césaire was the co-founder of a review called *L'Etudiant Noir* when he was a student in Paris in 1935-1936. His collaborator was Léopold Senghor, the poet who later became the President of Senegal. Senghor taught Césaire about African culture, and Césaire shared with Senghor his experience of the black soul in exile. Their journal was based on negritude as a common denominator. To Césaire and Senghor, it meant ". . . that there is a solidarity between all blacks . . . that we are suspended together in space" (Frutkin 1973, 16).

The aim of *L'Etudiant Noir* was to make blacks everywhere aware that their culture, although debased by colonialism both in Africa and in the New World, was a thing to be valued. It was different from, but certainly not inferior to, white civilization. The journal became a voice crying out against racial assimilation—although, of course, political realities meant that black intellectuals constantly had to preserve at least the mask of assimilation in order to get by. The ideal culture, then, remained "suspended in space," a thing of sometimes intangible spiritual essence perceptible only to those with the requisite soul.

It may be noted that the Spanish Antillean version of negritude (*Negrismo*) has been officially discouraged in Cuba since the Revolution, although it had previously been a very important literary movement there. The Castro government understands perfectly well that in celebrating a minority community, that of the Afro-Cubans, and by exalting that culture's intangible spirituality, Negrismo implicitly denied the basis for the unified state, as well as for an international solidarity based on Marxist economic principles (Moore 1986, 15).

The turning point of Césaire's career was the poem "Cahier d'un Retour au Pays Natal." This epic in blank verse was written in 1936-1937 when Césaire was on vacation in Yugoslavia. It was first published in an obscure Parisian literary review, and went almost unnoticed. However, after the war, it was resurrected and reprinted by André Breton, and came to be called "the supreme and original statement of negritude" (Frutkin 1973, 16). It is a great irony—and one of which Césaire himself was certainly not unaware—that this manifesto is so clearly the product of the very process of cultural assimilation that the poem sets out to deplore.

The poem is a declaration of Césaire's desire to return to Martinique, not because the island per se was to be the locus of his identity, but because it could be a useful political base from which to proclaim the doctrine of negritude, something that could be done only with great and ironic difficulty in Paris. It was therefore not only the inauguration of his literary career, but also the beginning of his political activism. The "Cahier" sets out the three principles of negritude which were to follow Césaire for the rest of his literary life. First, there was his personal identification with blacks everywhere and with their heritage of slavery. Second, there was his rejection of white civilization, because it was the progenitor of slavery and racism. Third, there was his hope for a future of universal fraternity.

In order to fulfill this vision, he had to return to Martinique and reestablish contact with *his* people. Césaire's poetic raptures were, of course, the product of a refined literary sensibility, and his language was standard French (he rarely used "antillea-nisms"). But the sentiments he expressed were certainly not beyond the experience of ordinary readers, and his poetic style was an attempt to imitate the strong rhythms of African music. He was essentially saying aloud and in the language of poetic metaphor what other blacks were feeling in their hearts—and would themselves begin saying out loud, in a more overtly political context, three decades later. Fanon himself sarcastically remembered the reception that greeted the publication of Césaire's early work. "For the first time," he noted, "a . . . professor, apparently a reasonable man, was openly saying to the Antillean society, 'it is good and beautiful to be black.' It was absolutely a scandal" (Frutkin, 21).

In sum, Césaire's poetry "is engaged with past suffering, but . . . is resolute upon revolt . . . a breaking away, a cleansing, and a freeing of the body, soul, and mind" (Cartey 1970, 183). So Césaire's mission was to cleanse and uplift the downtrodden. His aim was not so much to glorify Martinique or the Antilles, but to *transcend* his homeland. He was, in effect, an evangelist who led his people to the mountaintop of racial identification, just as Naipaul led *his* people to the slough of ethnic despair. From both of these head-clearing vantage points people could begin to come to terms with the realities of their circumstances. Caribbean readers had to live out in the symbols of literature the fantasies of escape to other cultures before they could deal with "home."

GEORGE LAMMING AND THE CULTURE OF CHILDHOOD

George Lamming, born in Barbados, has become a successful literary figure in the English-speaking Caribbean. Although he achieved early success in England, Lamming has opted not to remain an exile like his contemporary, Naipaul. He lives and works in the West Indies, where he is now as famous as a vigorous and influential polemicist as he is as a creator of fiction. Lamming was among the first prominent anglophone Caribbean writers to espouse the cause of "black consciousness" in the 1960s, and he has argued eloquently for a regional identity. He has been a vocal and scornful critic of Naipaul and others who have remained in permanent exile; his objections have rested less on their physical removal from the Caribbean than on their unwillingness to deal directly with West Indian subject matter.

And yet Lamming himself has been caught up in the typical West Indian need to escape to an ideal, although his evocation of that ideal is quite different from that of either Naipaul or Césaire. Like so many West Indian writers, Lamming returns to childhood, and his very first novel, *In the Castle of My Skin*, still stands as the classic of the quite numerous genre of West Indian childhood narratives.

Lamming's view of childhood, and the uses for which he mobilizes his image of youth, are, however, quite different from the common run. His distinctive tone is part of the source of his power as an opinion leader. Other famous Caribbean childhood novels, such as the Barbadian Geoffrey Drayton's *Christopher* or the Trinidadian Michael Anthony's *The Year in San Fernando*, take what might be the expected approach of dwelling on the innocence of childhood and the creation of a kind of magical, special world sheltered from adult fears and responsibilities. These novels are written in the first person, and preserve the point of view of the young boys who narrate them. Lamming, on the other hand, infuses his first-person narrative with the voice of the wise adult. The little village that is the setting of *In the Castle of My Skin* is not a place of refuge; the changes that were to happen in the course of time are already reflected in Lamming's descriptions of it as it was when he was a child.

Lamming is explicitly political in a different way from the other childhood escapists. Lamming has affirmed his belief that as an artist his responsibility is to his own consciousness, to his society, and to the "community of man," not necessarily in that order (Ramchand 1983, 6). Lamming expresses a particular disdain for the West Indian bourgeoisie, because in his view only the "peasants" (including, in his later formulations, the urban proletariat) are the true bearers of pure folk culture. It should be noted that Lamming's reference to "the folk" extends beyond those people who live in the West Indies. His use of the term is global, symbolic, inclusive, as was Césaire's use of "black." By the same token, the middle class is an artifact of colonial exploitation. He does not, therefore, depict the "coming of age" of his four young heroes as a psychological process. Rather, he sees the maturation of his protagonists essentially as a microcosm that symbolizes the evolution of rural, peasant society and the growth of consciousness among the formerly oppressed and ignorant peasantry. The village in *Castle* is "growing painfully . . . into political self-awareness," and Lamming's political aims generally serve to push his account of the boys' adventures to the background, so that he can concentrate on detailing "the complex shiftings in the community at large" (Ramchand 1983, 25).

The common problem is the confusion of West Indian identity. The solution again is to clear the heads of people so that they can start fresh. Naipaul did so by first setting up the romantic allure of the sophisticated world of the metropole, and then debunking even that myth; Césaire did it by exalting the race that transcends the locality and its specific sufferings. Lamming does it by equating the clear-headed, straightforward approach of childhood with the earthbound good sense of the immemorial peasant. The "folk" could be seen as "the ground of psychic wholeness and source of new community" (King 1984, 102). He was not one to mourn the passing of the old order. Rather, he wished people to greet the coming of the new order with the unabashed, can't-put-nothin'-over-on-us common sense of the common people. The peasants were no less confused than the intellectuals about their identity, but, Lamming suggests, they did not let their confusion hold them back. His was therefore a plea for the unashamed acceptance of the implications of local history and culture. His was among the first strong voices to suggest that the West Indies themselves had something valuable to contribute to the identity of its people.

HERBERT DE LISSER AND THE CULTURE OF THE PAST

One further image of escape must now concern us as a part of the local heritage Lamming spoke about. The historical novel has always been extremely popular in the West Indies. Europeans and North Americans, of course, have also thrilled to sagas of pirates and planters on "the Spanish Main," but we may be surprised at the extent to which these purple visions have also entranced Caribbean readers, given their closer familiarity with the realities of slavery, indenture, and colonial exploitation. Certainly the finest writer of Caribbean historical romance was the Guyanese Edgar Mittelholzer, but I would like to conclude this survery with reference to another romancer, the Jamaican Herbert De Lisser.

De Lisser was a most prolific writer. He was the founder, and, for twenty-four years the mainstay of a literary annual, *Planter's Punch*, and he faithfully turned out a book-length fiction feature for this journal every year until his death. Current critical opinion holds most of this vast output in disesteem, consisting as it does of stilted, formula-bound potboilers. De Lisser's style was "a heady mixture of instant love, sexual jealousy and intrigue, a delicious *frisson* of sadism, simmering racial tensions, black magic and explosive violence" (Chang 1985, 13). De Lisser was, in some ways, a spiritual godfather of the Harlequin Romance school of fiction. And yet he was wildly popular throughout his lifetime, and even after his death, his most successful novels continued to be reissued. *The White Witch of Rosehall*, for example, was originally published in 1929, and was into its fourth printing as late as the mid-1950s. In the career of such a popular hack, we may thus find some clues to the kind of escape craved by the masses. The audience returned the dialogue to the writer who, having nothing very different of his own to say, happily obliged with his version of what they seemed to want. We may note the difference from the previous artists who were intent on awakening the consciousness of their readers.

Mark McWatt (1982) has made the point that "the past exerts . . . an almost obsessive influence upon the creative imagination of the West Indian writer." But *whose* past? And *how* was it to be resurrected? De Lisser was writing for the tiny white colonial elite which read *Planter's Punch*, the pages of which were filled with social notes of the business and social upper crust as well as with De Lisser's blockbusters. These people liked to see themselves as the bearers of gentility and civilization, and, as their devoted servant, De Lisser was certainly not inclined to challenge their complacent self-image directly. And yet he could not avoid probing beneath the placid surface. De Lisser's waxworks planters and their ladies were all periodically swept by uncontrollable lusts. In *White Witch*, the devastatingly suave Robert Rutherford claps eyes on the fair Annie Palmer:

> It was as though an electric shock had passed through him. He felt himself gazing into a pair of eyes which he thought the most wonderful he had ever seen . . . intoxicated with her beauty and her evident liking for him, he felt at once inclined to live gaily, riotously, dangerously. (38-39)

But ravishing Robert also finds time to ogle black Millicent, just as his counterpart, Captain Thornton in *Morgan's Daughter*, dallies with the "mulatress" Elizabeth, whom he tells, "Do you know, you are the prettiest coloured girl I have seen in Jamaica? You are. I want to tell you so often. I have fallen head over ears in love with you" (28).

The proprieties of colonial society being what they were, Annie ends up strangled by the vindictive Millicent, and Thornton and Elizabeth are killed by outraged citizens after they have at each

other and are discovered *in flagrante*. Long before such a notion
had become commonplace, De Lisser was saying that lust and
sexual jealousy were the driving forces behind racial oppression.
He could not possibly have said so in so many words without
losing his genteel readership, but his standard plots made the
point over and over. Blacks and their culture were essentially
melodramatic foils for the sexual problems of the white heroes
and heroines. His very earliest novels, of the pre-*Planter's Punch*
era, are far more sympathetic to black people. Two of these
novels, *Jane: A Story of Jamaica*, and *Susan: Mr. Proudleigh's
Daughter*, were originally serialized in the Jamaica *Daily Gleaner*
in 1913 and 1914 respectively. They were both reprinted, as *Jane's
Career* and *Susan Proudleigh*. Both deal with the then contemporary scene, rather than the romantic past. De Lisser's
encomiums for black characters (Maria, in *Susan Proudleigh*,
"though black was comely") would scarely win prizes for
liberality today, but they were certainly avant-garde for the time
and place—and quite different from the rather dreary stereotypes
of the later novels, written for the delectation of the *Planter's
Punch* in-group and designed to appeal to their views on race
and the colonial order.

Modern critics assume that black readers have always scorned
De Lisser's oeuvre. But it is almost certainly true that they read
his books, and did not remain immune to their lavender glamor.
For a people just emerging from slavery, the image of slave days
as a time of passionate, swashbuckling romance was certainly
more appealing—and more influential in terms of self-image—
than hard-edged sociological analyses. The white elite's view of
the past, when even the most hotblooded creatures bowed to the
niceties of social convention, was just as much a part of the
emergent West Indian consciousness of all West Indians as was
Césaire's impassioned negritude or Lamming's celebration of the
peasantry. Coming to terms with a regional identity means,
perforce, coming to terms with its history—not only the hard
realities of slavery and oppression, but also the fantasy past of
lurid melodrama. In symbolic terms, the enduring appeal of the
latter is just as significant as the political significance of the
former.

CONCLUSIONS

"Living in a borrowed culture," Naipaul (1962, 68) has
written, "the West Indian, more than most, needs writers to tell

him who he is and where he stands." It is not unusual for a
writer to think of himself as being in a position to lecture his
compatriots. But the history of Caribbean literature in the
twentieth century is a story of more than a small intellectual elite
"telling" the masses who they were. In fact, most of the writers
needed guidance themselves to tell them who *they* were. In their
very different ways, Naipaul, Césaire, Lamming, and De Lisser
all went back to "their people"—the communal ethnic group, the
universal race, the peasantry, the ruling elite—to define their own
identities and to formulate images of escape from the vexing
contradictions of their societies.

The writers' struggles were the conflicts of their fellows writ
large. Caribbean literature has been a grand, symbolic theater in
which intellectuals and the "common people" exchange ideas
about identity. Caribbean people worked through several decades
of doubt and confusion before they could begin to see that there
was something uniquely theirs—a wholly West Indian brew of
ethnic diversity, racial pride, metropolitan influences, and
healthy peasant skepticism. Far from being evidence of weakness,
this diversity could at last be seen as a source of strength, a basis
for choice.

It would be unfair to conclude this survey with the implication
that a synthesis of these disparate elements has been effected, and
that there is now a happy consensus about what a West Indian
identity is, and that a contemporary West Indian literature exists
to celebrate that identity. Indeed, it may truly be said that "West
Indian territory, both regional and insular, remains (in most
cases) unavoidably plural, perhaps perpetually so" (Clarke 1984,
132). But the elements are now recognized as part of the symbolic
repertoire of choice. The older need to deny and reject has been
replaced by an inquisitive desire to incorporate. After all the pain
of being deceived and disappointed in escape, the current West
Indian consciousness has begun the process of coming home.

As Lloyd Brown has put it,

> Literature, then, allows the West Indian to perceive the past not only in terms
> of its brutality and waste, but also with references to that creative sense of
> self-affirmation which salvages a cultural identify from that past. (1984, 9)

NOTES

[1]The full implications of this point of view are explored in Hugh D. Duncan
(1968). The uses of this "dramatistic" model for the study of modernization are
discussed in Peacock (1975). This perspective has been most convincingly applied
to the Caribbean setting by Manning (1978).

[2]By the "Caribbean" I mean all the islands of the Greater and Lesser Antilles, plus the territories on the mainland of Central America and northern South America which border on the Caribbean Sea, and whose history of plantation/mercantile economy is linked to that of the islands. By convention, the term also includes Bermuda and the Bahamas, islands in the Atlantic whose history links them with the colonial empires of the Caribbean proper. The term "Caribbean Basin," which has come into vogue among political economists in recent years, will be avoided. In some parts of the English-speaking Caribbean, "basin" is a euphemism for a toilet, and many Caribbean intellectuals resent having North Americans refer to them as inhabitants of a "basin."

The English, French, and Dutch have all used the appellation "West Indies" in official designation of their Caribbean empires. The Spanish did not do so. Moreover, the term "West Indies" has often referred only to the islands, not to the mainland territories. However, in this paper, I will use "West Indies" as if it were a synonym for "Caribbean" in the sense defined above, solely for the purpose of injecting some variety into the text.

WORKS CITED

Anthony, Michael. *The Year in San Fernando.* London: Andre Deutsch, 1965.

Apter, David. *The Politics of Modernization.* Chicago: University of Chicago Press, 1965.

Brown, Lloyd. *West Indian Poetry.* 2d. ed. London: Heinemann, 1984.

Carew, Jan. "The Caribbean Writer and Exile." *Caribbean Studies* 19 (1979): 111-132.

Cartey, Wilfred. *Black Images.* New York: Teachers College Press, 1970.

Césaire, Aimé. *Cahier d'un Retour au Pays Natal.* Paris: Présence Africaine, 1956.

Chang, Victor L. "The Historical Novels of Herbert G. De Lisser." In *West Indian Literature and Its Social Context,* ed. Mark McWatt. Cave Hill, Barbados: University of the West Indies, 1985, pp. 12-17.

Clarke, Colin G. "Caribbean Consciousness." In *Perspectives on Caribbean Regional Identity,* ed. Elizabeth M. Thomas-Hope. Liverpool: University of Liverpool Centre for Latin American Studies, 1984, pp. 122-34.

De Lisser, Herbert. *Jane's Career.* London: Methuen, 1914.

——. *Susan Proudleigh.* London: Methuen, 1915.

——. *The White Witch of Rosehall.* London: Methuen, 1929.

——. *Morgan's Daughter.* London: E. Benn, 1931.

Drayton, Geoffrey. *Christopher.* London: Collins, 1959.

Duncan, Hugh D. *Symbols and Society.* New York: Oxford University Press, 1968.

Erikson, Erik H. *Childhood and Society.* 2d. ed. New York: Norton, 1963.

Frutkin, Susan. *Aimé Césaire: Black Between Worlds.* Coral Gables, FL: University of Miami Center for Advanced International Studies, 1973.

James, C. L. R. *Party Politics in the West Indies.* San Juan, Trinidad: Vedic Enterprises, Ltd., 1962.

King, Lloyd. "Caribbean Literature: Aspects of a Nationalist Process." In *Perspectives on Caribbean Regional Identity,* ed. Elizabeth M. Thomas-Hope. Liverpool: University of Liverpool Center for Latin American Studies, 1984, pp. 97-108.

Lamming, George. *In the Castle of My Skin.* London: Michael Joseph, 1953.

MacDonald, Bruce. "The Artist in Colonial Society." *Caribbean Quarterly* 28 (1982): 20-31.

McWatt, Mark. "The Preoccupation With the Past in West Indian Literature."
    Caribbean Quarterly 28 (1982): 12-19.

Manning, Frank E. *Bermudian Politics in Transition*. Hamilton, Bermuda: Island
    Press, Ltd., 1978.

Moore, Carlos. "Race Relations in Socialist Cuba." *Caribbean Review* 15 (1986):
    12-15.

Naipaul, V. S. *The Mystic Masseur*. London: Andre Deutsch, 1957.

——. *The Suffrage of Elvira*. London: Andre Deutsch, 1958.

——. *A House for Mr. Biswas*. London: Andre Deutsch, 1961.

——. *The Middle Passage*. London: Andre Deutsch, 1962.

——. *An Area of Darkness*. London: Andre Deutsch, 1964.

——. *The Mimic Men*. London: Andre Deutsch, 1967.

——. *Guerrillas*. London: Andre Deutsch, 1975.

——. *Bend in the River*. London: Andre Deutsch, 1979.

——. "Michael X and the Black Power Killings in Trinidad." In *The Return of
    Eva Peron*. New York: Vintage Books, 1981, pp. 1-98.

——. *Finding the Center*. New York: Vintage Books, 1984.

Peacock, James L. *Consciousness and Change*. New York: Wiley, 1975.

Ramchand, Kenneth. *The West Indian Novel and Its Background*. 2d. ed.
    London: Heinemann, 1983.

Walcott, Derek. "Review of *The Mimic Men*." In *V. S. Naipaul: A Critical
    Interpretation*, ed. Landeg White, 180-81. New York: Harper & Row, 1975.

LITERATURE AS ETHNOGRAPHIC EVIDENCE: THE CASE OF MEXICAN NARRATIVE

Barbara Jo Lantz

ABSTRACT

This paper compares three kinds of narrative in Mexico: conversational storytelling, the narratives of mourning, and drunken narrative. In Mexico, the life stories of heroes and dead loved ones, and even one's own life experiences are infused with an interpretive tension that derives from the persistence of Christian norms in a Modernist climate. The epic structure of conversational storytelling contrasts with the novelistic self-revelation of drunken narrative. Narratives of mourning combine these two narrative possibilities. This paper draws on both ethnographic and literary evidence and makes a case for the structural continuity between the narratives of social life and literary narratives by demonstrating the social and moral risks of life stories in Mexico.

> The storyteller: he is the man who could let the wick of his life be consumed completely by the gentle flame of his story.
>
> Walter Benjamin, *Illuminations*

In 1950, in his much acclaimed treatise on Mexican character and culture, *The Labyrinth of Solitude*, Octavio Paz used the example of the Day of the Dead (*El Día de los Muertos*—the Mexican counterpart of our Halloween and All Saints' Day) to comment on Mexicans' love of fiestas. He begins his analysis in this way:

> The solitary Mexican loves fiestas and public gatherings. Any occasion for getting together will serve, any pretext to stop the flow of time and commemorate men and events with festivals and ceremonies. We are a ritual people . . . . (47)

He points out that the State and Church provide a multiplicity of fiesta occasions and that national fiestas are supplemented by fiestas for local village and city patron saints, festivals for neighborhoods and trade unions, and individual saints' days and birthdays. In Paz's view, all this celebrating is not amusement so much as a kind of escape from the solitude of daily life. Paz explains:

> In all of these ceremonies—national or local, trade or family—the Mexican opens out. They all give him a chance to reveal himself and to converse with God, country, friends or relatives. During these days, the silent Mexican whistles, shouts, sings, shoots off fireworks, discharges his pistol into the air. He discharges his soul. . . . This is the night when friends who have not

exchanged more than the prescribed courtesies for months get drunk together, trade confidences, weep over the same troubles, discover that they are brothers, and sometimes, to prove it, kill each other. (49)

Paz's characterization of fiestas as an occasion for "solitary Mexicans" to "open out" relies on a kind of psychological portrait of Mexicans as silent, reticent, withdrawn, somber, closed up in themselves. On fiesta night, these silent, solitary Mexicans commune in an original chaos and freedom whereby

> [s]ocial structures break down and new relationships, unexpected rules, capricious hierarchies are created. In the general disorder everybody forgets himself and enters into otherwise forbidden situations and places. The bounds between audience and actors, officials and servants, are erased. Everybody takes part in the fiesta, everybody is caught up in its whirlwind. Whatever its mood, its character, its meaning, the fiesta is participation, and this trait distinguishes it from all other ceremonies and social phenomena. Lay or religious, orgy or saturnalia, the fiesta is a social act based on the full participation of all its celebrants. (52)

These passages from *Labyrinth* combine the rich metaphors and philosophical speculations of Paz's poetry with spirited ethnographic analysis. In the best tradition of interpretive anthropology, he outlines a theory of ritual that provides a native ontology to boot!

Living and working in Mexico City at the commencement of the 1980s, I wondered about an apparent discrepancy between Paz's 1950 analysis of fiesta frenzy and what I observed and came to participate in as an enthusiast of Mexican social intercourse. The account that I share here of conversational storytelling, narratives of mourning, and drunken narrative takes its inspiration from Paz but also makes use of his writings as native exegesis. I do the same with other articulate Mexican commentators who, through newspaper reports, biography, fiction, or informant testimony, convey the moral ramifications of participation in the narratives of social life.

The element of Paz's rendering of fiesta participation that did nor ring true with my own experiences in an urban, middle-class *milieu* was his characterization of Mexicans as silent and solitary. In fact, I found them to be quite the opposite.

CONVERSATION AS NARRATIVE

Social life in Mexico City is essentially conversational. Chance encounters with friends or neighbors on the street, the regular encounters with fellow workers in the office, parties and social gatherings in the home, and coffee or drinks in bars and restaurants provide opportunities for lively and richly textured conversational embellishment of ordinary situations. Even brief encounters with strangers such as taxi drivers, sales people, or others in service occupations require conversational pleasantries. Social encounters are governed by an expectation that they be enjoyable, engaging, and animated. Mexicans enjoy *un buen cotorreo* (a good bull session). Conversation is the key to a successful social encounter. It unites people in a kind of perpetual dance that joins individuals in a sense of brotherhood and goodwill without making undue demands on individuals to reveal themselves. To be part of the group, one must join in the conversation.

Just any kind of talk will not do. Content and style are interwoven in such a way that a topic's acceptability depends very much upon the spirit of its delivery. Politics and current events are popular topics, as are the problems of urban life, such as inflation, the price and availability of goods and services, the exigencies of work and family life, and the like. People discuss common friends or family members along with their problems or life strategies. They narrate the story of a trip or vacation that they have taken, a movie or television show that they have seen, a sporting event or concert that they have been to, or a newspaper article that they have read. People also describe anomalous occurrences that they have witnessed, such as political gatherings, traffic accidents, robberies, assaults, or fires, or they share accounts of events that they have heard from others. Finally, they enjoy telling and hearing jokes, and evening social gatherings can become joke telling sessions.

The mutual propriety of recounting tragedies and jokes is neither fortuitous nor paradoxical. Nor does the tragedy or joke succeed in engaging the group by its theme alone. The effectiveness of the narrative depends upon the rhetorical charisma of the teller. To be successful, the story must stand on its own apart from the biography of the individual. It should not be too punctuated with editorial comments or interrupted by references to the emotional state of the teller. The impact of the story and the relationship of the teller to it must be conveyed in the description of the events themselves. The events should be told in such a way as to allow the force of them to fall over everyone. The ego or individuality of the teller is important, then, not as the person to whom a thing has happened or even as the possessor of a certain knowledge of an event, but rather as the vehicle through which the event can be shared and experienced by the gathering.

In fact, too much insertion of the teller's self into the story is a cause of embarrassment. By removing himself from the focus of attention of a story, the teller can dispel the discomfort that would otherwise accompany the recounting of a tragedy or off-color joke. Both the group's and the teller's embarrassment are at stake. When the story can thus stand on its own apart from the teller, then it can be appropriated by any listener to be recounted again to someone else. Authorship, *per se*, is not of particular importance. Anyone can tell anyone else's story as long as he or she tells it well. Stories are not, therefore, for soul-baring or confession, nor should they be encumbered by the personal tribulations of the teller. The individual fuses with the story. The self of the teller is obscured behind the words, as participants shed their identities, however temporarily, to become talkers and listeners.

The telling of stories should be an exchange, if not of the spotlight, at least of comments relating to the story being told. In any gathering, there is a tendency for some to do the telling and others to do the listening, but all must participate in some way. Listening means laughing or expressing surprise at the correct moment, making eye contact with others present, and inserting comments as often as possible to convey that you are present and participating. Silence is taken for boredom or intransigence, and it is indicative of an unwillingness to join in the spirit of the group. A silent person is assumed to be out of sorts with the situation, and a consistently silent person will tend not to be included in future gatherings.

A typical session is one in which stories are traded, whether the exchange be of jokes, accounts of death, news items, childhood reminiscences, or whatever. Someone will tell a story that introduces a theme, and another will follow up with a second story on that same theme. The theme itself can take some twists and turns, so that a conversation that begins with a news item can move on to death incidents, movies, moments from childhood, local politics, etc. Although the theme can slowly transform itself in this way, it remains nevertheless the focus of attention. Interruptions in the storytelling occur to refill drinks, accommodate a new member, or change topics, but not to take stock of the conversation, the group, or the person talking.

Ideally, conversation accompanies any contiguity of persons in space. Waiting in line or riding in an elevator is much more pleasant if spent in conversation. It alleviates the embarrassment of silence and creates a mood of affability.

Being able to converse in this way becomes part of everyone's personal repertoire. Some people may be better storytellers than others, but everyone must know how to converse. Parents worry, for example, about children who are shy or reserved. Because they are not garrulous, they are assumed to lack skill in dealing with the world and to be unprepared for life. A withdrawn adolescent may be slow to make a career decision and may be considered to lack ambition. Not to pick a career (a decision that entails both *that* and *what* one will study) is taken as a reluctance to throw oneself into the stream of life, and this timidity is likely to be associated as well with verbal restraint. People size each other up on the basis of their participation in engaging conversation. After making a new acquaintance, you decide whether or not that person merits the ascription *una buena onda* (a good time) largely by the animation of their conversation.

The Epic Form of Conversational Storytelling

The conversational storytelling of Mexican social life displays some of the structural characteristics that Walter Benjamin (1968) imputed to the art of storytelling, which he perceived to be on the wane in Europe between the two World Wars. In Benjamin's historical typology of literary genres, storytelling as an art competes with the novel, which has somewhat different aims. The storyteller supplements one story with another in a string of narrative that, when all of the stories are considered together, forms a web. Benjamin contrasts the storyteller's series of "reminiscences" to the remembrance that characterizes the novel. The former is short-lived, whereas the latter is perpetuating. The aim of the story is to convey a lesson, whereas in the novel, the meaning of an individual life is revealed. Whereas the storyteller relates many diffuse occurrences, the novel as remembrance "is dedicated to *one* hero, *one* odyssey, *one* battle" (98).

Benjamin has drawn on a distinction in literary forms made by Georg Lukács (1971) in his work *The Theory of the Novel*, written in 1914 and 1915. Lukács differentiates the epic from the novel and places them in dialectical opposition by virtue of their different treatments of time, memory, and character. Written at the outset of the Great War and in opposition to it and to the enthusiasm for that war, *The Theory of the Novel* is often cited as a seminal work pointing in the direction that the modern novel had only begun to take at that time.[1]

In Lukács's analysis, epic time is homogeneous. It has no power to transform by intensifying or diminishing the meaning of things. And despite his guise as an individual, the hero of the epic is not an individual at all, but rather the representative of a community. Thus his story is not a personal story but the story of the community's destiny. In the novel, on the other hand, an individual with a personality faces the problem of self-discovery. Memory of the past is what allows the problem of the novel to be solved:

> The inner form of the novel has been understood as the process of the problematic individual's journeying towards himself, the road from dull captivity within a merely present reality—a reality that is heterogeneous in itself and meaningless to the individual—towards clear self-recognition. (80)

In the novel, the individual sets out to find self-recognition in a journey that comprises the events of his life. Thus the form of the novel is biography, with a beginning and end that delineate a segment of life, whether this segment of life coincides with a particular human life or not. This "segment of life" defines a relationship of past to present whereby the present emerges from the events and experiences of the past through memory. Separated from the rest of the world by a chasm that the individual fills with a sense of his own interiority, he can find the meaning in life through the hope or memory that makes the present the result of the past.

Benjamin (1968) carries Lukács's analysis of the problematic of the novel one step further by identifying death as the occasion for the revelation of the meaning of life. Lukács proposes that it is at moments of loss that memory can transform the fragmentary and meaningless into revelation. What Lukács articulates about memory may occur at other moments of loss as well, but his analysis reveals what is essential about the moment of death. In the novel, the structure of narrative leads inexorably to an end in which the protagonist completes his journey to self-recognition, the aim of novelistic revelation.

The reading of a novel, then, involves accompanying the protagonist on this journey in the hope that the meaning of life will be revealed. Benjamin tells us that, as readers of novels, we "must, no matter what, know in advance that [we] will share [the characters'] experience of death" (101). The characters that people novels are psychologically round, complex individuals who experience life through what Walter Ong (1982) has called a "highly interiorized stage of consciousness" (179). Storytelling, on the other hand, relies on the self-forgetfulness of the listener for its perpetuation. As Benjamin (1968) says, "There is nothing that commends a story to memory more effectively than that chaste compactness which precludes psychological analysis" (91). Because storytelling is the art of repeating stories, their authorship and the experience they relate do not define an individual self but a larger shared experience.

Mexican conversation conforms in some interesting ways with Benjamin's characterization of the art of storytelling. Conversational storytelling is like what Frederic Jameson (1978), following Durkheim, has called "ideological representation," the "indispensable mapping fantasy or narrative by which the individual subject invents a 'lived' relationship with collective systems . . ." (394). While talkers at a social gathering steer clear of intrusive or implicating comments, and listeners are careful not to reveal boredom or reticence, the material for discussion can include the most public and the most private of topics, ranging from the day's newspaper headlines to the President's most recent amorous affair. This social chatting permits the participants' contemplation of issues and events that highlight both the sensible and the untoward in daily life. While the specific incidents themselves may change from session to session, the general themes do not. And the most talkative participants carry with them a repertoire of stories that they tell to different gatherings, so that repetition and elaboration of stories is common.

The structure of stories is "episodic" in Ong's sense. He points out that the stories of oral narrative begin *in media res*, and episodes and descriptive asides can be added on without strict regard to chronological order. The stories of conversational storytelling also begin seemingly in the middle of things, and they are strung together by a kind of memory in which one incident reminds the teller of another, or one teller's story might inspire a listener to share one of his. Thus stories are added on to each other without regard to a chronology and without the expectation of a fixed beginning or ending. Conversation is pleasurable precisely on account of the seeming multiplicity of tales or incidents recounted. It is most engaging when one tale bumps up against another in an animated stream, and to *dar ánimo* to a group is to provide an unstoppable flow of conversation that puts "life" or "spirit" into the social occasion. The abundance of tales and the multiplicity of narrators prevent the formation of a single coherent narrative.

This quality of conversation contrasts markedly with the expectations of narrative coherence assigned to novels and histories. Literary theorist Frank Kermode (1979) in *The Genesis of Secrecy* traces this standard for narrative coherence to early Christian writing in which the apostles drew upon passages in the Old Testament and the Apocrypha to serve as generative models for the events they recorded in the New Testament. That earlier events could prefigure later ones depended upon a view of the world in which time had come to a stop, that is, in which the Messiah had come. The narrative coherence that we seek in the novel parallels that of the Christian Bible, as we sit in expectation that the end, that last page, will finally expose both the fates of the characters and the formal unity of the text.

Thus Christian narrative form selects as its domain the journey of a human life toward revelation and death. In Mexico, this form provides the narrative model for the lives of saints, heroes, and dead loved ones. Unified, coherent narratives characterize the recounting of lives at death. Narrative provides the means for remembering the dead. Ideally, death marks the resolution of a life. It transforms the indeterminate, unfixable, uncontrollable life into a remembered life. Death is an occasion for biography, and both the structure and content of biography are modeled after the Virgin mother and the martyr Son of Catholicism. Life becomes a journey through trials and adversity with death as the revelation of one's true identity.

THE NARRATIVES OF MOURNING

The story of the life of Beato Sebastián de Aparicio illustrates this narrative form. The pleas by the Franciscan order in Puebla to canonize him rely on the narration of his life of innocence and generosity. Fray Alejandro Torres's (1975) biography emphasizes his fortitude in the face of repeated intercessions by the devil to tempt him into sin and applauds his dedication to his work both as a lay person and as a monk. Torres sums up his life this way:

> Toda la vida de Aparicio es una infancia continuada derramando en toda ella el perfume de la sencillez y la inocencia. [Aparicio's whole life is a continual infancy permeated throughout with the perfume of simplicity and innocence.] (65)

The sanctity of his life is revealed at his death, for his body does not stiffen or decay. Instead, it emits a sweet odor that penetrates the entire convent and that lasts during his interment of nearly 200 years. In 1790, his still intact remains were unearthed and put on display in the Convent of San Francisco in Puebla, where they lie today.

His body has curative powers which it acquired at the moment of his death. Today, pilgrims visit his shrine where they pray for his intervention in childbirth, schooling, and illness. The image to which they pray is the body wrapped in a monk's shroud, with its peacefully sleeping face turned toward them and one foot protruding from beneath the shroud. The *reliquia* is evidence of his saintliness, for the natural processes of decay are interrupted and his body retains its life-like quality. To this miracle is added the supernatural power of the body to heal, but only those who are good, true believers can invoke this power.

Narrative apotheosizes the dead by transforming lives into destinies. We can find this model for death in literary and anthropological commentary about the sacrificial quality of the Mexican hero. Carlos Fuentes, for instance, notes:

> [T]he defeated have been glorified. Why? Because Mexico is a country where only the dead are heroes.... Our heroes are heroes because they were sacrificed. In Mexico, the only saving fate is sacrifice.... The nostalgia for the past in Mexico is a direct result of the original defeat. (quoted in Brodman 1976, 70)

Anthropologist Victor Turner has pointed out that some Mexican heroes have chosen the road to death in order to fulfill this requisite of herohood. In his view, a "religious myth" dictates the steps that certain Mexican heroes have taken to their own demise. That Zapata knowingly exposed himself to assassination and that Maximiliano remained in Mexico to face death in order to redeem himself in Mexican eyes derive from the model of the Christian martyr's death. Turner's point that religious myth penetrates life by presenting a standard for moral behavior as well as a strategy for political action suggests that narrative can itself take on the status of deed, as I will explore further.

The religious myth inspired by the death of Christ applies as well to deaths by natural causes. Manuel Arellano Zavaleta (1972) recounts the events of the death of President Benito Juárez, who died of a heart attack. In an effort to save him, his doctor applied boiling water to his chest. Arellano Zavaleta notes several times in his account that Juárez never uttered a single word of complaint during the course of his illness. As befits his stature as hero, he suffered stoically.

Apotheosis is not reserved only for saints and heroes, however. Anthropologist Luis Alberto Vargas G. (1971) points out that death brings absolution for the sinner. When someone dies, his defects disappear and his positive qualities remain. Death restores respectability and allows the recognition of one's merits. Narrative, with the standards of coherence that turn lives into destinies, makes apotheosis possible.

Still, the narration of lives on the occasion of death reflects on mourners as well as the deceased. To make this point, I will rely here on two literary treatments of the moral ramifications of grief and memory. I have chosen to present data from literature because I have found articulated there ramifications of narrative that remain implicit in social intercourse. These short stories, one by Emilio Carballido and the other by Carlos Fuentes, make the narration of the lives of dead loved ones social acts that can enhance or diminish the prestige of the teller. To narrate someone's life, then, entails a kind of social and moral risk. What this means in social life is that such stories can be quite cryptic or avoided altogether.

At the several funerals that I attended, and in social interaction with individuals in mourning, I observed a reticence to discuss a recently deceased loved one, but sometimes a desire to discuss other loved ones laid to rest in the past. At times, however, individuals refrained from talking of even long-dead loved ones if the circumstances of death implicated the survivor. The highly personal nature of mourning prevents my supplying data of a more direct nature. Yet these two short stories provide rich documentation of the potential power of narration to establish social and moral credibility. In the first, the telling of the life is a kind of cleansing expiation. In the second, such expiation has damaging implications.

Emilio Carballido's (1980) story, "La paz después del combate" ("The Peace After the Battle") explores the survivor's urge to bring order to memory through recounting life experiences shared with the deceased. At Adalberto's wake, his widow, Marión, anticipates with trepidation the arrival of her husband's first wife and children. Her marriage with Adalberto resulted from a love affair that disrupted her first marriage as well as his and brought a desire for vengeance from each injured party. Paloma, Adalberto's ex-wife, sued Adalberto for a large sum of money, as did Marión's former husband, Julio, leaving them to live in penury as well as scandal. At Adalberto's wake, Marión reminisces privately, aware that Adalberto's death has removed any reason to continue the conflict with his first family.

Nevertheless, when her niece Esther, an aspiring writer, invites Marión to sit with her, it occurs to Marión to recount the story of her life with Adalberto so that Esther might write it. "Podrías hacer una novela . . . tan bonita . . ." (126) ["You could write . . . such a beautiful novel . . ."], she tells Esther.

Even though the battle is over and done with now that Adalberto is dead, Marión needs to set the record straight. By relating her memory of Adalberto for Esther to write, she can quell the scandal that stalks her memory and perhaps put Adalberto (and her own past) to rest in her mind. His death makes it possible to transform his life and hers into a narrative. In this story, the wake is the scene of this transformation.

The tension between grief as social obligation and as moral testimony is played out in Carlos Fuentes's (1980) story "Mother's Day," which, through the interlocked lives of three generations of the Vergara family, explores the continuites and discontinuities in social values that have accompanied the transformation of Mexican society since the Revolution. General Vicente Vergara, who fought during the Revolution, became rich through riding the right political currents in its aftermath. His son Agustín faces ruin for having planted his Sinaloa lands in poppies and defrauded investors. Young Plutarco, approaching manhood but yet to embark on a career, contemplates the figure of these two progenitors and the meaning of their legacies for the course his life will take. His loyalties lie with his grandfather Vicente, who quarrels bitterly with Agustín over his failures in fortune and family. Plutarco listens eagerly to his grandfather's stories of Revolutionary valor and conquest and chastises his father for leaving him out of the drama and the pain of life.

Fuentes's tale suggests that despite changing historical circumstances, the images of past generations determine the terms in which their successors' lives will be played out by defining the standards that the young must meet. Because modern life does not present the same tests, it becomes more difficult to prove oneself by the old standards, which nonetheless maintain their power.

The three men's lives are overshadowed by two dead women: Clotilde, General Vicente's deceased wife and mother of Agustín, and Evangelina, wife of Agustín and mother of Plutarco. Every Mother's Day, the three men mourn their passing with a visit to the mausoleum where the two women are buried. Despite their absence as actors on the scene, these women have a continuing influence in the lives of their male survivors.

Vicente devotes an entire wall of his room to the memory of Clotilde. The wall bears a single photograph of her as a young woman and a table with a vase of flowers. The other walls are covered with a jumble of photographs of revolutionary leaders and the General himself as a young man in their company. He surrounds himself with mementos of her—the furniture from their first house, the wardrobe that still smells of her clothes. He delights in recounting the tale of how he saved her, orphaned by the war, from the low life of a vaudeville entertainer or a whore to the soldiers. Eventually, she learned to love him.

In contrast, there are no mementos of Evangelina in the house, not a single photograph. She died when Plutarco was five and his first encounter with her recorded image is through a photograph of his mother as "Queen of the Mazatlán Carnival" that his school friends deride. Plutarco questions his grandfather:

> —What was my mother like, Grandfather?
> —Beautiful, Plutarco. Too beautiful.
> —Why aren't there any pictures of her in the house?
> —Too painful.
> —I don't want to be left out of the pain, Grandfather. (40)

Later, on a night of carousing together that takes them to a brothel, Plutarco asks his grandfather to compare his mother to the whore who entertains them.

> "Is this what my mother was like, Grandfather?
> a whore like this? Is that what you meant?"
> . . .
> He muttered: "I hope so, Plutarco, I hope so."
> "Did she put the horns on my father?"
> "He looked like a stag when she got through with
> him." (48)

When Plutarco defends her infidelity by blaming his father for not satisfying her needs, the General replies, "I only know she dishonored your father" (48).

Agustín's account of these events differs. Unlike the General, who had to teach his Clotilde to love him, Agustín finds in Evangelina a woman who chooses his love over that of other suitors. Recognizing this victory of Agustín's, Vicente sets out to rob him of its sweetness by holding up Clotilde as a model of womanhood that Evangelina fails to match. In Agustín's version, Evangelina is driven to seek another man. When she does so, he still sees her as innocent, but while he does not hold her responsible, he cannot forgive her either. He strangles her.

As befits the sainted status Clotilde has in the General's mind, her memory is preserved not only through mementos and photographs, but through the General's constant references to her purity, to her good deeds. Agustín sees this reverence as a means for the General to sanctify his own "heroic" past.

> [H]e gave us everything on a silver platter as he always says, and there wasn't going to be another Revolution where a man could win at a stroke both love and valor, not any more, now we have to prove ourselves in other ways, why should he pay for everything and us for nothing? he's our eternal dictator, don't you see? see if we dare show we don't need him, that we can live without his memories, his heritage, his tyranny of sentiment. (55)

His recollections of Clotilde intertwine with the stories of his career as war hero. While the General is now an old man and his penchant for reminiscing is therefore "natural," Agustín considers it excessive to the point of tyranny. The General's memories have become an emasculating challenge to Agustín that leads him to kill his wife in order to prove his own manhood.

Moreover, the General's memories hide the truth that Clotilde was part of his war booty. They hide other truths as well, among them the ambiguity of Evangelina's culpability. Another Fuentes story, "These Were Palaces," enriches our sense of the selectivity of the General's memory. This story takes up the thread of the life of Manuelita, servant to the Vergaras for many years. Now Manuelita lives out her last years in a poor *vecindad* in the old center of the city. General Vergara fired her when she was only fifty, after the death of Evangelina and before the Vergaras's change of residence from Colonia Roma to the new luxury suburb of Pedregal. He told her he was firing her because she reminded him of too many things, especially of his dear Clotilde. Later she ponders this decision.

> That's why she'd felt so bad when the General fired her. She'd survived Doña Clotilde, she remembered too many things, the General wanted to be left alone with his past. Maybe he was right, maybe it was better for both of them, the employer and the servant, to go their own ways with their secret memories, without serving as the other's witness, better that way. (99)

By firing Manuelita, the General can remember things in his own way. The past which they once experienced together as ongoing, bawdy, seething, conflictive life fraught with moral turpitude and culpability, can be appropriated by each in his own way.

Like memory, grief is a solitary, individual experience, and the memory that prompts it is likewise personal. Yet both grief and memory have their public side. That the General can grieve on the annual Mother's Day visit to the cemetery and Agustín cannot reflects the unassailability of the patriarch's memories. The General has fought hard for his right to mourn Clotilde. As Evangelina's murderer, however, Agustín is not permitted to grieve openly. Nevertheless, as Plutarco tells us, his hand "blazes like fire" (57), a sign that perhaps he grieves in silence. Plutarco's retrospective musings about whether the General's tears are, in fact, for Clotilde or Evangelina suggest that perhaps even for the General sentiments cannot be contained in their proper place.

The intricacies of grief and culpability that Fuentes contemplates in this story aid in understanding the repercussions for the living of the memory of the dead. Apotheosis brings with it certain consequences. If the deceased is held up as a saint by survivors, the memory can protect the living, as in General Vergara's case; oppress the living, as in Evangelina's case; or incite the living to destructive action, as in Agustín's case. While the apotheosis of mourning usually satisfies a desire to lay the deceased to rest in memory, General Vergara's reminiscences abuse the memory of Clotilde by prolonging the apotheosis of mourning to transform his own life into an object lesson for his progeny. His wife's memory contributes to his own apotheosis.

At the same time, we see that the tears of grief for the loss of a loved one must not only be a sincere expression but must also represent a clear conscience. Mourners grieve, that is shed tears, because they *can*. Their tears are not contained by culpability. There is, then, a necessity to engage in the display of grief as a public statement of one's own moral uprightness. Surprisingly, the presumed interiority of grief is what permits it to stand as a public declaration. In this sense, tears become testimony. Tears that express the pain of loss also indicate that loved ones can make peace with the dead. Thus Agustín, culpable in the eyes of the General, is denied the right to cry in front of him.

We have seen that apotheosis of a loved one can present a challenge to survivors, one that requires more than a facile application of a Christian martyr's suffering. It is when apotheosis is problematic, that is, not immediately achievable through piety, that narrative telling of a life enters in. Narrative provides a way of bringing memories into line with the Christian model. Narrative helps fix the life in memory. It helps stop the flow of ambiguity by tracing a path that assigns fixity, coherence, and meaning to the unruly life. We find out about Evangelina's life and death through Agustín's confession to Plutarco; and Marión wants Esther to hear her tale of life with Adalberto.

But narrating the life of a loved one can entail a risk as well if it reflects negatively on the moral and social status of the teller. Like the tears of grief, the ready narration of lives testifies to a clear conscience. But when the story to be told implicates the survivor, then it takes on the tone of confession. Thus the story of Evangelina's life and death, suppressed so long in the shadow of Clotilde's saintliness, emerges in Agustín's confession to Plutarco.

THE RISKS OF SELF-REVELATION

The apotheosis of loved ones through narrative telling of their lives has a counterpart in the telling of one's own life troubles in drunken confession. As we saw in Fuentes's story, Plutarco learns the truth about his mother's death from a drunken Agustín.

Conversation does not always stop with the kind of epic storytelling that animates a social gathering. Storytelling sessions among male friends can last several hours, beginning in the early evening and ending at dawn. They might begin at a bar after work, continue at dinner, and then move on to someone's house, and these protracted sessions usually involve the consumption of large quantities of alcohol. Participants who do not want to drink a lot usually drop out of the group to leave a core of those who will carry on late into the night. After many drinks and many stories, the laughter and conviviality can give way to lamentation. Then the conversation becomes more personal. Talking no longer seeks to entertain but to release an emotional burden. The bond created by drinking together permits the carousers to take this step toward intimacy. Talking then becomes more self-revelatory, although out of deference to the speaker, companions do not hold him to his declarations the next day. Drinking can intensify the emotions of anger, despair, or romantic love, and inebriation permits their expression in part by allowing their subsequent denial. The alcohol takes over and it removes the talk from the domain of obligatory social life. Friendships that survive a night of drinking without temper flair-ups are strengthened by the intimacy that occurred. But friendships can terminate in one of these sessions, precisely because the constraints on emotional expression are removed, allowing conflicts to arise. In this state, the stories become the teller's own, and they are about betrayals, lost loves, or other disappointments. Not all evenings of reveling reach this kind of mood, but they can, and such sessions are important for the formation of friendship among men.

Even in these contexts, the stories need not be true, although they are related as if they were. Telling your troubles can be a kind of seduction or a kind of drama to win a listener's friendship. Betrayal and disappointment are common experiences. In fact, life failures often become encoded as betrayals, that is, the conventions for talking about failure convert it into betrayal. They assign guilt to others and protect the teller's honor. When you tell others of your disappointments, you invite them to participate in the common experience of hard luck. The hard luck of life makes people equal in a freedom from blame.

Sometimes the lamentation occurs through singing the drinking songs of loves lost, longings for rural places of origin, and masculine honor. Whether singing or talking, carousers punctuate their stories with exhortations to drink and with toasts, and they drink in unison. Sometimes the relationships thus reinforced are business relationships as well as friendships. To be willing to join someone in a drinking session of this kind constitutes a show of goodwill.

The narrative of conversational storytelling has many of the episodic qualities of epic poetry and orality with a focus away from individual self-revelation. When storytelling gives way to self-revelation, these more personal tales are conventional in casting the teller as the victim of bad luck if not treachery. By relating the events in this way, the teller is absolved of guilt at the same time that he expresses an emotional unburdening. This self-revelation in the atmosphere of social drinking invokes the conventions for the narration of individual lives. When self-revelation encodes personal experience as losses, it converts them into a kind of shared experience, but it does so in the face of a risk that such tales become "literary," revealing a psychologically complex, round character alienated from the community. The narrative of personal disappointments as betrayals, then, becomes a means to recover a sense of communion and to save oneself from the threat of solitude and culpability.

The self-revelation of drunken conversation is the possibility that polite socializing seeks to avoid. The narratives of grief and drunken narratives share this interpretive dilemma. When narrating their lives in this way, people risk humiliation in others' eyes. The potential for complicity in martyrdom can cast the teller as an all too willing victim. Late night carousing permits this kind of narrative by invoking the conventions of Catholic confession, for witnesses to such a self-revelation are kind enough to avoid reference to it afterwards, when the glow of the alcohol has worn off.

By contrast, the power to speak well is the power to put listeners at ease. A respectability accrues to those who can transcend the social and existential discomfort of silence while avoiding the embarrassment of self-revelation. Thus conversing becomes a magnanimous act if not a moral imperative. Chatting can decrease the distance of social class, dispel the fear of negative judgment, demonstrate respect for another person, and transcend self-consciousness. The communion of conversation allows one to forget responsibilities, limitations, boundaries, and personal pain. A good story transports all of the group outside themselves and into the flow of life.

CONCLUSION

To recapitulate, Paz's "silent" Mexicans have available to them at least two modes for social participation and narrative discourse. Each mode brings with it an expected set of consequences wherein its opposite stands as an implied alternative. Thus conversational storytelling holds narrative self-revelation at bay, while drunken conversation breaks through to provide the expiating completion of failure and loss. Each mode is defined by a set of formal conventions that restrict yet give expression to a particular content.

I have drawn on the typologies of literary genres of Lukács, Benjamin, and Ong because they set the epic and novelistic narrative forms in a concurrent, competitive frame. Each of these theorists has included in his scheme a historiographic component that I have chosen to ignore in preference for the analytical device of structural opposition and dialectic, because, in my view, it is precisely this coexistence of competing expectations for narrative form and the accompanying potential for interpretive possibilities that characterize the modernist climate of social, political, and historical discourse in Mexico today.

Lukács categorized literary works through a Modernist view of society in which shared meaning and consciousness were supplanted by alienation of the individual from the community. Like their twentieth-century contemporaries in social theory, the early Critical Theorists perceived a radical difference between traditional society, in which members are embedded in a social web for their definition, and modern society, in which individuals must look inside themselves for self-identity. They proposed that in traditional societies, where epic narratives and storytelling unite listening audiences, people enjoy a sense of community, whereas in modern society, the province of novelistic and historical narratives, individuals must *seek* community. This quality of traditional societies has become the nostalgic alternative to Modernist alienation and doubt.

In Mexico, apotheosis is variously applied to the lives of saints, national heroes, political and social protesters, dead loved ones, and even one's own life experiences. One must die or encounter hard times in order for one's life to take this form. Apotheosis then redeems the life. Otherwise, the life is a loss, an *unproductive expenditure*, as Georges Bataille (1984) pointed out earlier in this century. Bataille identified such losses as the obsession of Christian humiliation in his polemic against the interpretation of death and torture as martyrdom. This political critique of Christian martyrdom finds its way into Mexican historical discourse when the subject is cast as victim. Such political criticism constitutes an effort to recover from the epic uniformity of apotheosis the suppressed and forgotten acts of injustice against individuals.

Perhaps Octavio Paz (1950) has peopled his fiestas with otherwise silent participants the better to dramatize their communal quality. Recalling this characterization, we notice that, whereas in the course of normal social life, people exchange only polite courtesies, in festival occasions they can "converse with God, country, friends, or relatives, . . . whistle, shout, sing, shoot off fireworks, and discharge pistols into the air" (49). They can commune in an "original chaos and freedom." But even here, they do so not without risk, for as they "get drunk together, trade confidences, weep over the same troubles, and discover that they are brothers, [they] sometimes, to prove it, kill each other" (49). In *The Labyrinth of Solitude*, Paz attributes these killings to "violence and frenzy," "lightning and delirium," and to a kind of communal eruption of latent violence. In *The Other Mexico: Critique of the Pyramid*, which he wrote in response to the killing of protesters and spectators at Tlatelolco in 1968, violence has become specifically the submerged presence of the Aztec past in the Mexican sensibility.

In Mexico today, political debates frequently involve historical references. More than a simple invocation of historical precedents, this discourse oscillates between epic apotheosis and political criticism against injustice to individuals. I think when Paz conjures up for us the ritual release that fiestas represent, he does so to offer to the modern Mexican the hope of a return to the lost communal sense of epic experience, the nostalgic alternative to modern novelistic alienation. As regenerative events, the deaths that result become part of the explosion that releases emotions and hidden selves. He is less complacent about the killings at Tlatelolco in 1968, the event that motivates the later work, *The Other Mexico*. In that work, he denounces the tyranny of an apotheothetic interpretation of those deaths as sacrifice and exhorts Mexicans not to so condone them. This movement in Paz's analysis from a celebration of fiesta frenzy to a critique of complicity in martyrdom demonstrates his participation, indeed his leadership role, in the shaping of the modernist social, political and historical discourse of twentieth-century Mexico.

NOTE

[1]Paul de Man (1971), among others, points out that this work falls into Lukács's premarxist period and that it, in fact, substantiates the need to differentiate the nonmarxist from the marxist Lukács.

WORKS CITED

Arellano Zavaleta, Manuel. *Agonía y muerte de Juárez*. México: Comisión Nacional para la Conmemoración del Centenario del Fallecimiento de Don Benito Juárez, 1972.

Bataille, Georges. "The Notion of Expenditure." *Raritan* 3, (no. 3) (1984): 62-79.

Benjamin, Walter. "The Storyteller." In *Illuminations*, ed. Hannah Arendt. New York: Schocken Books, 1968.

Brodman, Barbara. *The Mexican Cult of Death in Myth and Literature*. Gainesville, FL.: The University Presses of Florida, 1976.

Carballido, Emilio. "La paz después del combate." In *Jaula de palabras*, ed. Gustavo Sainz. México: Editorial Grijalbo, 1980.

Fuentes, Carlos. *Burnt Water*. New York: Farrar, Straus, Giroux, 1980.

Jameson, Frederic. "Imaginary and Symbolic in Lacan." *Yale French Studies* (1978): 55-56.

Kermode, Frank. *The Genesis of Secrecy: On the Interpretation of Narrative*. Cambridge: Harvard University Press, 1979.

Lukács, Georg. *The Theory of the Novel*. Cambridge, MA: The MIT Press, 1971.

de Man, Paul. *Blindness and Insight: Essays in the Rhetoric of Contemporary Criticism*. New York: Oxford University Press, 1971.

Ong, Walter. *Orality and Literacy: The Technologizing of the Word*. London: Methuen, 1982.

Paz, Octavio. *The Labyrinth of Solitude*. New York: Grove Press, 1950.

———. *The Other Mexico: Critique of the Pyramid*. New York: Grove Press, 1972.

Torres, Alejandro. *Vida del Beato Sebastián de Aparicio*. Puebla, México, 1975.

Turner, Victor. *Dramas, Fields and Metaphors*. Ithaca, NY: Cornell University Press, 1974.

Vargas G., Luis Alberto. "La muerte vista por el mexicano de hoy." *Miccalhuitl: El Culto de la Muerte* 18, no. 145 (1971).

THE CASE OF *SITT MARIE ROSE*: AN ETHNOGRAPHIC NOVEL FROM THE MODERN MIDDLE EAST

Elizabeth Fernea

ABSTRACT

The genre of the *ethnographic novel* has become a new subject for both literary and social science analysis. Yet, what is an ethnographic novel? It is a text that, in the course of telling a fictional story, creates setting, characters, and action that the audience judges to be *authentic* in terms of a particular cultural, social, or political situation.

In these terms, new novels appearing in the Arab world and translated into English can be seen as suggesting to Western readers that traditional views about women and their roles in society are being challenged and criticized. In this paper, I propose to look carefully at a modern Lebanese novel, *Sitt Marie Rose*, by Etel Adnan, which has recently been translated into English.

Until recently, written works of the imagination, such as novels, short stories, and poetry, have seldom been studied as ethnographic documents by social scientists. This neglect seems strange, given the anthropologist's and the ethnographer's interest in myth, legend, and proverb as reflective of values and attitudes present within a particular society. Such disregard for imaginative literature as an expression of culture may be traced to two factors.

First, myth, legend, and proverb have been considered as group products and hence more likely to represent societal values than a single-author text, which has been viewed more as an expression of individual imagination. Second, until recently, the oral tradition has been seen as associated with "primitive" societies and the written word with so-called advanced societies. The canon of literary masterpieces in English is a list of great works considered as products of a written tradition, whatever their origins in orality may have been.

New approaches are apparent, however, in the analysis of language and its effects, the examination of the relationship between writer and reader, and the concern for voice and point of view. Furthermore, women's writing everywhere and the writings of men and women in non-Western cultures are emerging as subjects of serious study, which has helped to stimulate a reevaluation of old literary codes and criteria for artistic excellence. The value of the oral tradition and the links between oral and written traditions are being recognized. The literary canon has been called into question. It is difficult to see how texts can be ascribed permanent merit and meaning when, as modern critics point out, the meaning of any text seems to lie no longer in the text itself, but in how and when it is read and who reads it. Ethnographies are beginning to be treated as literary texts, and the boundaries between the humanities and social science disciplines are blurring. In such an intellectual climate, the novel as cultural text has aroused a new interest. Social scientists and humanists, in studying other cultures, have begun to see imaginative forms of writing as cultural products as well as individual texts. From such a perspective, the term *ethnographic novel* has emerged.

What exactly is an ethnographic novel? It is a text, like other literary texts, that in the course of presenting a fictional story creates a setting (or physical and social context), characters (or people), plot and action that the reader judges to be authentic in terms of the particular cultural, social, or political situation portrayed. If the reader judges the text to be *authentic*, he or she then not only will accept any messages explicit or implicit in the text itself but will also find information about matters outside the text itself: matters of love and death, the appropriate conduct of life, and the proper direction of culture and society. One must also make the distinction between an ethnographic novel, written by an outsider about an *other*, and an ethnographic novel written by an artist from within the culture. The latter genre has been referred to as the *auto-ethnographic* novel (Marcus and Fischer 1986, 74).

The ethnographic novel has some advantages over the standard ethnography. The novelist need not shun conflict, anger, hatred, or passion, and may often become a participant in the drama of the novel in a way denied the ethnographer, who has in the past been at pains to observe carefully and not to become too involved. Such involvement, existentially or textually, has been seen to mar the scholarly value of the work and violate the code of objectivity by which the ethnographer/researcher has been expected to abide. It is the relative freedom of the novelist that makes this form so fresh a source of insight into the cultures of others.

Sitt Marie Rose by the Lebanese poet Etel Adnan is an ethnographic novel that is outstandingly subjective. Reviewed as a feminist novel, winner of the France-Pays Arabes award, *Sitt Marie Rose* was first published in 1978 in French (the second language of Lebanon) by Des Femmes, Paris. The Post-Apollo Press, Sausalito, California, produced the English translation by Georgina Kleege in 1982, and the novel has appeared also in Arabic, Dutch, and Italian.

The work certainly deserves the term feminist novel, for it is about a woman who becomes a sacrificial victim when she breaks the rules of the Mediterranean code of honor. But it is also an anti-war novel, an antireligious novel, and, above all, it is an ethnographic novel, conveying information about the persistent, troubling conflict in Lebanon while giving us a sense of what that conflict feels, smells, and looks like to the people of Lebanese society. Through Etel Adnan's artistry, form and substance, content and style are joined, thus achieving the goal of all imaginative literature, as well as the recently stated goal of the new, experimental ethnographies (Marcus and Cushman 1982).

The dust jacket of the novel states that *Sitt Marie Rose* is "the story of a woman abducted by militia during the Civil War in Lebanon and executed." Marie-Rose is in her early thirties, divorced, Christian, and the mother of three children. She has been living for seven years with a young Palestinian doctor, who is high in the councils of the PLO, and this has brought a good deal of criticism upon her from the rich, upperclass Christian community of which she is a part. She has been involved in community and charitable causes, we are told, and teaches in a school for deaf-mutes. One morning on her way to work, she is abducted at a checkpoint while crossing from the Muslim zone into the Christian zone of the divided city. Her capture arouses indignation and concern since she is known in both zones for her nonsectarian humanitarian service.

> The news of her capture had the impact of a submarine missile in the camps. . . . Even in families accustomed to tragic news that was repeated with the monotony of weather reports, there rose a kind of death-rattle. (72,73)

Intercession with her captors is unsuccessful. She is interrogated, tortured, and finally killed.

The facts of this tale, not unusual in what is left of Lebanon today, unfold in a most unusual manner. The heritage of Scheherazade, the Arab storyteller par excellence, retreats into the dim past as Etel Adnan tells her story, not in traditional linear, narrative form, nor even in the *lozenge* form ascribed by folklorists to the tales of the East, but in a charged composite of many different forms of discourse: conversation, news bulletins, participant observations, monologues, life histories, interviews, and commentary. Within this multilayered text are found character, action, plot, fantasy, and prophecy, those aspects of the novel so gracefully delineated by E. M. Forster in 1927, but in combinations that Forster might not have recognized as novelistic. Etel Adnan utilizes techniques of ethnographic description as well as artistic forms from the oral and written literary tradition, and also draws upon narrative conventions from journalism and film. The influence of the distinguished Arabic poetic tradition, of which she herself is a part, is also evident.

The characters in this novel are Marie-Rose (Sitt is the formal, polite title like Mrs. or Madame given to married women in the Arab world); the three young men who are her captors—Tony, Fouad, and Mounir; a local friar-priest, Bouna Lias; and the class of deaf-mute children whom she teaches and who are witnesses to her death. An omniscient third person narrates the first brief section of the novel and is briefly present in the second, more extensive section of the text. And the war itself assumes the dimension of a character as the novel progresses.

The structure of the work is disarmingly simple and consists of two sections, presented like acts in a drama or a screen play. "Time I: A Million Birds," the opening segment, is in the narrator's voice and sets the stage for the action that follows. First, the characters are introduced:

> Mounir, Tony, and Pierre like to do a little of everything. They dabble. Mounir's family is extremely rich, and he includes Tony and Pierre in his projects and distractions. Fouad is a part of the "group". . . . [H]unting [is] the most noble occupation. It's more wholesome. It's also more intellectual. (2-3)

Mounir wants to make a film about Syrian workers in Lebanon, and asks the narrator to help him. The group of friends meet to discuss future plans and so the novel opens.

Next, the socioeconomic structure of modern Lebanon is established:

> In The City, this center of all prostitutions, there is a lot of money and a lot of construction that will never be finished. Cement has mixed with the earth, and little by little has smothered most of the trees. If not all . . . . [After dawn] a mean gray falls on this half-commercial, half-industrial city, and contrasts are affirmed: luxury apartment buildings next to hovels. (9)

The civil war breaks out.

> On the thirteenth of April 1975 Hatred erupts. Several hundred years of frustration re-emerge to be expressed anew . . . . The Palestinians avenge their thirty dead. The Phalangists counterattack. (11-12)

Up until this point, the tone of the narrator's voice is conversational, even calm, and this tone continues into the early stages of the war:

> This evening the sky is streaked with huge flashes of lightning that break it up from end to end. The streets I can see from my ninth floor are empty as in the work of a primitive painter. The song of a muezzin drifts from far away to this Christian quarter of Achrafieh, and has something unearthly about it, even if one knows it is only a record. (12)

But as the war progresses, the storytelling technique changes from traditional narrative description. A series of cryptic news flashes are presented to the reader, arranged on the page as bulletins, with large dots before each one and spaces to separate them:

> • The removal of the twelve bodies abandoned on the street at the Port, in Achrafieh, and Place Debbas, proceeded normally. (22)

> • A mortar shell fell in Hammana near the public garden, killing a little girl. (23)

Time II, titled "Marie-Rose" is divided into three sections, generally concerned with (a) the capture of Marie-Rose by members of the Christian militia, including Tony and Fouad; (b) her trial, conducted by Mounir, Tony, and Fouad, and attended by a local peasant priest, Bounas Lias; and (c) her execution by the group. These sections are further broken down into smaller parts, some only a paragraph in length, each devoted to a different narrative voice. Both character and action are conveyed by these voices, which tell us what is happening, and also how the different characters are feeling and thinking about what is happening. Here, for example, is Sitt Marie-Rose:

> I know, everyone warned me not to cross the line which divides the city into two enemy camps, to come back to this Christian zone where I've always lived. But there was a cease-fire, and normally they never bother women. (31)

Her old friend Mounir, with whom she was vaguely in love when both were teenagers, states:

> I had nothing to do with this abduction. In principle, I'm against any procedure that's not strictly military. I told them, at the Party's Direction, not to pursue this method. We will get our enemies. (33)

Tony, another of Marie-Rose's captors, and also an old acquaintance from school days, tells us:

> My name is Tony and it will never be Mohammed. It is as clear and inevitable as the succession of the hours. And no matter what anyone says, the will of the group rules. We are the Christian Youth and our militia is at war with the Palestinians. They are Moslems. (36)

Bouna Lias, the priest:

> I wonder why they wanted me to attend this indictment, me who's nothing
> but a friar and a peasant. And then, what did this woman do? (38)

The voice of the deaf-mutes, who speak as a group, operates as
a kind of chorus, giving information to the reader about
themselves, and also about the indictment, the trial, and the
execution, which is taking place in their classroom before their
eyes. Each of the three segments in Time II ("Marie-Rose") opens
with the deaf-mute chorus. Time II, I, sets the scene for the
events to follow:

> In this classroom, always occupied by the air and the few flies that can
> survive at the height of this hill, there's US, the deaf-mutes. . . . Because we're
> deaf, we can forecast earthquakes. Besides, there's one every day in Beirut.
> The civil war has been going on for almost a year, and they're still
> fighting . . . . She came this morning, Sitt Marie-Rose, followed by four men.
> What beautiful guns they have! (29-30)

Time II, II, describes the setting of the trial:

> Today is no ordinary school day. Sitt Marie-Rose is sitting before these three
> men who have guns that are bigger than rifles. (43)

And in Time II, III, the deaf mute chorus serves to alert the
reader to the impending execution:

> We're beginning to get the feeling that something really bad is going to
> happen. We're tired of waiting. Something really bad is going to happen.
> Those men . . . look at Sitt Marie-Rose with eyes like cats have in the dark,
> eyes that do more than just glow. (80-81)

Etel Adnan uses the technique of the "voice" also to indicate
the inaccurate information and confused thought patterns of the
characters. Tony's comment that all Palestinians are Moslems is
not true, but is widely believed. Mounir's mind moves swiftly
from Party regulations to an emotional assertion, "We will get
our enemies."

More information about the characters and their motives is
provided by the voice of Sitt Marie-Rose. Just after her capture,
she describes Mounir, Fouad, and Tony.

> [Mounir] . . . while the others believed that unless one resembled Europeans
> one was nothing, he spoke of Asia as an enchanted continent . . . . Eventually
> though, his friends did have an influence over him, and he too made fun of
> Arab cinema and everything else that belonged to the region. It was because
> they were taught by Jesuits who oriented them towards Paris and the quarrels
> of the French kings. (47)

Further ethnographic description follows:

> These young boys were exalted by the Crusades. Mounir identified with
> Frederick Barbarossa because he was himself slightly red-haired. He bitterly

regretted, as though it had happened recently, that Saladin had conquered
Jerusalem. It caused him actual pain. (47)

The voice of Tony enunciates an important bit of ethnographic
information: the traditional Mediterranean view of woman's place
and of the punishment to be meted out for transgressors of the
code of honor:

> It's a waste of time to try to reform a woman who takes herself seriously. She
> should not have had a Palestinian for a friend. She could have found
> someone better to sleep with. If she were my sister, I would have killed her
> long ago. (60)

The national conflict is debated by the voices of Marie-Rose
and the friar-priest, Bouna Lias:

> *Sitt Marie-Rose*: This war is a fight between two powers, two powers and two
> conceptions of the world [liberty and oppression]. You've made it into a
> religious war to reinforce your ranks, to cloud the issues.
>
> *Bouna Lias*: But Islam is behind them. Therefore we are at war with Islam,
> whether you like it or not. They can't separate their religion from their
> culture, from their heritage, and neither can we. We're fighting for the road
> that leads to the Divine. The best road. (63)

Another character slowly emerges in the novel, the war itself, a
character whose presence affects everyone, as Marie Rose tells us:

> Violence rises from every square meter as if from a metallic forest. During
> these days human reason appears like an insulating body, an impotent
> power. The city is an electro-magnetic field into which everyone wants to
> plug himself. It is no longer a place of habitation, but a being. (12)

The war slowly becomes a seducer:

> Violence is absorbed like a consumer product. I understood this need for
> violence one day in front of an electric wire torn from its socket. In the two
> holes there remained two little bits of brilliant copper wire which seemed to
> call out to me. And I wanted to touch them, to reunite them in my hand, to
> make that current pass through my body and see what it was like to burn. I
> resisted only with an extraordinary effort. (13)

Such long passages in the voice of the omniscient third person
narrator are found only in the beginning (Time I) and at the end
of each of the three sections in Time II: (1) the capture, (2) the
indictment and trial, and (3) the execution. In these three
passages, the longer sentences and the careful descriptive detail
contribute to a reflective tone that contrasts with the short
sentences and conversational fragments in the voices of Tony,
Fouad, and Bouna Lias. Mounir's voice is less sure, less
consistent in tone, a technique used by the author to suggest
Mounir's own uncertainty and conflict about his role in the
unfolding tragedy. He says:

Marie-Rose, you stand before me. Why did you come back to me from so far?
And at such a moment? I waited several months before joining the militia. I
hesitated, but the time came when I could no longer let my comrades
down . . . . I must be dreaming. Sixteen years could not have passed since I
left my first man's kiss in your hair . . . . Now I'm afraid that the nostalgia
you awaken in me will give me a reason to despise myself, and add another
torment to my soul. (53-54)

If the novel were analyzed as an experimental ethnography, one
might suggest that the author uses the short pieces, the voices, in
the same way that an ethnographer uses quotations from
interviews and field notes to give the reader not only the sequence
of events in the society, but also the reactions of individual
informants to those events. Stylistically, the quick shifts back and
forth between voices, and the short, choppy paragraphs like jump
cuts in film serve to reinforce the sense of terror, urgency, and
horror associated with the war; they help convey the human
emotions of the moment, the immediacy of different individual
experiences, and the texture of the time, place, and events.

Another quality of experimental ethnographies found here is
the placing of the ethnographer's or the informant's personal
thoughts about the text within the text, the statement of self-
conscious awareness that the ethnographer or the informant is
part of the text. Fouad says:

I didn't position artillery on the hills of the city to get myself mixed up in
some story about a woman. I did it to blow up things . . . . They said to me,
You Fouad, you're an anarchist. (37)

If one turns the analysis around, however, one can see a major
element that traditional social science would criticize, but that is
allowable in imaginative literature: the expression of value
judgments, based on subjective opinions. These are made, not
however, in the voices of the four characters, or the chorus of
deaf mutes, but by the omniscient third person narrator, who says
for example:

The Churches of the Arab East are those of the catacombs, those of the Faith,
of course, but also those of obscurity . . . . They have never gotten the knife in
the belly that the great reforms were to the Church in the West. They're not
concerned with human pain. They're not in actual communication with any
force other than the Dragon . . . . Set against these churches is an Islam that
forgets all too often that the divine mercy affirmed by the first verse of the
Koran can only be expressed by human mercy. (65)

Or, at the end of the novel:

They have separated the bodies, they have separated the minds, those who
govern as well as those foreigners brought on a wind from the West, those
from Iran and the Soviet Union, all, all have sown poison herbs in these

peasant mentalities . . . in these slum children, in their schizophrenic student logic. (98)

Although one could argue that these passages could be compared to the summation and analyses found in ethnographies, they are too emotional and ideological for that, and certainly they are not objective. At one level, they are scarcely needed. The mix of news bulletins, voiced monologues, and chorus tells the reader all: the novel works because it is a successful simulation of thought and action in everyday life and also because of the power of the voices in which the author-poet reproduces the tone, thought, attitude, and speech that differentiate one voice from another and one character from another.

I would contend that *Sitt Marie Rose* fulfills the criteria laid out earlier for an ethnographic novel; the author, Etel Adnan, has, "in the course of presenting a fictional story, create[d] a setting, characters, plot, and action" that the reader judges to be authentic in terms of a particular cultural, social or political situation. Because of the author's success, we then as readers also accept the commentaries, however ideological and passionate, as authentic expressions. Though we may have reservations about those commentaries artistically or politically, we accept them as constituting another voice from within the culture, another way of telling the story. For a western reader, however, the artistic effectiveness of the technique of character-voice over abstract commentary-voice may be demonstrated in the following passage in which Marie-Rose talks to us about Mounir. She tries to articulate his dilemma even as he sits in judgment upon her:

> He was fighting—that was all there was to it. For what? To preserve. To preserve what? His group's power. What was he going to do with this power and this group? Rebuild the country. What country? Here, everything became vague. He lost his footing. Because in this country there were too many factions, too many currents of ideas, too many individual cases for one theory to contain. (75)

Is this really a feminist novel (as well as an ethnographic one) in the western definition of the word? The following quotations illustrate that certainly Marie-Rose is depicted as an individual, expressing her right to equality and to choose for herself, her right not to give in to the wishes of the group.

> *Commentator*: "She was a woman, an imprudent woman, gone over to the enemy and mixing in politics" . . . . (100)

> *Marie-Rose*: "I continued to fight the visible and invisible things that thwarted me." (49)

> *Bouna Lias*: "You're a Christian and you went over to the enemy. Come back to the community." (64)

She is a woman who has broken the rules, defied the line between family and stranger, and declared her independence. She is also a sacrificial victim. We are told, however, that "Marie-Rose is not alone in her death" (104). Hundreds of persons, male and female, are listed in the news bulletins as sacrificial victims (22-23). As the novel progresses, the character of Sitt Marie-Rose transcends its individual feminine identity.

> *Mounir*: I can't say no to my comrades. They told me: here's some really special loot, a particularly bad sort we're bringing you. You want to see? . . . I saw. I saw Marie-Rose. I expected to find her beaten, maybe disfigured, terrorized. No. She stands before me as beautiful as she was long ago when we were both sixteen and going to high school in Beirut. . . . She's here before me. She's familiar to me. And yet it's up to me to decide whether she lives or dies. How can I? (33-35)

> *Fouad*: These children . . . we want them to see what happens to traitors. Sitt Marie-Rose? . . . They'll have to see with their own eyes what's going to happen to her. They must learn so that later they won't get any ideas about rebellion. You never know, nowadays, even deaf-mutes could be subversives. (61)

Sitt Marie-Rose emerges as an expression of a larger force within the *group*, the desire for freedom, which wars against other forces in the community.

> *Commentator*: Thus, when the impossible mutation takes place, when, for example, someone like Marie-Rose leaves the normal order of things, the political body releases its antibodies in a blind, automatic process. The cell that contains the desire for liberty is killed, digested, reabsorbed. (76)

Her death is "the explosion of absolute darkness among us" (105). By the end of the novel, Marie-Rose has become a kind of transfigured image of Lebanon. According to the deaf-mutes, "[S]he looks like the Blessed Virgin at church, the big one, the one that stares at us during Mass" (45). The symbol is charged with ethnographic as well as artistic meaning, giving the reader messages about the multireligious and political fabric of the area, torn by violence and revolutionary change.

How does this extraordinary novel compare with other contemporary writing by Arab women appearing in the West in translation? I view it as an excellent example of a group of new works that have emerged in the 1970s and 1980s and have been recently translated into English. Some of the new work available includes *A Distant View of the Minaret* by Alefa Rifaat and *Woman at Point Zero* by Nawal al-Saadawi (both Egyptian); *Wild*

Thorns, by Sahar Khalife (West Bank); and such stories as "The Charm" by Ilfet Idilbi (Syria); "The Aunt of Rafik" by Daisy al-Amir (Iraq); and "The Divorce" by Laila Abouzeid (Morocco). Hanan al-Shaykh's novel *The Story of Zahra* (Lebanon) has just appeared in England, and Nayra Atiya's *Khul Khaal: Five Egyptian Women Tell Their Stories* is a novelist's rendition of women's life histories. All of the works must be seen in the context of the long and distinguished history of imaginative literature in the Arab world. The new novels, poetry, and short stories might be seen also as attempts to come to terms artistically and ethnographically with a world vastly different from the society of the early twentieth century.

In the final analysis, *Sitt Marie Rose* is less important as a feminist novel than as a document of social history, an ethnographic novel that chronicles not only feminist concerns, but also the end of a class—the urban Maronite Lebanese Christians, who were placed in power fifty years ago by colonial France. *Sitt Marie Rose* was a best seller in Paris as well as in Beirut. The author, Etel Adnan, reaches her audience both East and West through her highly charged combination of many forms of discourse. She uses traditional and modern literary conventions from both East and West and from oral as well as written traditions, as well as ethnography, journalism, and film. Given the challenges of a new Arab world, she has responded with a literary *bricolage*, a new kind of novel, that is ethnographic in terms of our response as much as because of the way it is written.

Sitt Marie-Rose, the focus of the novel, was a real person. The novel's extraordinary intensity is a result of the poet-author's careful observation, faithful detailing of everyday life, and a genuine concern for human beings—the characteristics of good ethnography and a basis for good imaginative literature.

WORKS CITED

Adnan, Etel. *Sitt Marie Rose.* Translated by Georgina Kleege. Sausalito, CA: Post-Apollo Press, 1982.

Alifa Rifatt. *Distant View of a Minaret.* Quartet Books. London. 1983.

Daisy al-Amir, "The Aunt of Rafik"; Leila Abouzeid, "Divorce" and Ilfet Idilbi, "the Charm" in Elizabeth Fernea, editor, *Woman and Family in the Middle East: New Voices of Change.* University of Texas Press. 1985.

Forster, E. M. *Aspects of the Novel.* New York: Harcourt Brace Jovanovich, 1927.

Hanan al-Shaykh. *The Story of Zahra.* Quartet Books. London. 1986.

Marcus, George E., and Dick Cushman. "Ethnographies as Texts." *Annual Review of Anthropology* (1982) 11:25-69.

Marcus, George E., and Michael M. J. Fischer. *Anthropology as Cultural Critique*. Chicago: University of Chicago Press, 1986.

Nawal al-Saadawi. *Woman at Point Zero*. Zed Press. London. 1985.

Nayra Atiya. *Khul-Khaal: Five Egyptian Women Tell Their Stories*. Syracuse University Press. 1982.

Sahar Khalifeh. *Wild Thorns*. Al Sagi books. London. 1985.

MOTHER EARTH IN AMAZONIA
AND IN THE ANDES: DARCY RIBEIRO
AND JOSE MARIA ARGUEDAS

Claudette Kemper Columbus

ABSTRACT

Darcy Ribeiro (1922- ; Brazil) and José María Arguedas (1911-1969; Peru) draw deeply on their fieldwork as anthropologists in writing fiction. The differences in the depiction of Mother Earth in Ribeiro's *Maíra* and in Arguedas's *Deep Rivers* and *All the Bloods* indicate some ways in which environment influences consciousness. Different topographical configurations impose some constraints that are obvious and some that are less so. In the *sierra*, shadows and dark utterances are valued attributes of Mother Earth. In the *selva*, darkness is feared, earth is threatening, and phallic signifiers enforce authority over the environment. In the Andes, Pacha Mama exercises marginalized power. There the sacred inheres in the touched, the damaged, the hurt. This phenomenon is exemplified by such female earth figures as the mumbling idiot, the *opa* in *Deep Rivers*.

Darcy Ribeiro (1922-) and José María Arguedas (1911-1969), noted anthropologists and novelists, not only bridged major differences between doing anthropology and writing fiction, but also built bridges between their readers and the other inhabitants of their countries, the indigenous peoples of Brazil and Peru. Arguedas fought, also, the separation of life from letters, the separation of reality from language. He wrote from within, submerged in indigenous life and in indigenous languages, that is, in realities experienced differently in the Quechua language than in realities shaped by Spanish.[1]

As artists or aesthetes of the anthropological, Ribeiro and Arguedas integrate mythological and indigenous configurations in their works to oppose a homogenizing, univocal "reality" manufactured by technologically advanced societies. Ribeiro and Arguedas belong to the aesthetes among whom Claude Lévi-Strauss counts himself, aesthetes he defines as setting themselves up against analytic and pragmatic reliance upon the hard sciences (Lévi-Strauss 1966, 247).

This paper focuses on Mother Earth as refracted through Ribeiro's novel *Maíra* and a selection of works by José María Arguedas, especially *All the Bloods*.[2] It draws on the Peruvian anthropologist, Alejandro Ortiz Rescaniere, who, after some years

gathering and analyzing *selva* and *sierra* myths, has begun to
suggest differences between Andean and Amazonian myths.
According to Ortiz Rescaniere, Andean myths are *exotic*,
eccentric, and elliptic. They are so dependent on context that he
uses the term *sedentary*. Their specificity is resistant to
generalization. In admitting many practitioners to magical
practices, they disperse authority over the word and control over
knowledge.

Ortiz Rescaniere argues the inverse pertains to Amazonian
myths. The Amazonian shaman concentrates power. Myths are
elaborated. And there is a far greater component of *threat* in
Amazonia: "daily life . . . is perpetually threatened by taboos:
prohibitions, avoidances, purifications, which provide assurances
in the hunt, in the social order, in rules for living together"
(Ortiz Rescaniere 1985, 64).

This paper makes further observations about conceptual
differences attributable to geography between the *selva* and the
sierra and therefore between the works of Ribeiro and Arguedas.[3]
Topological configurations impress on mythology certain constraints with results less obvious than might appear at first. I
argue, for instance, that the mountains have ears and that the
relative quiet of the *sierra* leads to a listening world view
differing from one of the noisy *selva*. I argue that, although the
Andes would seem to emphasize isolation, paradoxically individuals establish a familiar and familial relationship to earth, in
part because of the reach of horizontal and vertical visibility. In
the Andes, persons do not become easily lost in the environment
on which they depend. Despite aspects of her inwardness and
obliquity (the figure of Pacha Mama is not directly seen), even
when feared for her inwardness and obscurity, Mother Earth
remains beloved by people who perceive themselves simultaneously on earth and within her. Her presence is everywhere:
under foot, in the water, in the mountains, all around. Figure 1
conveys at a glance her enclosing and her *totalizing* powers. It
shows Pacha Mama at once everywhere and nowhere, a spacial
concept, a temporal concept, a climate, a cosmic vision, a fox
crossing the road.[4]

Her massive marginalizing properties are apparent in the
agglutinative visual activity necessary to read Figure 1. Terrific
vertical and horizontal reaches retain marginality; above is
represented as if below. The mountains do not dominate, nor
does the foxy cayman creature slipping along the inside circle,

Fig. 1. Drawing of Pacha Mama

right-hand side. Listening produces a marginalized responsiveness, a multiple-centered eccentricity.

Andean myths speak of opaque Mother Earth abandoned with her twins, the Willka, and seeking out beneficent shadow. Relatively helpless despite her vast powers, notably over liquids (blood, liquor, water), she depends on other forms of life as they depend on her. Pacha Mama and living beings inter-animate one another in contexts in which sacrifice is based more on hope and hospitable help than on propitiatory fear. So great is her need that her most understanding adherents today—and probably originally—are paupers and peasants, marginal people who survive through mutual generosity and alliance. What she represents remains open to interpretation; hers is a "word" "open to all events," not as revelation but as our "corporate body" (Urbano 1982, i-iii).

Fig. 2. Drawings by children of the *sierra*

Pacha Mama resides in every locale in a sacred spot. Sometimes, these sacred places are mountains (Brundage 1967, 170). Pacha Mama has been represented as a female mountain, and she has been represented as a postconquest concept. Commenting on the iconography of the image of the Virgin Mary impressed on Potosí in Bolivia, Teresa Gisbert argues that the virgin has been superimposed on and subjugates the mountain (1980). But the argument that Pacha Mama is a product of colonialism, that Spanish Catholicism in the time of the Inquisition tried to extirpate pagan ideas by resorting to a pagan idea, makes little sense to me. Unless the idea were already present and inviting assimilation, proselytizers would not have united Mary to Mother Earth.

Indeed, insofar as Joseph W. Bastien (1978) has argued for an Andean mountain as a metaphor of man, if the mountain can also be imaged as a woman by indigenous Andean peoples, then it follows, as the Pacha Mama sketch suggests, that Pacha Mama may be bisexual, a father-mother, as Bastien also hazards. R. T. Zuidema associates Viracocha, one of a number of cognate Andean creator gods, with seeds underground and with night (1977, 25).[5] Billie Jean Isbell sees in the Andes a great balancing in the scale of procreative powers, a sense of sexual complementarity reflected in myths of hermaphroditic animals as progenitors of herds (1978, 206-7, 211).

A relatively helpless and hungry deity, Pacha Mama has to be tough for her children to survive. One component of her toughness is her incorporative capacity. Another component of her capacity for survival is her relative muteness. In an interview with Ortiz Rescaniere in which I asked about the relationship of touched or mumbling or drooling female characters in Arguedas's work to Mother Earth, he replied that oral tales describe Pacha Mama as an idiot or *opa*, as mute or murmuring, as inarticulate but oracular (Columbus 1985). If so, her oracles or voices represent words and language without explanatory tyranny, without the bleaching out of bodiless intellectual light. Like the *opa* in *Deep Rivers* and like the fat woman urinating in *Amor mundo*, this mother of margins is base in two senses of the word. She is excremental, and she is the basic material for transformation. In that earth is broken, "kicked" and "cut," she is productive through the torture of the farmer's plough and the birth process (Jacob 1970).

Women characters in Arguedas's work associated with deformity (that is, associated with the sacred), however crude, teach resistance to oppression. They train the ear to hear the muted voices of the indigenous people. An adolescent taught by an idiot or a dwarf or a fat woman to accept women "monsters" learns protest through them and human solidity (Ernesto in *Deep Rivers* [1958] and Don Bruno in *All the Bloods* [1964]). A number of grotesque and/or violated women characters decultivate, decolonize, dehierarchize the impressionable young male and make renaturalization possible.

Arguedas's writing decenters the reader by wrenching authority over language from institutions and dispersing it eccentrically among a range of characters. Among the most eloquent are the powerless, who are receptive to the voices and rhythms of the natural world. These are primarily indigenous characters, who hear the songs in stones and water, the language of the pig and of the pine, the song of a high altitude duck, languages that help the marginal to survive. Their songs and sentences do not, however, suggest hypermediative music, inherently phallocentric, the orchestrated expression of constellations of powers. What Arguedas suggests is an alliance of "ears," of hearing and overhearing, the music of semi-mediation, the liminality of the half-heard.

In contrast to the sexual diffusiveness of Mother Earth in the *sierra*, sexual confusion and sexual ferocity pertain to Mother Earth in the *selva*, in Amazonia, and are reflected in *Maíra*. There is so much poorly defined space in the jungle that it is easy not to know where you are, easy not to be heard, or to be heard by the wrong creatures. Terrain struggles for visibility. The relationship between Mother Earth and living beings reveals a reciprocally defensive ferocity. This ferocity arises in part from a cluttered geography that spells exposure.

> The son of God was there, dispersed in the forest, when one day he saw passing close by our ancestor, Mosaingar, who attracted his attention. Maíra liked him and wanted to see the world through his eyes. He descended, dressed himself in the skin of Mosaingar, and, deep inside him, he made a hole for himself, a womb. . . .
>
> Enchanted, he then discovered the mobile head with its openings for seeing, hearing, smelling, and tasting. He stopped there more fully to enjoy Mosaingar through her senses. Through the eyes he saw the darkness of the world, the absence of color. Through the ears he heard and recognized the noise of the wind rustling in the forest. . . . He ended by feeling the entire body again, from the tips of the outspread toes to the bristly hair, from the grainy texture of the tongue to the dentulus vulva.
>
> Maíra was involved in getting to know the world of old when he saw, running through the bush and making funny faces, a little animal: that stinking little opossum Micura. Maíra found it amusing; he liked it and immediately thought: "Here is the one who will be my twin brother."
>
> He called with all his strength for the opossum to enter the hole in the belly of Ambir. But Mosaingar did not want Micura to enter; she tightened up, closed her legs, flexing the muscles of her thighs. Poor Micura, complying with the will of Maíra, struggled and struggled. Mosaingar was screaming no, beating Maíra in the stomach and biting Micura with the piranha teeth of her cunt. Maíra lost patience and had to break the teeth from inside to allow his brother to enter. (Ribeiro 1984, 121-23)

In time, male Maíra becomes the sun; his twin brother Micura, the moon. Mother Mosaingar, introduced as male, and even reverting to maleness in the middle of the chapter, and then back to female, leaves space and time, and even motherhood, preponderantly masculine. In the passage above, the violation and the subsequent forgetting of Mosaingar offers no curative, polyvalent marginalization. Mosaingar has been twice raped, once from within.

The Andean Pacha Mama bears twins, the Willka, which were ancient names for the sun and also, ambivalently, ancient names for places above and below where foxes speak, in Francisco de Avila's compilation of Quechua myths in *Dioses y hombres de huarochirí*. Indeed, a word for sky in Quechua suggests "above earth" as an other earth, Earth-Above, High-Earth (*hanaq-pacha*). But Pacha Mama is not raped by either her husband or her son, unlike Mosaingar (although in some versions of the myth, she is captured by a lustful monster and even killed). Her children are both male and female; the male becomes the sun; the female, the moon.

The Willka resemble twins far more familiar to the West, Apollo and Artemis. But differences between the sets contribute more to understanding modulations attributable to geography. Three seem especially significant. Unlike the Willka, Apollo and Artemis are not children of a representative of Mother Earth, such as Gaea or Rhea or Demeter, although Leto or Latona is a little like Pacha Mama in being left indistinct, in the shadows, though thought to be kind. Second, Apollo and Artemis, helpless as children, are helped, protected from the wrath of the legitimized. Yet they grow up in an ambiance of the aristocracy of light and become the lord and lady of arrogance and sexual threat, whereas the Willka connect the sky to earth-in-need-of-help. The clarity of stars in the Andes brings the heavens intersectingly close to earth and the "Milky Way is therefore an integral part of the continual recycling of water throughout the Quechua universe" (Urton 1981, 60). The interconnectedness of earth and heaven includes human beings. To celebrate the spring solstice, indigenous Andean groups light fires on the mountain, "because spring never comes to a cold bed." Third, unlike Maíra and Micura, and Apollo and Artemis, the Willka are neither vindictive nor idly mischievous.

The chapter "Maíra-Poxî" in *Maíra* provides a sort of parodic illustration of male dominance, of Jacques Lacan's description of the phallus as king of signification in the symbolic domain:

Maíra had always thought that the world of our Creator, the Nameless One, wasn't of much use. Without wanting to, he found himself imagining and inventing in his mind the world as it ought to be; a world good for his favorite people, the Mairuns of the Iparanã; a world that was truly a joy to live in.

One day he decided that the hour had come. He began the work of reforming the world by bringing together all the Ambir people who existed and dividing them into two groups—those over here and those over there. He ordered those over here to build a very large hut that would become the Great House of Men, and he showed them right there how to construct it. When it was ready, Maíra went inside, sat on the ground, and tapped the ground three times to cause God's prick to emerge. When it rose in front of him, as hard as it could be, he cut it off at the base with one stroke, grabbed it firmly, and thrust it between the legs of those who were standing around. At the end of this task, all were now men with their own pricks, and they went out to fuck the women there outside on the dancing ground or wherever they liked. What a feast of copulation. . . . (150-51)

The scene continues the sexual confusion typical of Mairun creation myths. Elsewhere, earth is represented as female, but in this passage seems undifferentiatedly intermixed with Old Ambir. In the myth cited, the son castrates not only father, but also mother.

Mairun myths are interjected amidst scenes from the life of Alma, a dissolute woman from Rio who enters a convent, who hopes to join a mission in the jungle, who goes native and becomes a tribal whore, and who dies during childbirth. Myths are also taken from the life of Avá/Isaías, a Mairun hereditary chieftain, taken to Rome to train for Holy Orders, but who returns to his tribe. As Alma awaits childbirth, Avá tells her the Mairuns will never accept her, doubly burdened as she is by gender and lack of tribal status. The tribe cannot classify her, because of the phallocentric organization of their social relationships. The tribe cannot accept Avá, either. He lacks initiative, confidence, and aggressiveness.

To the degree that geography's visceral effects are translated into correspondent symbols that shape consciousness and mythology, and even cosmology, Alma is a stranger to that world and does not know where she is. Her sense of herself shifts from third person "too distanced" in "The Alien World" (220-26) to the interior monologue of Mosaingar (301-8), in which the streaming of her consciousness deludes her into feeling conjoined to Mother Earth ("I had never before had this feeling of the world as a nest."). Had she deep contacts with her environment, or had she read her Lévi-Strauss, Alma would not have happily conceptualized herself as a yellow macaw in a chapter entitled "The

Opossum and the Public Woman." Subject to "the allegedly self-evident truths of introspection" (Lévi-Strauss 1966, 249), she is not cautiously perceptive about what she sees as living "a season of long blue days" to "the rhythm of the Mairuns" (Ribeiro 1984, 238). Macaw, however, is food for jaguar (Lévi-Strauss 1973, 36). She is the body of Mosaingar, to be consumed (Ribeiro 1984, 197).

Implicitly Avá also will succumb to the ferocity of *selva* mythologogy, in which only the aggressive survive. This fate befalls his only close associate, the ineffectual sorcerer who once had sung "with the voices of all people and all animals: plaintive," frightened, ominous, or "soft enough to lull whomever listens to sleep" (245). When he can no longer mediate among deities, culture, and nature, the sorcerer is torn to pieces. Avá also fails to empower himself. Maíra-Coraci, the Sun, ruminates, "How sorrowful that my true son Avá cannot be guide of souls. He could never be: he has been stripped of his soul" (233).

Impotent Avá loves though does not voice his love for Alma. Placed as they are in interstices of cultures and nature, Avá and Alma could have *in potentia* grasped "the essential function of totemic classifications . . . to break down this closing in of the group into itself and to promote an idea something like that of a humanity without frontiers" (Lévi-Strauss 1966, 166). They could have brought a "myth dream" into experience by combining the rhythms from the world of the others and from nature, the hypermediative rhythms that suggest correspondences despite opposition, as in canon inversion, the hypermediative music necessary in the *selva*, where "everything must have its jaguar" (Cook 1980).

On-going transformative relationships to the environment can restore the group, if it becomes a poetic echo "of the cadences that guide the innermost course of the world. Magic takes language, symbols, and intelligibility to their outermost limits, to explore life and thereby to change its destination" (Long 1986, 109). Alas, the ferocity Maíra shows includes the destructiveness of the clash between tribal values and the West. Even Isaías/Avá cannot be integrated nor can he integrate Christian concepts with pagan ones. From the tribal point of view, he is insufficiently masculine. He lacks the phallus-tongue (presence/speech/rattle) necessary to survive in the *selva* (Lévi-Strauss 1973, II, 352).

Avá's nephew, Jaguar, who has killed a jaguar and worn its skin and slept with many of the women of the tribe, will assume

the chieftainship. But Jaguar as chief will throw the tribe back
into the past, with detrimental repercussions inversely correspondent to the self-absorbed savagery of urban life. As the urban
world does not assimilate but alters the Indian and steals his
tongue, so the resonant and receptive Mairuns ingest but do not
digest people. Alma and Avá are swallowed by aggressive
standards of presence, of potency.

The novel does not explain the death of Alma's twins in
realistic terms, but only inferentially. On the mythic level, the
reader may suppose that mother and children could have perished
because there was no man from the tribe to stand in *couvade* for
them. Or it may be that Alma herself lost confidence in the tribe
and sought Western medicine. Symbolically, however, once again
birth has been forced upon Mosaingar's body and once again the
teeth have been knocked out. Only this time, in the final part of
the novel, "Corpus," the death of Alma's twins implies the death
of Maíra and Micura as well.

A few Andean ideas conflated may effect the transition back to
Pacha Mama. The Andean sense of the sacred, what it attributes
to the holy, is strangeness. *Huaca* is the blessing the gods confer
on the eccentric, on the marginal, on the "half-created," "half-
understood." What is *huaca* is not always a site that conveys the
radiant power of the sacred, but anything "other"—deformed,
odd, unusual, eccentric, whether it be a rock (Brundage 1967), a
bird's nest, a one-eyed llama, a monstrous birth, the spirit of the
place—partakes in its "otherness" of the divine. Another
Quechua word, *ususi* ("girl") is derived from the root word *usu*:
to be lost (Isbell 1978). To be a girl is in some way to be lost. As
already indicated, most myths of Pacha Mama, abandoned and
represented as needing help, show her "lost," running with her
twins the Willka from threatening starvation, violation, and
death. In one sense, Pacha Mama is "lost girlhood," sacred, yet
"mumbling," affrighted by light, *terra lumine territa*, inarticulate
although not silent (Columbus 1985). For when, in *All the
Bloods*, the dwarf Gertrudis sings, "lost" to civilized life, the
ancient timbre of her song, the strangeness and profundity of her
voice cause Anto to hear her as the whole earth, complaining
(53).

Not to be too confident, clear, and complete about what one
knows or how one speaks distinguishes not only the *huaca*
oracles, but also Quechua speakers and the oral tradition in the
Andes. Humility gives the telling of tales an extraordinary

tenderness, as in the tale-tellers of *huarochiri*, who "forget" parts, or whose refrain is, "and that is all that I know," or "that is what they say," or who say, "we will more or less speak of that matter" (6), and who worry that *"el doctor Francisco de Avila . . . acaso no pueda llegar hasta el corazón lo que él diga"* (*the doctor* may not understand what he says *to its heart* [59]). Contemporary storytellers still use the refrain heard by Baumann: "And now I know no more than that, I, the old weaver of Paracas" (1963, 130).

But Pacha Mama is not threatened from within. She finds allies she needs among foxes, deer, shadows, human beings, *et alia.* Although it seems to result from transient encounters, the help offered her represents, nevertheless, mutual dependency. Unlike Mosaingar, Pacha Mama never becomes recessive. Rituals on her behalf are performed almost automatically, and it is worth citing Ernest Becker: "Let us not rush over these words: ritual is *a technique for giving life* [sic]" (1975, 6). Pacha Mama may be deserted, but her blood is preserved in pots, by ritual. She never disappears. Merely sprinkling blood or liquor on the ground revives her. Unlike recessive Mosaingar, who disappears (though she may reappear), Pacha Mama spells survival and a different order of language, an order that does not control rhetoric, but seeks expression obliquely, peripherally. Unlike *hypermediative* music and myth, her music is *feminized.* The pre-Hispanic *harawi* or lamentation Gertrudis sings in *All the Bloods*, for example, in its horizontal and analogical depiction of space, in its evasion of binary and hierarchical distinctions rather than a hypermediative transcendence of them, expresses the *feminization* Pacha Mama represents.

> Where are you going, blind dove,
> Where are you going; it is already night.
> Place your cold feet within my breast,
> Your wings rest on the beat of the heart.
> Drink my blood, blind bird . . . .
> (409)

If we conceive of Mother Earth as she is represented in the work of Arguedas, then, slim though it may be, there is a chance for the marginal (us) to survive. Survival is conceived neither in *selva* (ferocious, paranoid) nor in capitalist and consumer terms (ferocious, schizoid), but in harsh yet tender (musical, manic-depressive) *sierra* terms. Survival comes from an attitude toward anguish and toward loss that is odd, that takes concrete advantage of what is available and that can endure because of an "odd" generosity beyond calculation and beyond exchange (as in tit for tat), that comes from earth-all-around.

The figure of Pacha Mama corresponds to the cooperative ethic of *competencia*, collective achievement rather than individual success. In *All the Bloods*, uncontaminated Indian *colonos* or hacienda-owned Indians, with no more rights than slaves have, preserve in their illiteracy the old ways. They perform a *competencia*, a collective task when one of the "Cain" brothers, Don Bruno Aragón de Peralta, sends them to work for his brother, Don Fermín Aragón de Peralta, in his mines. Although led by natives, even their leaders are presented as cooperators in a body social. In the *colonos*, the sense of Mother Earth remains strong and *"la tierra muda"* (60) helps them endure death itself. The Indians from communities are led by their chosen elders, whose actions are ritualistic and symbolized by the *vara* or symbol of authority each carries. The quiet, collective correctness of their comportment forms a marked contrast to the depredations of multinational corporations and the Peruvian government. They are better able to understand the Western world for what it is than are the Mairuns.

Ribeiro braids realistic and mythic stories in Maíra. Occasionally, he slips his reader into the mind of a character or a demiurge. Occasionally, the reader sees through the eyes of indigenous characters who inhabit an already elaborated system of belief. But Arguedas almost never evolves the narrative element of plot along the line of an already established myth. Neither does Arguedas use "the great voices": the omniscient narrator, the stream-of-consciousness interior monologue of the self-absorbed. Little sense of privacy is conveyed in Arguedas's work. Scenes speak. Characters speak to nature. Characters speak of one another's affairs. Readings of one another are shared in conversations between people, making the demarcation line between public and private sketchy. Particularly in *Deep Rivers* and *The Fox Above, the Fox Below*, the plot line jumps so that powers of association are constantly called upon to make connections. The author in the latter and the character Ernesto make oblique, associational leaps that connect the world in contrast to the divisive declarations made by those believing they shed light.

To read the logic of *Deep Rivers* and *The Fox Above, the Fox Below* is to think in landscapes. Thinking in terms of the figurative earth provides the rhythmic logic of the connections among the narrative elements and the associations that motivate the indigenous characters. This understanding does not entail knowing the stories of Andean myths or being told them. Rather, it entails thinking with the concrete, imagistic associativeness of indigenous peoples. Arguedas recreates discursive rhythms through concrete image clusters and harmonizing or musical discourse built up by opposition balanced by correlation, permutation, and transformation. Arguedas creates the consciousness that gives rise to mythologies. So the Willka of myth appear in *All the Bloods* only indirectly, through the name of the Indian protagonist, Rendón Willka.

In Arguedas's earlier works, certain characters confer mythic status on the world: on flies, dancers, flowers, pigs, and people. These characters are invariably drawn from the mass of the oppressed, not from the ranks of any who might be regarded as privileged, except insofar as tribal leaders and indigenous musicians embody the spirit of the people. In his later work, characters move as themselves in the halo of the mythic dimension, their lives reverberating beyond their historical situation. In *All the Bloods*, neither of the protagonist/antagonist brothers, Don Bruno nor Don Fermín Aragón de Peralta, attains the mythological resonance of the "ex"-Indian Rendón Willka. The names Willka and Aragón indicate that Arguedas is contrasting indigenous, opaque, collective being against heroic, Castillian, Catholic, guilt-ridden competitiveness.

Early in the novel, Don Bruno performs a ritual obeisance *to* Pacha Mama (*"voy a dar a mi madre Pacha [Tierra] un traguito,"* 83). But his seignorial, Hispanic heritage takes him first from hysteric and melodramatic attitudes and secondly to vigilante actions. Finally and prophetically for Peru, it results in terrorist acts, an apocalyptic river of blood or sea of slaughter that differs *in kind* from Rendón Willka's willingness to pay for his decisions by risking the shedding of his own blood. The "ex"-Indian—like Isaías/Avá, he has been educated in Western ways—has not been decultured, that is, denatured. His acts are concrete demonstrations of the qualities of dignity, humility, humanity, endurance, resistance, and adaptation, learned in the *ayllu*, in the communal world rather than the colonial world. He moves to a mental music infused with the elemental. Living in two cultures does not divide Willka against himself, as it does Isaías/Avá. On the contrary, he becomes more himself, more infrastructural.

When he is introduced, he has returned from his travels in time for old Andrés Aragón's funeral (35-36). A *colono* servant worries about where the suicide's soul will go, and Willka provides serenity in replying, "To the earth, that is all, brother Anto; to the wee earth, that is all." Willka orients what he learns about Spanish speakers to his relationship to his people and his birthplace, where he returns not as a chief nor as a savior, but with the natural energy of one who understands himself part of the character of the autochthonous environment. By drawing the character of Willka who experiences "from within" a mythic orientation to the world, Arguedas avoids the problem of understanding the nonliterate by studying their chroniclers. *The Fox Above, the Fox Below* solves the problem of written language in a different way: Quechua experience *in* its language, its specificity almost untranslatable, is captured by imitation of the Quechua (or Aymara) speaker *in situ*. In contrast most indigenous speakers who translate old myths into Spanish superimpose a context not present in the original.

Raised in an *ayllu*, Rendón Willka lives animated by communal values, needs, and customs that he does not articulate except insofar as his own story performs the myth of the marginal man who must live like a fox. In the scene in which Willka is humiliated and finally expelled for daring to attend a Spanish school (61-66), Willka shows himself confronting oppression with generosity and dignity. He listens silently. Rather than flinging down gauntlets when he returns as a man, in the heroic, masculine style of Don Bruno, with whom Willka eventually allies himself, Willka copes quietly. When he is forced to speak, he speaks obliquely. Although executed almost randomly for political convenience, he lives, because he *is* Willka, son of Pacha Mama, part of a collective cosmic vision, a semiarticulate metaphysic, a cavernous sense of time ritualized toward survival rather than verbalized toward hierarchical verbal dominance. Even his execution is concretized in terms of his surroundings and shows Willka's life figuratively *transferred* to the blood-red blooms of the pisonay tree (Cornejo Polar 1973, 246-47), to his mother place, of which he has always been a part, and hence to the future of his people.

In *All the Bloods*, the further Don Fermín's wife is from the stones in the mountain stream that her eyes reflect, the less contact she has with what she knows to be true about life. The crying of *Amor mundo*'s violated Gabriela becomes nature crying, the sounds like "those hidden threads of water that can sometimes be found falling thousands of metres between black precipices of stone without vegetation" (I, 223). Willka speaks like this, "with" nature, "from within" his "hidden" mother, his language dark but moving, oracular, deep as the beat of the heart.

As the ways of life of indigenous peoples are threatened, these two authors see all life threatened through dissociation from the rhythms of nature that revitalize life and language. To save ourselves means to preserve these people and to re-create relationships to earth, to remediate language through reapproaching nature and the peoples close to nature. Their "fiction" shows cultural survival dependent on the mythopoeic sensibilities of indigenous peoples. Reattunement to biological rhythms and to the languages of earth's other inhabitants preserve the deep background of the deep past.

NOTES

[1] *Primer encuentro de narradores peruanos, passim.* Arguedas's friend, Emilio Adolfo Westphalen, remembers ". . . it was his luck to experiment in his own flesh, 'from within,' as he used to say, the cultural dichotomy basic to his country . . . ." (1).

[2] The translations from *All the Bloods (Todas las sangres)* are my own, but the University of Texas Press, Austin, has published *Los ríos profundos* (1958) as *Deep Rivers* in 1978 and *Yawar Fiesta* (1941) as *Yawar Fiesta* in 1984, both brilliantly translated by Frances Horning Barraclough, who is now translating *All the Bloods.*

[3] The influence of geography on mythology has been noted by such scholars as the Frankforts (1977) and, in respect to Arguedas, by such scholars as Rouillon (1966).

[4] The two drawings by *sierra* children (figure 2) also express a sense of protective enclosure (de la Torre, 1985, 103). Note especially the use of space; these children are not driven to fill up the entire paper.

[5] Zuidema elaborates on *suyu* as suffix by contrasting it to the prefix *saya* (1977, 17). *Saya* admits vertical, phallic, hierarchical, and binary distinctions. *Suyu* is non-excluding, feminine. See also his work with Gary Urton on the sex of the *ur*-shaper, *camac*, as feminine (1976, 69).

WORKS CITED

Arguedas, José María. *Amor mundo*. Montevideo, Uruguay, 1967.

———. *Primer encuentro de narradores peruanos*. Lima, Peru: Casa de la Cultura del Peru, 1969.

———. *Deep Rivers*. Austin: University of Texas Press, 1978.

———. *Obras Completas*. Lima, Peru: Editorial Horizonte, 1983.

———. *Yawar Fiesta*. Austin: University of Texas Press, 1984.

de Avila, Francisco. *Dioses y hombres de huarochirí*. Translated by José María Arguedas. 2d ed. Buenos Aires: Siglo XXI, 1975.

Bastien, Joseph W. *Mountain of the Condor: Metaphor and Ritual in an Andean Ayllu*. St. Paul, MN: West Publishing Co., 1978.

———. "Literature and Anthropology." Panel comments presented at the Twentieth Annual Comparative Literature Symposium, Texas Tech University, Lubbock, Texas, 1987.

Baumann, Hans. *Oro y Dioses del Perú*. Barcelona: Editorial Juventud, S.A., 1963.

Becker, Ernest. *Escape from Evil*. New York: The Free Press, 1975.

Brundage, Burr Cartwright. *Lords of Cuzco*. Norman, OK: The University of Oklahoma Press, 1967.

Columbus, Claudette Kemper. "Los Labios Resumaban Saliva: ¿ Una Imagen Arguedeana de la Pacha Mama?" *Antropológica* 3 (1985): 291-94.

———. *Mythological Consciousness and the Future José María Arguedas*. New York: Peter Lang, 1986.

Condori, Bernabé, and Rosalind Gow. *Kay Pacha*. 2d ed. Cuzco, Peru, 1982.

Cook, Albert. *Myth and Language*. Indiana University Press, 1980.

Cornejo Polar, Antonio. *Los Universos Narrativos de José María Arguedas*. Buenos Aires: Editorial Losada, 1973.

Frankford, Henri, and H. A. Frankfort. "The Emancipation of Thought from Myth." In *The Intellectual Adventure of Ancient Man*. Chicago, IL: The University of Chicago Press, 1977.

Gisbert, Teresa. *Iconografía y Mitos Indígenas en el Arte*. La Paz, Bolivia, 1980.

Isbell, Billie Jean. *To Defend Ourselves: Ecology and Ritual in an Andean Village*. Austin, TX: University of Texas Press, 1978.

Jacob, H. E. *Six Thousand Years of Bread*. Translated by Richard and Clara Winston. New York: Greenwood Press. 1970 [1944].

Lacan, Jacques. *Écrits A Selection*. Translated by Alan Sheridan. New York: W. W. Norton, 1977.

Lévi-Strauss, Claude. *The Savage Mind*. Chicago, IL: The University of Chicago Press, 1966.

———. *From Honey to Ashes: Introduction to a Science of Mythology* II. Translated by John and Doreen Weightman. 2d ed. New York: Harper, 1973.

———. *Structural Anthropology* II. Translated by Monique Layton. New York: Basic Books, 1976.

Long, Charles. *Significations*. New York: Fortress Press, 1986.

Ortiz Rescaniere, Alejandro. "Símbolos y Ritos Andinos: Un Intento de Comparación con el Area Vecina Amazónica." *Antropológica* 3(1985): 61-86.

Ribeiro, Darcy. *Maíra*. Translated by E. H. Goodland and Thomas Colchie. New York: Aventura, Vintage Books, 1984.

Rouillon, José Luis. "Notas sobre el mundo mágico de José María Arguedas." *Mercurio Peruano*, May-June 1966.

Urbano, Henrique. "Introduction." In *Kay Pacha*, 1-5. 2d ed. Cuzco, Peru: 1982.

Urton, Gary. *At the Crossroads of the Earth and the Sky: An Andean Cosmology*. Austin, TX: University of Austin Press, 1981.

Westphalen, Emilio Adolfo. *Amaru* 11, *dic.*, 1969.

Zuidema, R. T. *Allpanchis* 10 (1977): 15-52.

Zuidema, R. T., and Gary Urton. *Allpanchis* 9 (1976): 59-113.

THE POET AS ANTHROPOLOGIST

Celia A. Daniels

ABSTRACT

Both the poet and the anthropologist have the same goals: first, to gain a deeper understanding of the world and humanity; second, to capture and communicate this to others. Although their techniques for exploring the world are often quite different, there are similarities. Both poets and anthropologists act as participant observers, and at times they undertake material culture studies. Their methods of communicating their findings are obviously quite different. The anthropologist's reports are ethnographies or articles, whereas the poet's reports are poems. The fact that many poets write about anthropological topics and cross-cultural experiences illustrates that anthropology has had a very personal effect on their lives. Conversely, many anthropologists' lives have been enriched by the personal experiences captured in poetry. Poetry can be a tool that leads to a better understanding of anthropological ideas such as rites of passage, cross-cultural comparison, and differing concepts of time. Throughout this paper, poems are used to exemplify these points and illustrate the pertinence and power of anthropological poetry.

The poet often wears the mask of the anthropologist as he studies the world around him and attempts to come to a better understanding of his existence. As anthropologists strive to break through their cultural biases and ethnocentric perceptions, poets try to break through the limitations of their own reality. In this excerpt from "Arrowhead Hunting, A Guide" (1980), poet Steven Hind offers advice on how to achieve this:

> First, be willing to look foolish
> in the eyes of the world . . .
>
> Second, walk with arms bent
> behind your back, getting
> all of yourself out of the way.
>
> Third, love the broken
> as well as the whole stones . . .
>
> Fourth, accept the signature
> of a thousand years' seeing
> with none of the self in the way.
>
> Fifth, go, knowing nothing
> you've lost will last.
> You hunt for things that last.

(74)

Hind sees the normal everyday self as an obtrusion that must be removed in order to perceive the world in a new way. As the poet breaks the barriers of his traditional perceptions of the world, he opens himself up to new possibilities. He allows his life to be changed by what he discovers. Like all students of anthropology, the poet finds his life enriched both intellectually and emotionally by coming into contact with other peoples and cultures. In "New Cambria, Kansas: Indian Burial Pit," Midwestern poet Denise Low (1984) writes about a visit to an archaeological site that enhanced her life:

> Farmers pitched a garage
> over the eroded burial mound.
> Cornfields stretch to the river.
>
> Inside, a hundred nests of bones
> rest in the pit,
> river sand troweled and brushed away.
>
> Skeletons curled
> in a vast mother.
>
> The farmer says
> they lived here one thousand years
> without murders or wars.
>
> Tonight as I climb down
> an endless ladder into dreams
> I will sleep better,
> thinking of them.

                                                            (67)

For Low and other poets, the sensual, physical experience becomes fieldwork. The poet is an observer who, through research and a wealth of imagination, becomes a participant in another culture. Thus, walking around the Taos Pueblo, tracing the fingerprint etched in a potsherd, holding a silver ring, and standing near a mummy in a museum case, all become experiences that increase the poet's depth of understanding of other peoples. Through its concern with the tangible, the poem often becomes a simplified material culture study. The poet, then, responds to the object, delving into its origins and seeking its cultural context:

> Four candles burning
> and grain rising in water
> in the near darkness
>
> They close the door on you
> and seal it forever—
> so short a time

Inside the painted hieroglyphs
and carved women dancing
are motionless.

First, they come to steal
your golden skin
your pectoral and rings.

Centuries later they tear
away your linen wrapping
to soak and grind and make
into books and broadsides.

Finally, they carry off
your half-wrapped body
to another continent.

Here in this museum
they have entombed you in glass
while we stand and stare
in silence.

Dusty pyramids rise
out of desert stone
while
toppled temple columns
of granite
are resting beside the Nile.

Somewhere
far away from the cities
the carved women
are waiting
alone
in an empty tomb.

(Daniels, "Empty Tomb")

In another example of "poetic fieldwork," Gary Snyder (1969)
draws on his impressions of the Anasazi homeland. Snyder
concentrates less on a specific object, but uses a number of
sensual descriptions to evoke a feeling for the early cliff dwellers
of the Southwest:

Anasazi,
Anasazi,

tucked up in the clefts in the cliffs
growing strict fields of corn and beans
sinking deeper and deeper in earth
up to your hips in Gods
        your head all turned to eagle-down
        & lightning for knees and elbows
your eyes full of pollen

        the smell of bats.
        the flavor of sandstone
        grit on the tongue.

> women
>   birthing
> at the foot of ladders in the dark.
> trickling streams in hidden canyons
> under the cold rolling desert
>
> corn-basket wide-eyed
>   red baby
>   rock lip home,
>
>   Anasazi
>   (3)

Poets of anthropology include a broad range, from those professionally trained in the field, to those whose understanding of anthropology is intuitive. In any case, their work can be interpreted and better understood using anthropological concepts—such as cross-cultural comparison, the universality of the rites of passage, or the idea of cultural *emic/etic* (insider/outsider) views. Poets may use these concepts consciously or unconsciously in their work.

Through cross-cultural comparisons or by focusing on a single culture, the poet is able to explore the rites of passage. The common experiences of birth, growing up, old age, and death, which we share with all humanity, offer a sense of connectedness to others.

"Amulet," Cynthia Pederson's poem (1983) about birth and childhood among North American Indians, was inspired by a small beaded lizard found in a museum:

> soon after birth
> the life cord is cut
> and swallowed by the beaded lizard.
> tied to the cradleboard
> with swinging pendant limbs,
> it crawls close to the Crow infant.
> a seed bead tongue flicks out
> to touch the tiny face.
>
> days grow old,
> counting the sunsets
> she slowly
> loosens her hold.
>
> black hair hides
> a cradle-flattened head
> as the child plays among
> the sun-warmed rocks
> catching lizards,
>   letting them go.

she guards the amulet.
tucked in
among her bundles
a buckskin beaded lizard
still sucks
on a black and brittle cord
and flickers out its tongue.

(14)

Throughout the life cycle, culturally conditioned responses dictate how the individual deals with personal changes. Stanley Diamond (1981) explores the final rite of passage in his poem, "The Laying Out," thus adding a new dimension to our understanding of death through his cross-cultural comparison:

The face hardens in the mold of youth
The body curls to an apostrophe
Jews bury their dead in business suits
Anglicans in unction and misery
Vestments of the elect
Catholics where they fall
As shadows intersect
The Crow, Apache, Arikara
Raise the corpse to cauterizing winds
And escort the spirit with buffalo gongs
While hawks congregate
In a corner of sky

(93)

An aging Loren Eiseley (1979) uses a more emotional tone than Diamond when dealing with death, for he confronts his own personal rite of passage. Eiseley incorporates the imagery of an Indian legend as he considers the future in "The Songs for Weeping":

The Indian who learned to fly south with the Crane
                              people
came to where they lifted the sky curtain and passed
                              under it.
There are many stories about that country, but no one
seems clear about it, no one
in the winter lodges can tell you. Only the birds
return in the springs, and the autumns
are sad with footprints departing; no one since
has lifted the sky curtain and returned among men.
                              No one
knows the way there on borrowed wings. Those who go
do not return. Those who stay are filled with longing.
                              Bird country
is not made for men. The songs are for weeping
   or for new things coming—spring

that forgets the old person in the tipi, autumns
                                        that cause tears to start.
I am not the one who joined the Crane people.
I hear the geese in the night, but cannot follow them.
Sky curtain is impenetrable except to bird magic.
All magic is sad to me, Old-man-sitting.
One pays too much for lifting the sky curtain.
No one returns in the spring though they say one man did
I do not believe—I, Old-man, who have lived many
                                        winters.
Sky curtain is forever. Watch carefully. The birds
                                        will inform you.
                                                                (93)

The emic perspective, such as Eiseley has adopted, conveys an understanding of a culture from an insider's point of view. The etic perspective, the outsider's viewpoint, tends to be more abstract and less emotional. The anthropologist recognizes the dichotomy established by the two views and attempts to incorporate both perspectives by playing the role of a participant and an observer during research. The poet, too, is caught between the two roles. The poet is asking the same questions as the anthropologist: about the world, humanity, and himself. But the level of understanding he seeks and the way he communicates this is different. The anthropologist, as a scientist, tends to find himself viewing the world from the etic perspective, which is more objective, intellectual, rational, scientific. The poet is drawn to the subjective and the emotional. He seeks to achieve and capture in words an emic understanding of another culture. The effects of these efforts are sometimes surprising. As the poet draws nearer to another culture, he begins to separate himself from his own culture and his own traditional conceptual framework. The poet begins to feel like an outsider, emotionally distant and experientially distinct from his own culture. At once, he seems more objective about his own culture and more subjective about the culture he seeks to understand. What would be considered emic poetry written by a participant about his own culture begins to take on an etic viewpoint. In the following excerpts, Richard Shelton (1975) offers a mini-ethnography about his own town of Santo Tomas:

Walk down Main Street at midnight
when the only places open
are two bars in the same block.
Turn the corner and walk past
the homes of the good people
of Santo Tomas . . .

Years ago some desperate
farmer took this land away
from the desert, and every summer
the desert wants it back.
In the heat, everything
stops moving, even the dogs.
All night cicadas drill out teeth.
Water gets scarce
and what little there is
is warm and bitter, but we learn
to drink our liquor straight.

New people come here
sometimes, but don't stay long.
I'd like to know what attracts them.
Maybe the need to suffer; . . .
Some people think that if you
suffer enough you'll get to be
better, even noble, but I've lived
here forty years and I get
meaner every day.

Because of the way they dress
it's getting hard to tell
the whores from the female
schoolteachers, which probably
means that whoring isn't
as well paid a profession
as it used to be, what with
all the enthusiastic
amateurs around here.

I used to think this bar
was the center of the community
and if I sat here long enough
I'd learn everything worth knowing
about the people of Santo Tomas.
But this afternoon I went
to the funeral of the richest
man in town and watched his two
widows fighting over which of them
would follow his coffin to the grave.
Now I realize that all
significant social events
still take place in church.

The earth is moving several ways
at once, but sometimes I wonder
if we are going with it.
And when the drive-in movie
shuts down for the night,
the stars remain over Santo Tomas
like holes in the darkness

through which we can see
a cold, enormous light.

(3-6)

Shelton captures the isolation the poet sometimes feels from his own cultural ties. Yet poets can also draw nearer to their peoples and gain a greater understanding of their way of life through their poetry.

Native American poet Robert J. Conley (1979) also writes of isolation, but through his poetry, he is beginning to come to terms with the two cultures he is caught between. These stanzas express a new understanding of his personal cultural connections:

When I go to the supermarket
and buy some meat
pre-cut and wrapped
how do I apologize
to the spirit of the animal
whose meat I eat
and where shall I build my fires?

My poems are my fires.
oh gods forgive me all
the things I've failed
to do. the things I should
have done. forgive me the meat
I've used without a prayer
without apology forgive
the other prayers I haven't
said those times I should
but oh ye gods both great
and small I do not know
the ancient forms. my poems
are my fires and my prayers.

(69)

For many Native American poets and others in tune with their cultural heritage, the poem does not separate but connects. Gladys Cardiff (1975) writes about the simple, yet almost sacred act of combing hair in "Combing":

Bending, I bow my head
And lay my hands upon
Her hair, combing, and think
How women do this for
Each other. My daughter's hair
Curls against the comb,
Wet and fragrant—orange
Parings. Her face, downcast,
Is quiet for one so young.

I take her place. Beneath
My mother's hands I feel

The braids drawn up tight
As a piano wire and singing,
Vinegar-rinsed. Sitting
Before the oven I hear
The orange coils tick
The early hour before school.

She combed her grandmother
Mathilda's hair using
A comb made out of bone.
Mathilda rocked her oak wood
Chair, her face downcast,
Intent on tearing rags
In strips to braid a cotton
Rug from bits of orange
And brown. A simple act,

Preparing hair. Something
Women do for each other.
Plaiting the generations.

(50)

This expression of rich cultural traditions illustrates the wide
scope of poetic themes. The poet does not limit his potential
topics, but considers such diverse themes as myth, music, beauty,
beliefs, and kinship. Neither can the influence of time be ignored
by either the poet or the anthropologist; anthropology is a science
concerned with the temporal. Indeed, the effects of time through
evolution—physical, social, linguistic, technological—are of
major concern to the discipline. The poet deals with time in a
number of ways. Often the poem is like a snapshot—a frozen
moment. Or it might cover a short temporal period such as a few
years or a lifetime. Sometimes the poem is intended to capture a
great passage of time as in Langston Hughes's (1979) "The Negro
Speaks of Rivers":

I've known rivers:
I've known rivers ancient as the world and older than
        the flow of human blood in human veins.

My soul has grown deep like the rivers.

I bathed in the Euphrates when dawns were young.

I built my hut near the Congo and it lulled me to sleep.
I looked upon the Nile and raised the pyramids above it.
I heard the singing of the Mississippi when Abe Lincoln
        went down to New Orleans, and I've seen its muddy
        bosom turn all golden in the sunset.

I've known rivers:
Ancient, dusky rivers.

My soul has grown deep like the rivers.

(4)

Hughes illustrates the progression of linear time, but the poet recognizes also that time can have a cyclical nature. In capturing this nature, the poet has the power to make the past present. Dave Smith (1975) reconstructs an incident of the past in "Pietas: The Petrified Wood":

> As old cottonwood has jeweled, my piece
> the bruise of a warrior's first spear
> hurtled, retrieved as the sun circles
> and a boy hardens to a man.
> I touch it to see him learn the art
> of killing, and a man grows
> to a boy in the presence of scars.
>
> It does not live, on my desk,
> in its warm grains, would not burn
> though it is filled with smoke,
> or slowly bear the agonizing green
> of a desert spring. But as heartwood
> I keep it for its weight, its shape
> showing where the lance entered
> and currents of sap loosed, shone,
> broke the winter bark each year
>
> as a man and a boy run down an arroyo
> illusory with heat, tufts of dust
> growing under their feet, the haze
> of spring spreading like a sweat.
> My finger sees the spear cocked
> up like a bird toward the horizon
> and I know his angle is still wrong
> where a man grins up at the light
> leaves, his arms open as if to soar,
> and I feel the gouged bark fall, and
> fall again, already beginning to be
> mine, a spice in the hot dry air.

                                                                (214)

There are some problems in equating poetry with academic forms of anthropology. The most obvious weakness is the poem's lack of scientific or quantitative basis and its dependence on emotion to communicate. The poem must be understood by the reader as a personal, highly interpretative expression.

Although a poem gains strength and power through its simplicity, this simplicity is also its greatest weakness in terms of a poem's potential usefulness for understanding anthropology. The poem, by its nature, is fragmentary; it offers only a part of the whole picture. The reader cannot even begin to gain a holistic understanding of the culture through the isolated artifact/incident illustrated in the poem.

Further, the author himself often has only a superficial understanding of the culture he seeks to interpret. Indeed, a poet's knowledge about a culture may be so limited that his perceptions are actually distorted. His poetry is shallow and speculative, that of a tourist rather than a scholar. Even a knowledgeable poet, like a professional anthropologist, is limited and influenced by his own cultural biases in topic selection and the nature of his interpretations.

Once its limitations are recognized, however, poetry can be a valuable means of learning about people and cultures. Culture is a highly complex system. Yet, when understanding any system, we must first understand the elements that make up that system before we can begin to understand the complex whole. Poetry can help explain these elements—material culture, ideology, social organization, and language.

For the beginning student of anthropology, a poem can stimulate an interest in the field and instill the desire to learn more about a culture or tradition. For the professional, poetry has been called "subjective anthropology." The language of poetry can be an alternative way of communicating research results to both a traditional and nontraditional audience. On a more personal level, poetry can help integrate the impact of our confrontation with other cultures and our search for our own cultural identity. For the writer, anthropological poetry can provide a distinctive poetic voice and a chance to explore and communicate another dimension of the world around us.

A poem, like an ethnography, an ethnographic film, an archaeological site, or a museum exhibit, is just one of the ways anthropology can be explored, understood, and communicated. Poetry offers an insight that goes beyond intellect: that is its power. The poet as anthropologist invites the reader to experience a greater understanding of humanity than facts alone can offer.

WORKS CITED

Cardiff, Gladys. *Carriers of the Dream Wheel*. Edited by Duane Niatum. New York: Harper and Row, 1975.

Conley, Robert J. *The Remembered Earth*. Edited by Geary Hobson. Albuquerque, NM: Red Earth Press, 1979.

Daniels, Celia. "Empty Tomb." Unpublished.

Diamond, Stanley. *Totems*. Barrytown, NY: Open Book Publishers, 1981.

Eisely, Loren. *All the Night Wings*. New York: Times Books, 1979.

Hind, Steven. *Familiar Ground*. Lawrence, KS: Cottonwood Review Press, 1980.

Hughes, Langston. *Selected Poems*. New York: Alfred A. Knopf, 1979.

Low, Denise. *Spring Geese*. Lawrence, KS: University of Kansas, Museum of
    Natural History, 1984.
Pederson, Cynthia. "Signals." Thesis, University of Kansas, Lawrence, KS, 1983.
Shelton, Richard. *You Can't Have Everything*. Pittsburgh, PA: University of
    Pittsburgh Press, 1975.
Smith, Dave. *Heartland II*. Edited by Lucien Stryk. De Kalb, IL: Northern Illinois
    University Press, 1975.
Snyder, Gary. *Turtle Island*. Newton, NJ: New Directions, 1969.

THE SHAMAN, LIGHT AND DARK

Ann Daghistany

ABSTRACT

Anthropological studies of the shaman illuminate the literary manifestations of this mysterious figure. This chapter attempts first to define the shaman using scholarship from anthropology and interpretive patterns from comparative religion. The shaman stories *Bless Me, Ultima* and "The Burning," show a benevolent or light use of power acquired through initiation, sacrifice, and harmony with nature, a power that is manifest through its relation to deity and community. By contrast, the sorcerer story "Historia and Tale of Doctor Johannes Faustus" reveals a similar power used for dark purposes. Myth scholarship also clarifies the literary shaman through the archetypes of Asclepius, Orpheus, and Hermes.

Anthropology, myth studies, and comparative literature all look for—and find—in their respective subject matters recurrent images of forms and aspects of human life and of its environing forces, factors that condition and shape it. The term *archetype* is used widely to signify such images. I assume here that such images are not simply made up by individual persons, but are given by society and have, moreover, the power of acting upon individuals in various ways. This assumption provides a basis for understanding how anthropologists, comparative mythologists, and students of literature can be regarded as having something important in common: if such images and their relationships to the persons whose lives they shape and whose experience they inform are in this sense objective, they are subject to descriptions that can be more-or-less accurate, penetrating, or comprehensive.

Let us consider the case of the shaman archetype. Anthropologists have described shamanism in many different cultures, and the shaman figure seems to be of more than local interest. Furthermore, a shaman archetype seems to occur in literary and mythic sources long before the modern descriptions of shamanism by anthropologists. This chapter focuses on the shaman archetype in several stories that exhibit varying relationships to the three categories of anthropology, myth, and literature. The discussion of these stories offers some materials for reflection upon the relationships of these three disciplines and should thus serve to clarify what *interdisciplinary* might mean in this connection.

Let us see how the literary portraits of two women—Lela in Trambley's story "The Burning" and Ultima in Rudolfo Anaya's novel *Bless Me, Ultima*—and the earliest recorded medieval version of Faust show how the anthropological and mythic shaman images coalesce and diverge. In his book *The Shaman: Patterns of Siberian and Ojibway Healing*, anthropologist John Grim states:

> Among tribal peoples the shaman is the person, male or female, who experiences, absorbs, and communicates a special mode of sustaining, healing power. For most tribal peoples the vital rhythms of the world are manifestations of a mysterious, all-pervasive power presence. This power presence is evoked by a shaman in ritual prayers and sacrifice to guide tribal hunts, perpetuate sacred crafts, and sustain human life in its confrontations with the destructive forces of the surrounding world. (3)

The words of María Sabina, a Mazatec shaman born in 1894 and described by ethnomycologist Gordon Masson as "an artist in her mastery of the techniques of the vocation," add concreteness to the anthropologist's definition:

> There is a world beyond ours, a world that is far away, nearby, and invisible. And there it is where God lives, where the dead live, the spirits and the saints, a world where everything has already happened and everything is known. That world talks. It has a language of its own. I report what it says. (Halifax 1979, 130)

The type of control exerted by the shaman image over the individual is rigorously demanding. This may be seen in the religious experience of initiation that utterly transforms the shaman and through which he acquires his powers. The initiation into the role separates itself into several stages: the summons, the solitary experience, suffering, death, and re-creation. According to the comparative mythologist Mircea Eliade, the young person may receive his summons in the form of a call through dreams or visions, through hereditary transmission, or by personal quest. Alone, he is required to undergo a harrowing experience during which he is stripped of his mortal identity and recreated as a new being. This change of being gives the shaman access to the world of the spirit (Eliade 1979, 21). Eliade says:

> To see into the very far distance, to ascend to heaven, to see spirit beings (souls of the dead, demons, gods), means, in the final analysis, that the medicine man is no longer confined to the universe of profane man, that he shares the condition of Superior Beings. He attains this condition thanks to an initiatory death . . . .. (25)

The meaning of the initiation is this: through his own crisis and suffering, which he must resolve in order to become a shaman, the individual acquires a power over death. Thus the shaman image, in drawing the individual into itself, bestows upon him the reflection of deity. It is because of his power over death that the shaman earns his status among his peers. (Drury 1982, 2) In their citation of the Siberian Yakut shaman's sacrifice of personal self, anthropologists Joan Halifax and Andreas Lommel illustrate the extraordinary degree of suffering that the shaman must undergo:

> Here is another account of the shaman's sacrifice of self to the spiritual forces that will guide as they consume: "They cut off the head and place it on the uppermost plank of the *yurta*, from where it watches the chopping up of its body. They hook an iron hook into the body and tear up and distribute all the joints; they clean the bones, by scratching off the flesh and removing all the fluid. They take the two eyes out of the sockets and put them on one side. The flesh removed from the bones is scattered on all the paths of the underworld; they also say that it is distributed among the nine or three times nine generations of the spirits that cause sickness, whose road and paths the shaman will in future know. He will be able to help with ailments caused by them; but he will not be able to cure those maladies caused by spirits that did not eat of his flesh. (Lommel 1967, 60)

The initiation pattern is so common that it can perhaps be regarded as universal (Eliade 1970, 2546). In her short story "The Burning," Trambley portrays an old woman whose shamanic pattern includes the calling, the suffering death of the old self, the descent, and the sacrifice. The story opens upon a group of pueblo women who condemn the main character Lela, an old woman, to death by burning because her different beliefs have incensed them (despite her benevolent healings). Lela, ill inside her hut, remembers her youth and the sequence of events that brought her to the pueblo. She had inherited the sacred artistic occupation of creating clay figures of household rural gods from her mother. One day, in search of the larger self, she followed "the command of dreams" to the lake. She swam to the waterfall and then was led to leave the world of her childhood for the people outside. Her initiation begins on this journey. She feels great hunger and thirst in the cold night desert wind. Her fall into a crevice between two large boulders leaves her foot wounded, and she suffers from fever all night. Her departure from her people reflects the death of her old self, whereas the wound represents the suffering that accompanies shamanic initiation. The fall can be seen as a descent. In the new village, she is never accepted. Lela lives in isolation, giving up the comfort she would have enjoyed among her own people because of her dedication to her occupation:

> The people in her new home needed her, and she loved them in silence and from a distance. She forgave them for not accepting her strangeness and learned to find adventure in the oneness of herself. . . . Many times she wanted to go back . . ., but too many people needed her here. (Trambley 1986, 422-23)

During Lela's initiation, the power of the shaman image had so utterly transformed her into a new being that she willingly sacrificed the security and comfort of her old identity.

Lela's relationship to the community acquires a special meaning because of the particular setting identified in the story: she is named as a Tarahumara from Batopilas, in the northwest corner of Mexico. The plot of the story seems to reflect the historical pattern of the Tarahumaras in relation to Spanish intruders who, from the early seventeenth century, attempted to Christianize the Tarahumaras. The pattern shows the features of acceptance-disillusion-withdrawal on the part of the Indians and exploitation-brutality-murder on the part of the Spanish.[1] (Kennedy 1978, 17) Lela's gentle character, willingness to help, and withdrawal from contact into solitude and isolation, even her ultimate death at the hands of the pueblo women, show the traits of the Tarahumaras described by the anthropologist John Kennedy in his book *Tarahumara of the Sierra Madre*. He notes, "the present day Tarahumara traits of passivity, withdrawal from confrontation, avoidance of aggression, and introversion are at least partially institutionalized responses to their contact with the Spanish in the seventeenth century" (19).

After initiation, a second requirement of shamanism is a harmony with nature. "The experience of resonance with the natural world distinguishes the shaman as a religious type from the prophet, priest, yogi, and sage" (Grim 1983, 207). The novel *Bless Me, Ultima* develops this aspect of the shaman fully. Ultima is a wise old woman who guides the development of the young narrator, Tonio. When they walk together in the hills seeking herbs, Ultima seems to become more vital, reflecting the reciprocal bond: nature's strength flows through her, as she serves others with its powers. Her vitality comes from the fact that, like other authentic shamans, she "perceives the link between humans and earth processes, and it becomes the means for experiencing constellations of energy in the natural world and channeling those forces into the tribal community" (207).

The shaman's close connections with nature are effected at initiation, whereupon the novice may take upon him/herself the powers, attitude, and identity of an animal. "Often the shaman finds a new identity in an animal form, taking possession of the animal to acquire its natural strength and rhythms" (204). Ultima's animal spirit is the owl, which always accompanies her. It is identified with her closely as an ally and seeks to protect as well as to warn her. It blinds Tenorio, the enemy who tries to kill her. It also wounds his daughters, who haunt her dwelling as wolves, and it shares her spiritual strength. Although separated by continents and centuries, another tradition linking the owl and the modern female curer is described by the anthropologist Douglas Sharon in his study of a Peruvian Shaman entitled *The Wizard of the Four Winds*. In the early Peruvian *Moche* art period (100 B.C. to A.D. 700), "a shawl-clad female figure in a curing scenario . . . often has the features of an owl, the alter ego of modern female curers, a wise old woman associated with traditional wisdom and herbal lore" (42). The young Tonio hears the owl frequently in times of trouble.

Lorene Carpenter notes the anthropologist Benson Saler's comments on the guardian animal spirit, observations that illuminate Ultima's death when Tenorio kills her owl:

> The animal is the individual human being's alter ego. Should the alter ego suffer harm, the individual whose destiny is linked to it is likely to suffer harm in the corresponding degree. (1981, 48)

In addition to the harmony with nature and the identity with an animal, "the shaman experiences natural symbols as revelatory of cosmic power" (Grim 1983, 185). Lela, the main character of "The Burning," does so: her shamanic call at the beginning of her story is accompanied by the insight into nature's message. The earthly phenomena speak to her and beckon her: "The soft breath of wind was the breath of little gods, and the crystal shine of rocks close to the lake was a winking language that spoke of peace and the wildness of all joy." (Trambley 1986, 423).[2]

As the powerful image of the shaman draws the individual into itself, so too does it control the relationship between the individual shaman and others, notably deities, but the general community as well. That the shaman has a relationship with deities, and that this relationship is a controlled one, is and has been the subject of much scholarly inquiry. In this section we shall focus on what the relationship is, how it is effected with the deities, and why it is sought by the shaman. In the history of the scholarly study of shamanism, there are three stages. The early studies investigated the origin of religion and took shamanism to be a primordial religious experience, the source of religions

(Grim 1983, 16). The second stage saw "anthropological efforts to collect ethnographic data from particular cultures," while in the third stage, of hermeneutical studies, shamanism is interpreted in its multicultural context (15). During the first and second stages, it was common to regard the shaman as a psychopath because of the disturbed behavior that preceded and accompanied his/her initiation (Eliade 1970, 2547). Today, however, the attitude taken toward the reality of his encounter with deity, or supernatural forces, is elusive: the scholar will comment only on the content and implications of the shaman's role (Drury 1982, 18). Infrequently it will cautiously affirm the "reality" of the spiritual contact (Eliade 1960, 87-89). In either case, the distinction between the shaman and the psychopath is seen to be the control that the shaman has over his visions. That is, he can move at will between the upper, Earth-level, and lower cosmological zones. Important distinctions between the medium and the psychopath are drawn; for unlike the medium he can *remember* what he experiences (Drury 1982, 14), and unlike the psychopath, he makes contact with the spirits for *specific purposes*, which we will soon examine. Before we do, however, we need to understand something of what happens in the contact between the shaman and the spirit. First, the shaman becomes identified with the power during the contact itself. Second, he experiences a mystical illumination, an inner light "felt throughout the body but principally in the head and accompanied by the experience of ascension." The spiritual contact

> involves vision into the distance and clairvoyance at the same time: the shaman sees everywhere and very far, but he also sees invisible entities (souls of the sick, spirits) and also sees future events . . . , sees through the flesh, in the manner of x-rays. (Eliade 1979, 23)

The method of attaining contact is through trance, which may be aided by drums and songs. During trance, Halifax maintains, "the soul of the ecstatic leaves the body and flies into the realm of spirits and gods" (1979, 18). There is danger for the shaman in these quests, for he can be killed while in the other worlds and never return. The specific purpose of the shaman in undertaking these journeys is to become one with the source of power, "to relay requests to his or her guardian spirits" (Grim 1983, 206), to retrieve a lost soul, to guide the soul of the dead to its resting place, (Eliade 1960, 206) and above all to heal.

Both Lela and Ultima use natural elements as instruments of healing. Lela discovers fine, crystalline sand at the bottom of the crevice where she falls during her symbolic "death." She uses this sand in healing. Various cultures have believed that sand of crystalline quartz has supernatural powers: to produce clairvoyance, to fly, and to bestow upon its possessor the divine qualities of its sacred origin.[3] Lela calls it the sand of the little gods and sees it assume their shapes. She uses it to cure skin diseases, sores, and open wounds.

The shaman's role within the community is governed by his mediating function between others and the gods, and by his healing powers. An actual shaman is often given respect and support by his or her group, who see him as a focus of sacrifice and a ritual contact figure with their gods. In these fictional representations, however, the healers Ultima and Lela experience tension between themselves and their communities because of the groups' dogmatic Christianity. The stories criticize indirectly the group's limited knowledge of Christianity, for the communities do not tolerate the competition with natural forces as a form of deity. Hence, unlike the actual shaman whose tribe worships the same gods, the stories represent the conflict arising from culture contact. This fact heightens the sacrifice made by the shaman. Lela's adopted people enjoy her healing powers, but do not tolerate her refusal to join their faith. Ultima, on the other hand, worked within the Christian faith as a member of the community. Yet the people, and particularly the young narrator, Tonio, experience the church as too dogmatic, conceptual, and abstract; the message of mercy is forgotten. In Tonio's mind, Ultima, with her powers of nature and her simple belief in goodness, is a stronger influence. She is understanding and kind, and intercedes in his behalf. Her blessing shows her synthesis of a shaman's natural powers and Christian beliefs:

> Even my father knelt for the blessing. Huddled in the kitchen we bowed our heads. There was no sound.
> "En el nombre del Padre, del Hijo, y del Espiritu Santo—"
> I felt Ultima's hand on my head and at the same time I felt a great force, like a whirlwind, swirl about me. I looked up in fright, thinking the wind would knock me off my knees. Ultima's bright eyes held me still. (Anaya 1983, 51)

Both Lela and Ultima are referred to as *curanderas*. In their book entitled *Curanderismo*, the anthropologists Robert T. Trotter and Juan Antonio Chavira (1981, 90-93) outline the types of problems cured by curanderos as fright, loss of soul, and various physical ailments. They show that in South Texas, curanderos are a specific form of shaman who practice mediumship, or the mediation between earth and spirit worlds. In the following passage, they make a distinction between the curandero and the brujo that Anaya also makes in *Bless Me, Ultima*:

> Curanderos are viewed from many different social perspectives within their communities. Some people seek them out as their sole or major health resource, while others view them as quacks, fakes, or even the Devil's emissaries on earth. All of these people view the curandero as a person set apart from the rest of humanity, either by his gifts or his actions. The curandero is considered different from ordinary people, and this difference produces respect, distrust, and even fear. Sometimes it produces the accusation that the curandero is a brujo, a witch, doing antisocial magic, so not everyone feels drawn to this profession. (Trotter and Chavera 1981, 110)

A useful contrast to the shaman image is provided by the sorcerer. The sorcerer seeks a power equal to the gods, not in order to benefit others, but for his own gain. Although he traffics with supernatural spirits, his dedication to his own selfish *earthly* aims places him frequently into close cooperative contact with "demons." Such a sorcerer is the ancient medieval Faust from the oldest surviving manuscript of 1580. As we shall see, Faust possesses all of the anthropological shaman's powers, but pursues them in the context of defiant disobedience to orthodox, medieval Christianity. It is helpful to remind ourselves that only a small fraction of the medieval population—scarcely five percent—were literate; hence, the tales of the period concerned themselves with their aristocratic readers primarily. They were written against an assumed moral backdrop, "namely the concerns of the Christian living in an age in which the church was the arbiter of social practice and moral behavior. As a result, whether or not the Church as institution appears in medieval works, the moral theology of the Christian religion, which defines correct action, is present (Gentry 1983, xiv).

The anthropologist Michael Harner's (1973, xiv) definition of a shaman includes the following features:

(1) makes contact with the spirit world through a trance state,
(2) commands one or more spirits,
(3) bewitches or heals people with the help of spirits,
(4) influences the course of events,
(5) identifies (unmasks) criminals,
(6) communicates with spirits of the dead,
(7) foretells the future.

These seven powers are possessed by the Faust in the medieval German tradition. Faust makes contact with the spirit world, however, through magic by describing certain circles with his staff, and by his pact with the devil. In his first contact, the difference between the shaman and the magician may be seen: the shaman seeks to make himself a vessel or mediator, whereas Faust

> so admired having the devil *subserviently* to him that he took courage and did conjure the star once, twice, and a third time, whereupon a gush of fire from the sphere shot up as high as a man, settled again, and six little lights became visible upon it. Now one little light would leap upward, now a second downward, until the form of a burning man finally emerged. (Gentry 1983, 151)

Faust's initiation differs in content as well as in tone from the typical shaman, for instead of acquiring a power over death through the suffering experience of his own death, Faust bargains with the spirit. He agrees to give his soul in afterlife to the devil in return for the powers. Other shamans do not pay this price, for instead they surrender their personal body and identity at the *outset* of their careers. In addition, this version of the Faust legend underlines the theme of the devil's duplicity, or the treachery of evil, by bringing Faust repeatedly to the door of repentance only to have Mephisto slam it shut with the lie that God would never, at this point in his transgressions, forgive him. That Faust believes him shows total loss of faith. Thus, he contrasts sharply with Ultima, whose belief was strong and who taught Tonio that the smallest particle of good can triumph over the largest evil:

> "Are you afraid?" she asked . . . She put her bowl aside and stared into my eyes.
> "No," I said.
> "Why?"
> "I don't know," I said.
> "I will tell you why," she smiled, "it is because good is always stronger than evil. Always remember that, Antonio. The smallest bit of good can stand against all the powers of evil in the world and it will emerge triumphant. There is no need to fear men like Tenorio." (Anaya 1983, 91)

The character strength of Ultima is emphasized frequently in Anaya's moral vision. Ultima's commitment to healing is based upon a sympathy for people: Tonio's father points out, "Ultima has sympathy for people, and it is so complete that with it she can touch their souls and cure them" (237).

Faust possesses the remaining features of the shaman also, but the chosen details seem to deflate rather than to enlarge the effect of the shaman's powers. The most impressive passages in the Faust manuscript have to do with the descent into hell and the ascent into heaven. These passages are illustrative of the basic shamanic motifs. In Faust's case, however, the descent and ascent illuminate his primary goal, the acquisition of immortal knowledge, whereas other shamans seek metaphysical knowledge to "pierce duality by embracing opposites" (Halifax 1979, 28). Faust is an intellectual, bored by the limits of human inquiry. We see the seeds of the issues that the later Faust versions will emphasize in Faust's request to see hell "so that he might see and mark the nature, fundament, quality and substance of hell" (Gentry 1983, 169). The concrete additions and details of the following passage give a Dantesque medieval sense of the infernal regions:

> Well, just at that moment when he hurled himself head over heels and went tumbling down, such a frightful loud tumult and banging assailed his ears, and the mountain peak shook so furiously that he thought many big cannons must have been set off, but he had only come to the bottom of hell. Here were many worthy personages in a fire: emperors, Kings, princes, and lords, many thousand knights, and men-at-arms. A cool stream ran along at the edge of the fire, and here some were drinking, refreshing themselves, and bathing, but some were fleeing from its cold, back into the fire. (171)

By the same token, Faust's search for knowledge separates him also from the evil *sorcerer* who seeks power to make himself equal to the gods, and power to satisfy his desire for money. A literary example of such a sorcerer is the character Kalimake, in Robert Louis Stevenson's short story "The Isle of Voices." In this voodoo adventure story, the powers of Kalimake are great—he can prophesy the future, transform himself into a giant that can walk across oceans, make his enemies vanish without a trace—most of all, he can change seashells into silver dollars. Unlike Faust, Kalimake never uses his powers to rescue or heal others. Also unlike Faust, he maintains a cloak of secrecy so that he tries to kill his son-in-law for learning too much about his black arts. Kalimake is present as the servant of no one but himself, whereas Faust's relationship to Mephistopheles indicates clearly the deity-mortal distinction. Kalimake operates in the realm not of spiritualism but of magic, which is "concerned above all else with the acquisition and exercise of power. . . . Omnipotence unqualified, supreme power over all things, is the ultimate goal of magic" (Cavendish 1970, 1983).

We have seen thus far that anthropology describes the context of shamanism, illuminating its occurrence in the fictional world. It has enumerated the shaman's powers, crystallized the conflicts in the stories, and enriched the owl and sand motifs by providing their background. At the same time, the stories provide a sharper focus upon certain aspects of the shaman's experience. Archetypal myth also contributes understanding through myth scholarship, which has identified three shaman images: Asclepius, Orpheus, and Hermes. The different emphases to the myth images yield new insight. As the myth scholar, Joseph Campbell, states:

> In every society in which they have been known, the shamans have been the particular guardians and reciters of the chants and traditions of their people . . . . The realm of myth, from which, according to primitive belief, the whole spectacle of the world proceeds, and the realm of shamanistic trance are one and the same. (1969, 250)

The myth image of the healer, Asclepius, manifests a special kind of affinity with nature, the knowledge of herbs, and incarnation in "telling" dreams. Apollo gave his son, Asclepius, to be raised and taught by the centaur, Chiron, the horse-man who synthesized natural and rational powers. Asclepius, like Ultima, brings the human faculties of reason, memory, intuition, and dreams to effect cures through his capacity to gently extract nature's secrets: her physical remedies through herbs, her situational correctives through the visions of sleep. Just as Asclepius received his training from a unique teacher, so too does Ultima have an apprenticeship with a luminary curandero so powerful that his name makes Tenorio tremble. Ultima's reverence for nature, the special affirmation of the life force in each plant, makes her pray for its blessing before she picks it. After she places the herbs on Tonio's body, his wounds heal quickly, leaving only thin pink lines. (Anaya 1983, 113) The healings in the temples of Asclepius were sought in sleep: the patient would hope to dream that the god touched him and healed his affliction, or that Asclepius would speak through the dream to provide the correct therapy (Kerenyi 1959, 12, 26) Tonio, the narrator of *Bless Me, Ultima*, experiences Ultima's presence in his dreams as he seeks to unravel his destiny. In the following dream passage, indicating Tonio's subconscious understanding of his affinity with nature, Tonio hears Ultima reveal the meaning of cosmic unity behind the diverse manifestations of earthly water:

> Stand, Antonio, she commanded, and I stood. You both know, she spoke to my father and my mother, that the sweet water of the moon which falls as rain is the same water that gathers into rivers and flows to fill the seas. Without the waters of the moon to replenish the oceans there would be no oceans. And the same salt waters of the oceans are drawn by the sun to the heavens, and in turn become again the waters of the moon. Without the sun there would be no waters formed to slake the dark earth's thirst. (Anaya 1983, 113)

This passage shows Tonio's perception of Ultima's natural wisdom as the source of synthesis for his conflicting backgrounds.

Together with the Christ figure, whose miracles of healing acquired him the reputation that alarmed the authorities, Asclepius presents an archetypal pattern of healing that prevails among physicians in the literary traditions of the West. The literary shaman shares the major parts of the archetypal image cast by both Christ and Asclepius: these parts are compassion as a motive, challenge to authority as a model, and the sacrifice of one's human life as a price. These three elements are clearly visible in the anthropological shaman, as we have seen. Likewise, both Ultima and Lela offer a challenge to authority by practicing their healings without official sanction. This challenge leads finally to their deaths, the sacrifice of their own human lives; for those who kill them know that the authorities will look the other way. Whereas the Greeks perceived the source of sickness to be the ill will of the gods, the shaman—and Ultima—traces disease to the gods as well as to men. Because of her special affinity with nature, Ultima interprets evil as a disobedience to the laws of nature or an incongruence with its harmony. Thus, she deflects the evil death-wish back to the *brujas*, the daughters of Tenorio, who wanted to kill Tonio's Uncle Lucas because in the forest he stumbled upon their black mass. They use locks of his hair to poison him. Ultima's rescue of his soul, at the point of death, is the classic shamanistic rescue (Campbell 1969, 261) She uses herbal remedies, incantations, and clay dolls to heal him:

> "Let the devil come out!" Ultima cried in his ear.
>
> "¡Dios mio!" were his first words, and with those words the evil was wrenched from his interior. Green bile poured from his mouth, and finally he vomited a huge ball of hair. It fell to the floor, hot and steaming and wiggling like snakes.
>
> It was his hair with which they had worked the evil!
>
> "Ay!" Ultima cried triumphantly and with clean linen she swept up the evil, living ball of hair. "This will be burned, by the tree where the witches dance—" she sang and swiftly put the evil load into the sack. She tied the sack securely and then came back to my uncle. He was holding the side of the bed, his thin fingers clutching the wood tightly as if he were afraid to slip back into the evil spell. He was very weak and sweating, but he was well. I could see in his eyes that he knew he was a man again, a man returned from a living hell. (Anaya 1983, 95)

In this case, the raising of the living dead and the subsequent death of the *bruja*, Ultima resembles Asclepius once again. Both are killed for a perceived violation of the natural order when in fact they were working in harmony with it.

The mythic image of the artist-shaman Orpheus adds richness to the portrait of Lela. The pattern of the Orpheus image includes four parts: the healing art, the descent, the mission, and the sacrificial killing. The pattern first allows us to appreciate the quality of healing through art which links artists with priests and prophets. As the music of Orpheus enchanted all who heard it, and momentarily united his audience in a transport of delight, so the clay gods of Lela unite families in an affirmation of life's beauty:

> These were painted in gay colors and the expression on the tiny faces measured the seasons of the heart. The little rural gods of river, sky, fire, seed, birds, all were chosen members of each family. Because they sanctified all human acts, they were the actions of the living, like an aura. They were a shrine to creation. (Trambley 1986, 723)

In the work of both artists, Orpheus and Lela, we see the unique quality of art: to heighten life as experience and to make its meaning more clear.

As art forms, both songs and clay figures share a method of healing and a living quality. Both open the door to another, coexisting world of spirits revealed through art (Campbell 1969, 265). Both present images to be retained by the brain as aesthetic models of healing radiance. For the shaman,

> the song word is powerful, it names a thing, it stands at the sacred center, drawing all toward it. The word exists and does not exist. It both awakens an image and is an awakened image. The word disappears, the poetry is gone, but the imaginal form persists within the mind and works on the soul. Poesis, then, an action and an interaction in its primary sense, is the process of creation. (Halifax 1979, 33)

The figures of the songs, and of the clay gods, imitate the shaman's spiritual visions (Campbell 1969, 265). The shaman sings, without composing, when his illumination is achieved. He later sings to heal others, in a reenactment of the original event that he experienced (Halifax 1979, 31). The function of repetition adumbrates the power of both song and statue: each time either is consulted in a healing situation, its archetypal value is affirmed. Lela molds the clay figurines and also looks for them in the townspeople, seeking the identity between the particular individuals and their models in the universals. "In her mind, she had molded their smiles, their tears, their embraces, their just being. Her larger self told her that the miracle of the living act was supreme, the giving, the receiving, the stumbling, and the getting up" (Trambley 1986, 427). Both songs and statues are "personified comrades, . . . living as men are living and as the

world of spirit is also living" (Halifax 1979, 31). Second, the
Orpheus model is reflected in Lela's descent as she spends the
cold desert night on the mountaintop after leaving her childhood
village behind her and then falls or descends into the crevice.
Eliade (1974, 391) comments that Orpheus is the archetype of the
artist shaman: his descent into the underworld is most significant, though he also possesses healing art, love for animals,
charms, and the power of divination. Orpheus's death at the
hands of the crazed Maenads is also like Lela's sacrificial death at
the hands of the fanatic pueblo women.

The Faust figure as shaman reflects the image of Hermes,
whose mythic pattern adds tonal clarity to his unique combination of attributes. Joseph Campbell (1969, 274) identifies Hermes
as a shaman figure, citing particularly his psychopomp function
of guiding souls to the underworld in his book *Primitive
Mythology*. The tone of whimsicality, which predominates in the
Faust story, notwithstanding, the obvious attempt to warn
Christians against sin, captures the Hermes spirit, which is

> the chaos principle, the principle of disorder, the force careless of taboos and
> shattering bounds. But from the point of view of the deepest realms of being
> from which the energies of life ultimately spring, this principle is not to be
> despised. (274)

We recall that although Hermes is a god, he has a somewhat
questionable status among his Olympian kin, who often seem
exasperated with him. We remember his theft of Apollo's cattle,
yet learn with interest that Hermes also drove off a pestilence,
carrying a ram on his shoulders around the city's walls (Kereneyi
1976, 83). We also see in Hermes the same mixture of
opportunism and benevolence that the earliest Faust figure of the
medieval manuscript manifests. For fun, Faust will conjure a
flowering garden in the middle of winter to please his guests, he
will become invisible at the Vatican and steal the Pope's silver
after blowing in his face, and he will share the knowledge he
acquired during his ascent into the heavens with other scholars;
yet he will also transform himself into the spirit of Mahomet and
lie with all of the wives of a Turkish harem owner. Faust as the
Hermes-shaman never has any purpose beyond living fully in the
moment. Faust, the fun-loving trickster, who had caused antlers
to cleave to a knight's head and who had deposited a butler in a
tree, was himself tricked by Mephisto: we recall that each time he
wanted to repent, he believed the false news that God would not
forgive. Yet his story, in this early version that shows him to be

in possession of shamanic powers despite the dissociation of these powers from their proper belief structure, is perhaps the most entertaining of all the Faust legends.

NOTES

[1]According to Kennedy (1978, 15), "in the early seventeenth Century, the Tarahumara were at first very accepting of Spaniards in general, and particularly of the Jesuits." When disillusionment and epidemics began to spread in 1648, "leaders arose who blamed the widespread death from epidemics on the Spanish God, and they, in turn, were branded 'witches' by the Fathers" (16). In 1650, the Tarahumaras revolted, but were crushed in 1652. "After 1673, Jesuit Fathers Tarda and Guadalajara led a movement to establish a line of eight new churches linking the Baja Tarahumara with the missions in Sonora among the Opatas and Chinipas, and the cycle of acceptance—exploitation—disaffection was again in motion" (17). In 1696, Spanish Captain Retana beheaded thirty Indians gathered on a cliff near a cache of maize and poisoned arrows, sparking a general rebellion (18). The Tarahumara attacked a church at Echogita, whereupon "Retana then beheaded thirty-three more men, placing their heads on poles near Sisoquichi. The suppression of the uprising of 1698 permanently ended effective Tarahumara resistance to Spanish rule. Their mode of resistance from the beginning of the eighteenth century until the present has been largely one of avoidance of contact and withdrawal further and further into canyons" (19).

[2]The famous Lumholtz (1973) study of the Tarahumaras, done in the last century, and the recent Kennedy (1978) study of the tribe do not reveal in specific detail correlations between the fictional gods—of personified natural forces—worshipped by Lela in "The Burning" and the historical traditions of the people. However, an actual Tarahumara dream seems to evoke vague suggestions of Lela's little gods: "Rodrigo of Vararari recounted the following, which is a very commonly reported type of dream: 'Last night I dreamed about the "ancient ones," the first Tarahumaras who were here. They looked like us and were drinking Tesquino like us.' " (Kennedy, 130).

[3]The Lumholtz (1973, 300) study points out certain features of the Tarahumaras' nineteenth-century beliefs that bear tangentially upon "The Burning." The Indians believed that Tata Dios (Our Father) *drew* the deer first and then they came to life. They believed that rocks also grew because they have life inside them 287). Apparently the contemporary belief that ancestors were fashioned out of clay (Kennedy 1978, 130) was widely prevalent during Lumholtz's time (297).

WORKS CITED

Anaya, Rudolfo A. *Bless Me, Ultima.* Berkeley: Tonatiuh-Quinta Sol, 1983.

Campbell, Joseph. *The Masks of God: Primitive Mythology.* New York: Viking, 1969.

Carpenter, Lorene. "Maps for the Journey: Shamanic Patterns in Anaya, Asturias, and Castaneda." Diss. Univ. of Colorado, 1981.

Cavendish, Richard, ed. *Man, Myth, and Magic: An Illustrated Encyclopedia of the Supernatural.* 24 vols. New York: Marshall Cavendish, 1970.

Drury, Nevill. *The Shaman and the Magician: Journeys Between the Worlds.* London: Routledge and Kegan Paul, 1982.

Eliade, Mircea. *Myths, Dreams and Mysteries: The Encounter Between Contemporary Faiths and Archaic Realities.* Translated by Philip Maren. New York: Harper and Row, 1960.

———. "Shamanism." *Man, Myth and Magic: An Illustrated Encyclopedia of the Supernatural.* Edited by Richard Cavendish. 24 vols. New York: Marshall Cavendish, 1970.

———. *Shamanism: Archaic Techniques of Ecstasy.* Princeton: Princeton University Press, 1974.

———. *The Two and the One.* Translated by J. M. Cohen. Chicago: University of Chicago Press, 1979.

Gentry, F. R., ed. "Historia & Tale of Doctor Johannes Faustus." *German Medieval Tales,* Translated by Harry G. Haile. New York: Continuum, 1983.

Grim, John. *The Shaman: Patterns of Siberian and Ojibway Healing.* Norman: University of Oklahoma Press, 1983.

Halifax, Joan. *Shamanic Voices: Survey of Visionary Narratives.* New York: E. P. Dutton, 1979.

Harner, Michael. *Hallucinogens and Shamanism.* New York: Oxford University Press, 1973.

Jayne, Walter Addison. *The Healing Gods of Ancient Civilizations.* New York: University Books, 1962.

Kennedy, John G. *Tarahumara of the Sierra Madre.* Arlington Heights, IL: AHM Publishing Corporation, 1978.

Kerenyi, Karl. *Asklepios: Archetypal Image of the Physician's Existence* Translated by Ralph Manheim. New York: Pantheon, 1959.

———. *Hermes, Guide of Souls: The Mythologem of the Masculine Source of Life.* Translated by Murray Stein. Zurich: Spring Publications, 1976.

Lommel, Andreas. *Shamanism.* New York: McGraw-Hill, 1967.

Lumholtz, Carl. *Unknown Mexico: Explorations and Adventures Among the Tarahumare, Tepehuane, Cora, Huichol, Tarasco, and Aztec Indians.* 2 vols. [1902] Glorieta, NM: The Rio Grande Press, 1973.

Sharon, Douglas. *Wizard of the Four Winds: A Shaman's Story.* New York: MacMillan, 1978.

Stevenson, Robert Louis. "The Isle of Voices." *Voodoo! A Chrestomathy of Necromancy.* Edited by Bill Pronzine. New York: Arbor House, 1980.

Tremblay, Edna Portillo. "The Burning." *Images of Women in Literature,* edited by Mary Anne Ferguson. Boston: Houghton Mifflin, 1986.

Trotter, Robert T., and Chavira, Juan Antonio. *Curanderismo: Mexican American Folk Healing.* Athens, GA: The University of Georgia Press, 1981.

OLIVER LA FARGE, WRITER
AND ANTHROPOLOGIST

Philip A. Dennis

ABSTRACT

Anthropology and literature were intimately joined in the life of Oliver La Farge. Trained as an anthropologist at Harvard, he did fieldwork among the Navajo, and among the Maya people of Guatemala. His lifelong ambition was to be a writer, and he turned to his Navajo material for his first novel, *Laughing Boy*. It won the Pulitzer Prize and remains his most popular work. Later stories and novels that deal with other subjects were less successful; however, the part of his work that explores cross-cultural themes from his experiences as an anthropologist remains vital and interesting today. This paper suggests that it was the combination of anthropology and literature that led to La Farge's creativity and to the enduring contributions he made.

I have admired Oliver La Farge's work for a long time, and welcomed the opportunity to read more about the man himself, as well as more of his work. For instance, I was interested to find a book entitled *The Man With the Calabash Pipe*, a collection of La Farge's newspaper columns published originally in the Santa Fe *New Mexican*. I was even more interested to find that Tony Hillerman had been editor of *The New Mexican* when the columns were published. Hillerman reports that in those days he paid La Farge $10 a week as wages, a figure not out of line with professors' salaries in the state of Texas in recent years.

My first interest in La Farge came from reading *Laughing Boy*, a romantic novel about a young Navajo couple, which won the Pulitzer prize in 1930. It has been reprinted in paperback and is the only one of La Farge's books that still enjoys much popularity. Later in life, La Farge came to resent the fact that this romantic story, which he wrote as a very young man, was the main work for which people remembered him, in spite of his four other novels, two scholarly ethnographies, four historical works, several volumes of collected short stories, and various other works.[1] I think the public's judgment has been right, however. La Farge's best work, like that of Joseph Conrad and various other writers, came first. Friends who study literature tell me that it is not uncommon for a writer's best work to be produced earliest in life. In La Farge's case, however, I have a specific theory, which I will explain shortly, as to why his best work came first.

My second experience with La Farge was a book called *The Door in the Wall*, which I picked up completely by chance in the library. It turned out to be short stories about anthropologists, which provided delightful bedside reading because the characters and the settings were all directly from my own experience. I savored it and continue to re-read the stories today. I have even committed a few of them to memory to tell my classes on those occasions, hopefully not too frequent, when the regular class material for the day has become boring.

In fact, it isn't any wonder that La Farge writes so entertainingly about anthropologists; La Farge *was* an anthropologist by academic training. As a boy, he had been fascinated by arrowheads and American Indian folklore (an auspicious beginning for an anthropologist, as poet Celia Daniels would point out). At Harvard University, La Farge studied anthropology, and, in 1921, at the age of 20, he went on an expedition to the Navajo country. He was repelled at first by the stark, arid landscape, but soon came to love the land and its people, which he wrote about for the rest of his life. Later, he went to Guatemala as an ethnologist and wrote two scientific monographs and a number of scholarly articles about the Maya.[2] His ethnography of Santa Eulalia, in the Cuchumatanes mountains of northwestern Guatemala, is still of interest, particularly because the village has suffered in the genocidal violence that swept Guatemala in the late 1970s and early 1980s. Part of La Farge's interests as an anthropologist involved the linguistic relationship between Kanjobal, spoken in Santa Eulalia, and Jacalteca, spoken a short distance away. He might be surprised to learn that today there are large Kanjobal-speaking colonies in Miami and Los Angeles.[3] He would certainly be grieved to learn of their refugee status and their recent tragic history. Actually, in his novel *Sparks Fly Upward*, he described prophetically the background to the current conflict. He wrote about the ladino upper classes' use of the Guatemalan military as a tool of repression, and he noted the smoldering resentment among the Indian population at their exploitation by the ladinos. Indeed, reading the novel, set in the mid-nineteenth century, one is struck by how accurately it describes basic Guatemalan social realities today.

La Farge was a field anthropologist, then, in the tradition of Robert Redfield, Sol Tax, and other anthropologists of the time who were his friends. For anthropologists, a common kind of interaction with literature is to struggle with the materials collected during fieldwork, to distill and remember those unique experiences as recorded in one's fieldnotes. Then, as one faces the grind of writing about one's data for publication in academic journals, one discovers that fiction or other literature about "one's own people" really describes their way of life much better than ethnographic reporting. Michael Angrosino, in this volume, makes a similar comment, noting how the fiction about a region can express its sense of cultural identity better than hard-edged sociological analysis. I remember my excitement at finding a book about the Miskito people among whom I worked, published in 1899, with the delightful and paradoxical title, *Tangweera: Life and Adventures Among Gentle Savages.*[4] *Tangweera* is a wonderful book, better than any of the twentieth-century ethnography about the Miskito, including my own. For the anthropologist, then, it is a short step from realizing how accurate fiction can be, in some deeper sense, to trying to write fiction oneself. It appeals to many anthropologists as a fuller, more truthful way of communicating to others what one has experienced. One longs for a change of genres. Like the classic turn to the right in politics, in which the flaming young radical becomes a conservative established citizen, it seems to be predictable that an anthropologist, at some point in his or her career, will turn from the limitations of ethnography to some form of literature.

In fact, there was a period in early twentieth-century American anthropology when it was quite respectable for anthropologists to write fiction. In 1922 a book of short stories about American Indians was published. It was edited by Elsie Clews Parsons and contained stories by the most eminent anthropologists of the day. A. L. Kroeber wrote the introduction. He explained that the volume was a sort of by-product of anthropological fieldwork. It attempted to portray the thoughts and feelings of American Indians in a way impossible in scientific monographs. As in a monograph, however, the accuracy of the stories would be vouchsafed by the field experience of its authors. It had been written "by the men who know most, who have given a large block of their lives to acquiring intensive and exact information about the Indian and his culture" (Parsons, 1974, 13). This was true, but unfortunately it was also true that the eminent anthropologists were poor at writing fiction. The most charitable

thing that can be said about most of the stories is that they are
not very good.

La Farge, on the other hand, was a first-rate storyteller who
had been sharpening his writing skills since he was a boy. In
Laughing Boy, we come to see the whole traditional Navajo
culture through the story of a young man and young woman in
love, whose marriage goes against the wishes and advice of the
boy's family. Laughing Boy is a hero, traditional Navajo style: a
handsome gambler, strong and fearless, quick to anger, but
willing to forgive even the deepest hurts. He seems to be taken
directly from the characters of Navajo mythology, a subject that
La Farge had studied in some detail. Slim Girl, on the other
hand, is more complex; her personality is more carefully drawn.
She is assertive, independent, manipulative, and clever—also very
much like a figure from Navajo mythology. Their tragic love
affair provides the vehicle for sketching Navajo culture: the
extended kinship system; the economy based on sheepherding,
silversmithing, and weaving; the religious philosophy of life; and
the uneasy relationship to the encroaching white society. It is a
story to move the hardest heart, and it continues to charm and
entertain readers by the thousand, including all my students who
have read it.

Feeling a kindred spirit speaking to you from the page is
without a doubt the basis for much of our enjoyment of
literature. In the happiest reading experiences, we come to feel
that we know the author better through his written words than
we would in person. It is a close but not an obligatory
relationship, somewhat like a good friendship, in which we get
the best of the person without having to live with him and put
up with his irascible personality quirks on a daily basis. As I
read La Farge's books and later read about him, I realized that
part of my interest came from sharing some of the same life
experiences: prep school and an Ivy League university, the
Southwest, Indians, Mesoamerica, hispanic culture, and a
continuing love of the outdoors. La Farge had a remarkable
feeling for the Southwest, for its history and geography, its
people, and its unique spiritual qualities. Simple images from
his books bring back shared experiences of the outdoors:

> The sun was low. I went back, built a fire and cooked supper. Camp again,
> the restful little cañon, the sharpness of night air adding to my pleasure in
> the fire, the big sky, the irregular, jerky clanging of the bell on my lead horse
> as he grazed, all good things of which one does not tire. (1935, 90)

In some of his best stories, he captures the essence of the Southwest through the eyes of an anthropologist. "The Ancient Strength" for example, deals with an archaeologist who wants to excavate a Pueblo Indian trash dump near the village (1965, 105-31). The Pueblo people dump their trash, year after year, over the side of a mesa near the community, thus creating a rich store of evidence for the archaeologist. In the story, elders of the pueblo finally deny him permission to dig. By way of explanation, they invite him to a big summer ceremonial, called the "Eagles Return Rite." Through observing the ceremony, he comes to appreciate the strength and continuity of Pueblo life through the centuries. Duration and repetition, he realizes, are the essential elements of a Pueblo dance. Duration and repetition purposely frustrate the intellect and in doing so they allow access to areas of the subconscious not normally available. This is also one of the principles on which hard rock music is based. The duration and repetition in the dance help create and sustain the collective representations of Pueblo life, and it turns out that they are even related to such mundane things as the trash dump on the side of their mesa. Like the dance, the trash dump is part of what these people are made of, part of their sacred history, which would be desecrated by being poked into and analyzed. Miles Richardson (1984) has made the same point about archaeology in a recent story in *Southern Review*. In Richardson's story, an old archaeologist stands in the museum that he has built painstakingly over the years. He faces two modern Indians who are angry about his excavation of a mound containing more than a thousand burials and many artifacts, the remains of their people and culture, all of which have survived only as museum exhibits. In La Farge's story, the archaeologist at the ceremonial has been watching the eagles on the rooftops of the Pueblo. He has been thinking pleasantly of the time when they will be set free and soar off into the sky. But he is told that their spirits must remain in the Pueblo, illustrating the "inward-turned, castellated quality of Pueblo life down the ages" (125). When he learns that the eagle spirits have to remain in the Pueblo, he realizes that the trash has to stay there too. It mustn't be disturbed by archaeology. Surprised at his own reaction, in an unspoken, happy moment of agreement with the Pueblo elders, the archaeologist agrees: he should leave the trash dump alone; they should preserve the wholeness. This is La Farge the writer, or perhaps the humanistic anthropologist, arguing for the preservation of a people's own feeling about themselves, over and against the retrieval of objective information that might destroy that feeling.

At the same time, La Farge the anthropologist shows an understanding and a respect for the methods and aims of science, even when they seem petty or inconsequential from a layman's viewpoint. La Farge was a scholar, and he knew firsthand the long, lonely days spent as an anthropologist trying to understand a different language, to make sense of a totally different way of life. In "The High Plateaux of Asia," he ridicules self-styled explorers (the Indiana Joneses of their day) and juxtaposes them with the hardworking, lonely, dedicated anthropologists he had known and with whom he had worked (1945, 72-91): "Year after year they go out, usually on a shoestring . . . and they come back with data. They suffer from chronic tropical diseases, they occasionally encounter something vaguely resembling a romance . . . they carry out careful, exact work while malaria racks them, they suffer from hells of loneliness, and they experience peace and unflawed beauty" (90). Working on the relation of Kanjobal to Jacalteca, La Farge explains how fascinating and absorbing such an intellectual problem can be: "the only way to do such research is to roll in it, become soaked in it, live it, breathe it" (85). Because so few people understand or care about an anthropologist's research

> at his greatest strength, at the vital point of his life work, the scientist is cut off from communication with his fellow-man. Instead, he has the society of two, six, or twenty men and women who are working in his spe-cialty . . . with whom he corresponds, whose letters he receives like a lover, with whom when he meets them he wallows in an orgy of talk, the keen pleasure of conclusions and findings compared, matched, checked against one another, the pure joy of being really understood. (87)

All scholars have experienced this joy of communication about the esoterica of their work—but, of course, we should remember that so have religious cult groups, soccer enthusiasts, and stamp collectors.

La Farge, in the scientific volumes that he wrote about the Maya, is a forerunner of recent humanistic ethnography. In the foreword to *Santa Eulalia*, published in 1947, La Farge states that:

> there will be found in it a good deal of subjective, even opinionated writing . . . the writer believes that ethnology is an inexact science, inseparable from subjective, qualitative observations. The opinions and bias of the observer, therefore, are essential data which should be frankly presented. The colorless objectivity affected by many ethnologists is a deception and a suppression of data. (v-vi)

Recent critiques have echoed La Farge, suggesting that the ethnographic stance of an omniscient narrator and generalizations made from unreported personal observations are misleading. From a scientific point of view, they make it impossible to go from ethnographic generalization back to original fieldwork experience, thus preventing scientific replication (Marcus and Cushman 1982). By contrast, in some recent ethnographies, the anthropologist establishes a narrative presence from the beginning and focuses upon his or her own subjective experiences as a way of interpreting the other culture.[5] The resulting ethnography can also be analyzed as if it were a literary text (which it is), as well as read as a scientific monograph. All the conceptual tools of literary criticism then become available for textual analysis.

For La Farge, it was his experiences and his view of the world as a writer that moved him to insist on writing "humanistic ethnography." Although it was anthropology that provided the creative matrix from which La Farge the writer drew his inspiration, the process worked in reverse, also. It was literature, or the process of creative writing, from which La Farge was able to contribute to anthropology, predicting a new and better kind of ethnography, twenty or thirty years ahead of its general appearance.

One interesting way in which La Farge combined his humanistic inclinations and his scientific goals—one small but significant field technique—was through sketching. His field notebook from Santa Eulalia is apparently full of sketches from everyday life in that Maya village (Pearce 1972, 105). La Farge's grandfather had been a well-known artist, and La Farge himself had great sensitivity to line, color, and proportion. His prose at its best is finely crafted. It is the work of a wordsmith handling and appraising each sentence and looking at it from different angles with an artist's eye. We should remember that in the early twentieth century, before cameras became a universal presence, many anthropologists sketched in the field. Furthermore, they regarded their sketches as important parts of their field material. Older ethnographies are full of sketches, which often catch the contours and feel of material culture objects and social gatherings in a way the flat perspective of the camera misses. Here is another aspect of humanistic anthropology from earlier work that might be revived successfully. In this regard an interesting book is James Houston's *The White Dawn*, in my opinion one of the finest of ethnographic novels. Houston's many small drawings grace the pages of this detailed portrait of pre-contact Eskimo life.

La Farge wrote fiction for a living—remember the $10 a week he earned writing for Tony Hillerman! Consequently, he produced a great deal of prose. Many of his stories and novels are set pieces: love stories, stories about heroes with fatal flaws, and stories about men of action in difficult circumstances. What makes the best of them go beyond being trite is their cross-cultural component. The different cultural backgrounds of the protagonists and those around them bring them to life. Here are people acting from different premises and seeing the world in different terms. Laughing Boy, La Farge's best-known character, for instance, introduces the reader to a set of traditional Navajo traits and values: manliness, independence, kindness and humor, "walking in beauty," and living in harmony with the natural world. These traits are seen as alien to the imposing Anglo world, and the hero's final action is simply to retreat deeper into the canyons of Navajo land.

One of La Farge's favorite cross-cultural themes was the individual who successfully crosses cultural barriers. Esteban, in *Sparks Fly Upward*, is a Guatemalan Indian who through force of personality manages to become the country's military leader, but must hide his Indian identity to do so. Given ladino prejudices against Indians, he has to conceal the fact that his native language is Maya, but he manages to use his language to his own advantage as a cavalry officer dealing with angry villagers in the countryside. In his own intimate life, he finds that he must use Maya to convince the Indian woman he loves to come home:

> With Marta, as with the soldiers, he had always acted as though he spoke Spanish; now he put that aside. His native language was a refuge, a charm. 'Little mother, make your heart big. I am alone and my house is empty; at night I come home to a dark room. Marta, I need you. I am just Stevan and it is cold in my little house, and I need you.' (215)

In this novel, we find a sensitive understanding of the sociolinguistics of Spanish/Maya in Guatemala, which incidentally has close parallels with English/Spanish in our own Southwest. La Farge notes with an anthropologist's skill the nuances of language, the world of thought and meaning compressed into a phrase, and he translates it for us in a way that captures those cultural differences. Tony Hillerman, as James Pierson points out in this volume, is also a master at this art.

One general theory regards crossing disciplinary lines as the key to creativity. Seeing a set of material from a different perspective allows one then to go on and create something beyond both the original material and the new, introduced ideas. Immersion in one set of ideas, in this theory, leads simply to involution: $A + A = A'$, which in turn leads to A'', A''', and so on. As we all know, the academic world and Ph.D. programs in particular are built on this principle. On the other hand, $A + B$ (B being something different) may lead to C, which is something quite different from either A or B (and quite likely heretical!). I maintain that this is what happened with La Farge. Writing plus anthropology yielded something relatively new and interesting: ethnographic fiction.

La Farge wanted to be a writer from his boyhood days; he tells us he wrote avidly as a student at Groton and Harvard. Anthropology was something that crossed his path, appealing to his early interests and sidetracking him for a time. It gave him his experiences with the Navajo people in Arizona and with the Maya of Guatemala. Ironically, it was these cross-cultural experiences that made him a good writer. As long as he practiced it, field anthropology was the creative cauldron for La Farge the writer, providing the experiences, the point of view, the insights, and the discipline on which he could draw for his best fiction.

By contrast, some of his nonanthropology-based work is quite pedestrian. Although he wrote many stories and a novel, *The Copper Pot*, about Bohemian life in New Orleans, others have treated the subject more convincingly. He also wrote stories about school life at Groton and Harvard, and an embarrassingly super-patriotic history of the Air Transport Command in World War II (*The Eagle in the Egg*). These books make heavy reading today, and it takes some perseverance to get through them. Later in life, La Farge said once that he didn't want to be identified as someone who just wrote about Indians, but as a writer of more general scope. In his own words, he wanted to write not just about the thing observed, but about the thing experienced—Groton, Harvard, New Orleans, World War II, and so on (1945, 208). I believe, however, that La Farge's real genius was in his writings about the Navajo and Maya people among whom he had lived. In reality, these people and events had been not only observed, but both observed and experienced at the same time. This phrase, expressed somewhat differently, almost defines anthropological fieldwork.

In a story called "The Creation of John Manderville" in *The Door in the Wall*, one senses La Farge's nostalgia for the experiences of his youth (much like Joseph Conrad in his famous novelette *Youth*). In the La Farge story, a successful New York businessman drops his career and leaves his socialite family to return to the Hopi Indians of Arizona, among whom he had lived as a young anthropologist. Taking the name of a former student, now dead, Applegate the businessman (now transformed into Manderville the anthropologist) rediscovers his physical vitality, his zest for hard work in the outdoors, his respect for a more spiritual way of life, and his intellectual curiosity about his Indian friends. Unfortunately, he also discovers in himself the beginnings of the alcoholism that had destroyed his former student Manderville. He finds himself longing for a cold beer, with the nearest bar eighty miles away in Flagstaff. Furthermore, he must hide his craving from his puritannical Hopi friends! In the story, perhaps we can see some parallel between La Farge the older writer, grown rather stale, and the young La Farge, both writer and anthropologist, whose vitality and creativity were drawn from his dual intellectual background.

It is in *Laughing Boy, The Enemy Gods, Sparks Fly Upward*, and the best of his short stories that we find the flashes of insight into other peoples and their ways of life, the clear, simple literary translation of people from diffrent cultural backgrounds that still make La Farge a delight to read. He crossed cultural boundaries as an anthropologist and came back as a writer to explain what the experience had really meant to him.

NOTES

[1]La Farge's four other novels are *Sparks Fly Upward, Long Pennant, The Enemy Gods*, and *The Copper Pot*. His Maya ethnographies are *The Year Bearer's People*, with Douglas Byers, and *Santa Eulalia: The Religion of a Cuchumatan Indian Town*. The historical works include *War Below Zero*, with Bernt Balchen and Corey Ford; *The Eagle in the Egg*; *A Pictorial History of the American Indian*; and *Santa Fe: The Autobiography of a Southwestern Town*, co-edited with Arthur N. Morgan. Volumes of collected short stories include *All the Young Men, A Pause in the Desert*, and *Door in the Wall*.

La Farge wrote a mid-life autobiography entitled *Raw Material*, which contains much interesting information about his early life. Two useful biographies of La Farge are *Oliver La Farge*, by T. M. Pearce; and *Indian Man: A Life of Oliver La Farge*, by D'Arcy McNickle.

[2]Apart from *The Year Bearer's People* and *Santa Eulalia*, La Farge's best known scholarly work on the Maya is probably "Mayan Ethnology: The Sequence of Cultures," in *The Maya and Their Neighbors* (1940).

³Personal communication from Jerónimo Camposeco, a Kanjobal anthropologist living in Miami in 1987.

⁴*Tangweera* will be re-issued in a new, facsimile edition by the University of Texas Press in 1988.

⁵See, for instance, Jean L. Briggs, *Never in Anger: Portrait of an Eskimo Family.*

WORKS CITED

Bell, C. Napier. *Tangweera: Life and Adventures Among Gentle Savages.* London: Edward Arnold, 1899.

Briggs, Jean L. *Never in Anger: Portrait of an Eskimo Family.* Cambridge: Harvard University Press, 1970.

Houston, James. *The White Dawn.* New York: Harcourt Brace Jovanovich, 1971.

La Farge, Oliver. *Sparks Fly Upward.* Boston: Houghton Mifflin Co., 1931.

———. *Long Pennant.* Boston: Houghton Mifflin Co., 1933.

———. *All the Young Men.* Boston: Houghton Mifflin Co., 1935.

———. *The Enemy Gods.* Boston: Houghton Mifflin Co., 1937.

———. "Mayan Ethnology: The Sequence of Cultures." In *The Maya and Their Neighbors*, ed. Clarence L. Hay et al., 281-91. New York: Appleton-Century, 1940.

———. *The Copper Pot.* Boston: Houghton Mifflin Co., 1942.

———. *Raw Material.* Boston: Houghton Mifflin Co., 1945.

———. *Santa Eulalia: The Religion of a Cuchumatan Indian Town.* Chicago: University of Chicago Press, 1947.

———. *The Eagle in the Egg.* Boston: Houghton Mifflin Co., 1949.

———. *A Pictorial History of the American Indian.* New York: Crown Publishers, 1956.

———. *A Pause in the Desert.* Boston: Houghton Mifflin Co., 1957.

———. *Door in the Wall.* Boston: Houghton Mifflin Co., 1965.

———. *The Man With the Calabash Pipe.* Boston: Houghton Mifflin Co., 1966.

———. *Laughing Boy.* [1929.] New York: Signet Classics, 1971.

La Farge, Oliver, and Arthur N. Morgan, eds. *Santa Fe: The Autobiography of a Southwestern Town.* Norman, OK: University of Oklahoma Press, 1959.

La Farge, Oliver, Brent Balchen, and Corey Ford. *War Below Zero.* Boston: Houghton Mifflin Co., 1944.

La Farge, Oliver, and Douglas Byers. *The Year Bearer's People.* New Orleans: Tulane University Press, 1931.

Marcus, George E., and Dick Cushman. "Ethnographies as Texts." *Annual Review of Anthropology* 11(1982):25-69.

McNickle, D'Arcy. *Indian Man: A Life of Oliver La Farge.* Bloomington, IN: Indiana University Press, 1971.

Parsons, Elsie Clews, ed. *American Indian Life.* [1922.] Lincoln, NE: University of Nebraska Press, 1974.

Pearce, T. M. *Oliver La Farge.* New York: Twayne Publishers, 1972.

Richardson, Miles. "The Museum." *The Southern Review* 20 (Autumn 1984): 919-27.

NOTES ON THE AUTHORS

A. OWEN ALDRIDGE retired from the University of Illinois in June, 1986. Since then he has held the Will and Ariel Durant Chair in the Humanities at Saint Peter's College and has served as visiting professor of English and comparative literature at Pennsylvania State University. Aldridge has also served as visiting professor at the universities of Toulouse and Clermont-Ferrand in France, and Rio de Janeiro in Brazil, and at Kuwait University, and Nihon University in Japan. He has written two books on Thomas Paine and three on Benjamin Franklin as well as others on the Third Earl of Shaftsbury, Jonathan Edwards, Voltaire, and early American literature. His most recent, *The Reemergence of World Literature*, was published in 1986. He is former president of the American Comparative Literature Association and founder and editor of the journal *Comparative Literature Studies*.

MICHAEL V. ANGROSINO, a native of New York City, received his Ph.D. in anthropology from the University of North Carolina at Chapel Hill. He is currently Professor of Anthropology and Public Health and Chair of the Department of Anthropology at the University of South Florida, and Adjunct Professor of Epidemiology and Policy Analysis in the Florida Mental Health Institute. He has conducted fieldwork in the Indian community of Trinidad, and oral history research in the Dutch West Indies. He has published on the works of the Trinidad-born novelist V. S. Naipul, and on autobiography as a genre in West Indian literature. His current research concerns the development of identity among deinstitutionalized mentally retarded adults. His books include *Outside is Death: Ideology and Community Organization Among the East Indians of Trinidad; Do Applied Anthropologists Apply Anthropology?*; and *Medical Behavioral Science*.

PHILIP K. BOCK is Presidential Professor of Anthropology at the University of New Mexico where he has taught since 1963. He holds an M.A. from the University of Chicago and a Ph.D. in social anthropology from Harvard. His recent publications include *Rethinking Psychological Anthropology* (1988), *Shakespeare and Elizabethan Culture* (1984), and *The Formal Content of Ethnography* (1986). Bock is also the editor of the *Journal of Anthropological Research*. His long-standing interest in the theater has included acting and directing in community theaters; one of his recent roles was Falstaff in *The Merry Wives of Windsor*. In 1984 he participated in the NEH Summer Seminar on Shakespeare, Psychoanalysis, and Literary Criticism at the University of Massachusetts, where he gave a paper on dual unity in "The Phoenix and the Turtle," just published in the *Journal of Psychological Anthropology*.

BERNADETTE BUCHER is Professor in the Humanities at Fordham University at Lincoln Center, New York. A native of Paris, she studied at the Académie de Paris and the Sorbonne, where her work was supervised by Claude Lévi-Strauss and where she earned her doctorate in comparative literature. She has taught in Montreal and New York. Among her awards are grants from the Wenner-Gren Foundation for Anthropological Research, the Centre National de la Recherche Scientifique, and the National Endowment for the Humanities. She has published studies on both anthropology and literature. She is the author of *La Sauvage aux Seins Pendants* (Paris, 1977), which was translated into English as *Icon and Conquest: A Structural Analysis of the Illustrations of De Bry's Great Voyages* (University of Chicago Press, 1981). She is currently preparing a book on history, culture, and society in the Vendée.

CLAUDETTE KEMPER COLUMBUS, Professor of English and Comparative Literature at Hobart and William Smith Colleges, received her M.A. from Columbia University and her Ph.D. from the University of Pennsylvania. She has written articles on Dickens, Blake, Ruskin, Schumann, Browning, García Márquez, Arguedas, and J. M. W. Turner. She has delivered papers on Turner at Brown University and on Millais at the MLA. Recipient of several Mellon grants, she was awarded a senior Fulbright research grant to Peru in 1984-85. Her book, *Mythological Consciousness and the Future: José María Arguedas*, was published in 1986.

ANN DAGHISTANY earned the B.A. degree in English at Boston University and the Ph.D. in comparative literature at the University of Southern California, where she was an NDEA Fellow. She taught at USC, Cerritos College, and Valley Junior College in California. She has delivered professional papers on comparative literature, women's studies, romantic irony, spatial form, García Márquez, and the archetype of the priest figure. She has published book reviews, articles on women's studies and on romantic irony, and a book co-edited with Jeffrey Smitten,

Spatial Form in Narrative. She is currently writing a book on archetypes and stereotypes in literature, and teaches in the Department of English at Texas Tech University.

CELIA DANIELS recently completed a graduate degree in anthropology and museum studies at the University of Kansas, and a B.A. in history and anthropology from Washburn University in Topeka. Ms. Daniels has had her poetry published in the anthology *Kansas Women Writers* as well as in a number of journals, including *Anthropology and Humanism Quarterly*, *Kansas Quarterly*, and *Little Balkans Review*. She has served on the Board of the Woodley Memorial Press and has provided editorial assistance for several books of poetry. Having worked as a consultant and volunteer for several regional museums, Ms. Daniels is currently directing the public education program at the University of Kansas Museum of Anthropology.

PHILIP A. DENNIS is Professor of Anthropology at Texas Tech University. He grew up in the Southwest, graduated from the University of Arizona, and received the Ph.D. in social anthropology from Cornell. He has done fieldwork in Oaxaca, Mexico, and among the Miskito of eastern Nicaragua. He served as chairman of the Anthropology Department from 1981-86. In fall, 1987, he was Fulbright Professor at the Universidade Federal do Rio Grande do Norte in Natal, Brazil. His scholarly interests include the cross-cultural study of health, political anthropology, ethnohistory, and ethnographic fiction. His articles include "The Role of the Drunk in a Oaxacan Village" and "The Costeños and the Revolution in Nicaragua." His book, *Intervillage Conflict in Oaxaca*, was published by Rutgers University Press in 1987.

ELIZABETH FERNEA is Senior Lecturer in the Department of English and the Center for Middle Eastern Studies at the University of Texas, Austin. She has done fieldwork in Iraq, Egypt, and Morocco, and was recently elected president of the Middle Eastern Studies Association of North America. Author of *Guests of the Sheik* and *A Street in Marrakech*, she has recently produced a number of films on women and social change in the Middle East. *Some Women of Marrakech* was shown on PBS's *Odyssey* series in 1981 and 1983.

TONY HILLERMAN was born in 1925 in the Oklahoma farming community of Sacred Heart. He attended St. Mary's Academy, a boarding school for Indian girls, for eight grades; and Konawa High School. After World War II—during which he twice attained the rank of Private First Class—he received a degree in

Journalism from the University of Oklahoma. He worked as a police reporter, political writer, and newspaper editor, then earned an M.A. in English at the University of New Mexico, where he later served as Chairman of the Journalism Department and twice as special assistant to the President before resigning from the faculty in 1985. He is author or editor of 14 books and is best known for his mystery novels. He won the Edgar Allen Poe Award for the best mystery published in 1973. Five of his novels have been book club selections and six have made the New York Times "notable books of the year" listings. His books are also published in England, Germany, Italy, Spain, France, Japan, Holland, Sweden, and Norway.

BARBARA JO LANTZ received her B.A. in anthropology from the University of Rochester (1974) and her M.A. and Ph.D. (1985) in that field from Cornell University. A cultural anthropologist, she has done fieldwork in Mexico, Colombia, and the United States. Her doctoral dissertation deals with the apotheotic structure of historical narrative in Mexico and locates its contexts in social and political life. In addition to her work in Mexico, she has done research on cultural identity and aesthetics among the Guambianos of Cauca, Colombia, and on the cultural legacy in America of the Vietnam War. She has received grants from the Center for the International Exchange of Scholars and the National Endowment for the Humanities and has taught at Cornell University and Marlboro College in Vermont. In 1987-88 she was a Fellow at the Woodrow Wilson Center in Washington, D.C. She is at work on a manuscript entitled *Western Genres, Mexican 'Culture'*, which seeks to clarify the impact of literary, journalistic, and anthropological discursive practices on cultural politics in 20th century Mexico.

JAMES C. PIERSON is Professor of Anthropology at California State University, San Bernardino, where he has taught since 1971. He received a Ph.D. in anthropology from Washington University, St. Louis, in 1972. He has conducted research among Australian Aborigines in Adelaide, South Australia, and among members of a family-based religion in Southern California. His other research and teaching interests include sociocultural change, religion and cosmology, urban adaptations of native populations, cross-cultural child-rearing practices, and the cultural aspects of human development. His current writing projects include a monograph on urban adaptations among Australian Aborigines. He is a sometime participant in his campus' upper division writing program and frequently uses novels, including mystery stories, as required readings in his courses.

MILES RICHARDSON, Professor of Anthropology in the Department of Geography and Anthropology at Louisiana State University, is also editor of *Anthropology and Humanism Quarterly*, the journal of the Society for Humanistic Anthropology. Richardson is currently engaged in the study of the transformation of space into place, or how cultures come to achieve an experiential existence. Recent publications for which he served as editor include *Place: Experience and Symbol; The Burden of Being Civilized* (with Malcolm Webb); and *Africa and Afro-America: Views From Women in the Field* (with Gelya Frank). He is also a published writer of fiction and poetry.

JOHN STEWART is Professor of English and Comparative Literature at Ohio State University. He holds degrees in English and comparative writing from Stanford and the University of Iowa, and in social anthropology from U.C.L.A. He has done fieldwork in the Caribbean, Nigeria, and the U.S. His previous publications, focused mainly on Afro-American culture and the response to racism in Trinidad and the U.S., include *Last Cool Days*, a novel; *Curving Road*, a collection of short stories; and *For the Ancestors*, a life history of Bessie Jones; plus other short stories and articles on folk religion and the Trinidad carnival. His several interests all converge in the practice of narrative ethnography. A new collection, *Drinkers, Drummers, and Decent Folk*, his most recent contribution to the development of this form, will be released by the State University of New York Press in 1988.

JAMES WHITLARK, who holds the Ph.D. from the University of Chicago, taught at the Illinois Institute of Technology, Roosevelt University, and Loyola University. He is presently Associate Professor of English at Texas Tech University. Author of *Illuminated Fantasy: From Blake's Visions to Recent Graphic Fiction* (Fairleigh Dickinson University Press, 1987), he has published articles on Geoffrey Chaucer, T. S. Eliot, Matthew Arnold, Franz Kafka, Popular Literature, and Tantrism. Since receiving a university-wide teaching award at Texas Tech, he has participated in the Comparative Literature and Honors Programs, and served as sponsor of Sigma Tau Delta, the English Honors Society. He is currently working on a book-length critique of Jungian theory to be entitled "Behind the Great Wall: Kafkaesque Philosophy and 'Archetypal' Fiction."

ACKNOWLEDGMENTS

This volume derives from the Twentieth Annual Comparative Literature Symposium entitled, "Literature and Anthropology," held on the Texas Tech University campus January 28-30, 1987. The Symposium was made possible in part by a grant from the Lubbock City Council, as recommended by the Lubbock Cultural Affairs Council. On campus, the joint sponsors of the Symposium were the Office of Academic Affairs and Research, the Dean of Arts and Sciences, and the Departments of Anthropology, Classical and Romance Languages, English, and Germanic and Slavic Languages.

The activities of the Symposium were planned and directed by Wendell Aycock and Philip A. Dennis. Symposium sessions were chaired by Donald Haragan, Clyde Hendrick, Otto Nelson, Dale Cluff, Joe R. Goodin, Russell Hughes, Ulrich Goebel, Robert J. Morris, and Neven P. Lamb. Panel discussion members were Terry Grieder, Tony Hillerman, Frances Sage, Peter I. Barta, Ivan Brady, James A. Goss, James S. Whitlark, Neal Newfield, Jeana Paul, Elizabeth Winkler Sommerlad, Alice Portnoy, Nigel Rapport, John W. Samson, Marietta Morrissey, Harley Oberhelman, Charles Butler, Sydney Cravens, Phillip Mehaffey, Joseph W. Bastien, Matthias Schubnell, Laura Foster-Eason, Suzanne Gott, and Lynn Hoggard. Ann Daghistany chaired the luncheon session, and John and Rosie Alford generously offered the use of their home for the Symposium reception. Alice French moderated two programs about the Symposium on KTXT, one of which was an interview with Keynote Speaker Tony Hillerman. Mr. Hillerman also provided a very entertaining evening of stories and informal remarks for Symposium guests and participants. Special thanks go to the Texas Tech University Library for hosting the sessions in the Special Collections Room, as well as to the Southwest Collection and the Bookstore.

The editors would like to thank all the individuals and organizations that participated in making the Twentieth Annual Comparative Literature Symposium a success.